A Teacher's Guide to Preventing Behavior Problems in the Elementary Classroom

Stephen W. Smith
University of Florida

Mitchell L. Yell
University of South Carolina

Boston Columbus Indianapolis New York San Francisco Upper Saddle River
Amsterdam Cape Town Dubai London Madrid Milan Munich Paris Montreal Toronto
Delhi Mexico City São Paulo Sydney Hong Kong Seoul Singapore Taipei Tokyo

Vice President and Editorial Director: Jeffery W. Johnston
Executive Editor and Publisher: Stephen D. Dragin
Editorial Assistant: Katherine Wiley
Marketing Manager: Joanna Sabella
Editorial Production Service & Electronic Composition: Dhanya Ramesh, Jouve (India) & Jouve (India)
Production Manager: Tom Benfatti
Creative Director: Jayne Conte
Cover Design: Bruce Kenselaar
Cover Image: Iofoto-Fotolia
Printer: RR Donnelley and Sons

6   16

ISBN 10: 0-13-714741-4
ISBN 13: 978-0-13-714741-0

BRIEF CONTENTS

CONTENTS

CONTENTS

Contents xi

PREFACE

WHAT THIS BOOK IS ABOUT

Teachers and other school professionals consistently rank student misbehavior as one of the most persistent and troubling problems that they encounter. They report various types of disruptive and aggressive behavior that range from talking out in class to physical assault. To manage classroom behavior successfully, teachers need to provide structure and consistent, positive expectations in their classrooms that maximize instructional time and minimize problem behavior. Although how to address problem behavior is discussed frequently during faculty meetings, in-service trainings, and informally in the teacher's lounge, what is too often ignored is how to prevent unwanted and inappropriate student behavior.

Teachers and other school professionals should attempt to avoid future problems in the classroom by investing in the learning community from the start. Preventive strategies allow students to learn effective coping strategies with support from classmates and teachers and lead to greater time for academic instruction. The key to effective classroom management is increasing student involvement and engagement in the classroom so that when problem behaviors are prevented through the strategies discussed in this book, teachers can provide the learning environment that students deserve.

This book focuses on the research, strategies, and techniques that teachers may use to help prevent problem behaviors from occurring in the elementary classroom. A well-organized, systematic, and predictable teaching environment helps to prevent behaviors, and this book presents ways to achieve this type of classroom environment. Moreover, it provides ideas for interacting with students in ways that will increase their appropriate behavior and prevent the problematic ones.

HOW CONTENT IS ORGANIZED

The content of this book is organized to give readers a foundational understanding of prevention through a multitude of strategies and procedures. Chapter 1 explains how prevention is basic and fundamental to successfully managing a classroom and offers a chronology of early classroom research that, even today, provides useful information on how to prevent student behavior problems. Chapter 2 describes classrooms as communities of learners and distinguishes between a positive classroom approach and one built on the use of punishment. This chapter also compares and contrasts teacher management styles that either inhibit or promote the prevention of behavior problems, and it describes how an explicit teaching philosophy can support proactive approaches in managing behavior. Chapter 3 moves into immediate and effective ways to structure and organize the physical space of the classroom, including room arrangement, procedures, and transitions, while Chapter 4 emphasizes the importance of fostering teacher–student relationships in the classroom as foundational knowledge for preventive behavior management. Chapter 4 also highlights ways teachers can foster appropriate teacher–student relationships, gauge the quality of relationships with their students, and design a relationship-driven classroom that prevents behavior problems.

Meeting with students first thing in the morning is a way to build an atmosphere for preventing unwanted student behavior, and Chapter 5 provides readers with ideas and easy-to-follow tips for conducting morning meetings in the classroom. These meetings are designed to create a positive classroom environment where all students are connected to each other and valued. This chapter discusses the components of morning meetings, and it describes creative ways to have fun in the classroom while, at the same time, allowing students and the teacher to know each other and learn together.

Chapter 6 examines ways to prevent behavior problems through effective instruction by managing classroom time, providing clear directions about instruction, monitoring student attention, and maintaining student accountability. This chapter also discusses teacher behaviors, such as "withitness" and overlapping, along with instructional strategies that can prevent behavior problems such as smoothness and momentum. Chapter 7 moves into research-based prevention techniques for use in the classroom, such as teacher modeling of self-control, turning student reprimands into redirects, and increasing choice making for students. This chapter also addresses the use of behavior contracts and group-oriented interventions as positive ways to prevent or reduce behavior problems.

Despite all of the prevention techniques used in the classroom, misbehavior is a natural part of the classroom environment, and Chapter 8 focuses on ways to respond effectively so that such behaviors do not accelerate and get out of control. This chapter also identifies a number of ineffective approaches for responding to problematic behaviors, and it parallels those with effective techniques to use instead. Chapter 9 gives teachers an understanding of how to provide students with the skills necessary to make appropriate behavioral choices on their own and, thus, prevent student behavior problems. Teaching students self-management skills and how to solve their social problems through systematic social problem solving instruction are included. By reading this chapter, teachers will have a solid understanding of how to assist students to become effective managers of their own behavior.

Chapter 10 helps the reader put all the information together into a cohesive classroom management plan. Step-by-step directions for developing procedures and rules and for reinforcing appropriate student behaviors help teachers integrate preventive behavior management in their own classrooms. Finally, this chapter offers teachers a look into the future by incorporating ideas for implementation and the direction of effective behavior management. The last chapter also serves to solidify the concepts introduced throughout the text, and it ensures that teachers are on the forefront of the changing landscape of education and the prevention of student behavior problems in the elementary classroom.

CHAPTER FEATURES

The book is organized in a "user-friendly" manner and employs a balance between research-based practices and readily accessible classroom strategies. Each chapter begins with a list of chapter goals. These goals drive the organization and content of the chapter, and they give the reader an understanding of where the chapter is heading. Following the goals, each chapter incorporates a scenario depicting ways teachers commonly respond ineffectively to problem behaviors in the classroom. It is our hope that teachers can see readily the ineffective teacher behaviors in the scenarios, and we try to anchor the chapter information on how to be effective managers of behavior.

Figures, diagrams, and examples are intermixed throughout each chapter. We have also included questions that teachers may have about the concepts in each chapter, and we provide answers about ways to approach the situation. The questions offer teachers an opportunity to visualize how to implement the recommended strategies from the chapter in a meaningful and authentic way. Finally, at the end of each chapter, we include an *Additional Resources* section listing Internet sites and a few relevant professional articles so that teachers can expand their understanding of the chapter's content through additional information. By offering these additional resources, we hope to provide the reader with a clear and substantive picture of how to use preventative behavior management in the classroom.

NEW! COURSESMART eTEXTBOOK AVAILABLE

CourseSmart is an exciting new choice for students looking to save money. As an alternative to purchasing the printed textbook, students can purchase an electronic version of the same content. With a CourseSmart eTextbook, students can search the text, make notes online, print out reading assignments that incorporate lecture notes, and bookmark important passages for later review. For more information, or to purchase access to the CourseSmart eTextbook, visit http://www.coursesmart.com.

ACKNOWLEDGMENTS

We would like to thank the reviewers for this edition: Stacy Carter, Texas Tech University; Heidi Davey, St. Xavier University; Brenda Fogus, James Madison University; Gail Hartin, Southern Methodist University; Melodie Santana, Loyola Marymount University; and Richard Raymond Templeton, Falkville High School, Falkville, AL.

1

Preventing Behavior Problems: The Foundation for Classroom Management

GOALS

- Establish the importance of preventing problem behaviors in the classroom.
- Present the rationale that supports preventive approaches.

- Provide an introduction to research supporting prevention and effective classroom management.
- Provide brief examples of strategies for creating and maintaining proactive classrooms.

SCENARIO

Ms. Jansen

Ms. Jansen's classroom is chaotic. Students are frequently off task, and Ms. Jansen reprimands her students repeatedly to maintain student behavior. Students are often out of their seats bothering other students, and there are unproductive teacher–student interactions that add to a noticeable tension in the classroom. What is apparent is that Ms. Jansen has not communicated the need for behavioral expectations, rules, or a social contract for behavior to her students, so they are unaware of the behaviors that are unacceptable. When Ms. Jansen observes appropriate behaviors from her students, she fails to consistently reinforce them, and she is equally inconsistent when she observes inappropriate student behaviors. As one example, Ms. Jansen believes that students should always raise their hands and wait to be recognized before they comment about a class activity or answer a question. Upon observation, however, Ms. Jansen allows verbal comments from students with and without hand raising at seemingly random times. She harshly reprimands some students but fails to respond to others for speaking without being called on. Further, her warnings about students' behaviors are applied more often to some students and less often to others in the classroom, resulting in an ineffective response to inappropriate behavior because students are confused about classroom expectations. Thus, students engage in unwanted behaviors at an unacceptable rate, and time for academic work dwindles as Ms. Jansen spends excessive amounts of time attempting to gain control of the classroom.

Ms. Johnson

Ms. Johnson and her students have worked together to develop clear expectations for classroom behavior, create definitive classroom rules and a social contract for classroom behavior, and generate associated consequences for students who abide by the contract and for those that do not. She invested considerable time at the beginning of the school year by conducting numerous classroom discussions and devising collaborative learning activities so that students were clear about how the classroom was to operate. Ms. Johnson even created role plays for the students about learning appropriate classroom behaviors, especially during transitions between activities, so that she can teach effectively and students can learn efficiently. Ms. Johnson, in collaboration with her students, settled on five rules that guided their social contract for classroom behavior, such as treat others with respect, follow teacher directions, and be an effective problem solver. It was their communal sense that these types of behaviors were required to maintain an atmosphere conducive to learning and to ensure they can all have a fun and productive school day. Ms. Johnson understood there must be positive consequences for following rules as well as negative consequences when rules are violated, and she made sure there was common agreement about what happens when students follow the rules and when they do not. By doing so, Ms. Johnson created a fair and consistent classroom atmosphere. Ms. Johnson also conducted daily morning meetings, used precorrection strategies, worked to control her own behavior, thought carefully about her philosophy of teaching, understood "withitness," and used redirection rather than reprimands for her students' minor behaviors. In this way, Ms. Johnson was trying to build a foundation of trust in the classroom and, thus, prevent behavior problems from occurring. Her clear, consistent, continuous, and proactive communication and use of effective prevention strategies helped Ms. Johnson and her students have an orderly and caring classroom designed for a productive school year.

M s. Jansen and Ms. Johnson are teachers engaging in different types of classroom management. One uses a reactive strategy to address student misbehavior after it has occurred, and one uses a more proactive or preventive approach to managing classroom behavior. In your estimation, which classroom has the best foundation for effective and efficient academic and social learning to take place? Ms. Johnson has deliberately structured her classroom and her approach to prevent, as much as possible, student behavior problems that can create ineffective learning environments. When teachers create environments that foster appropriate behavior, they spend less time reacting to inappropriate behaviors, thus creating more time to effectively teach academic content (e.g., Bohn, Roehrig, & Pressley, 2004; Cameron, Connor, & Morrison, 2005; Emmer & Stough, 2001). Effective teaching and student learning will not occur in a poorly managed classroom where prevention of behavior problems is not a high priority (Marzano, Marzano, & Pickering, 2003).

For many years, the management of student behavior in the classroom focused almost exclusively on responding to a student's disruptive and maladaptive behavior to decrease the unwanted behavior. Reacting to inappropriate student behavior is not entirely inappropriate, but attempts to curb student misbehavior without requisite knowledge of effective prevention strategies, and well-thought-out plans for their use, can be costly in terms of lost academic instruction time and lost opportunities for students to develop self-control. In times past, little attention was paid to the notion that preventing student behavior problems is worthy of teacher time or effort.

Messages about preventing problems are all around us in our daily lives. For example, nowhere is the prevention of problems more ubiquitous than in the medical profession. Promoting good health and preventing disease and life-threatening conditions are the essence of good medical practice. In fact, what is constantly heard are messages about the benefits of proper diet, exercise, and health screenings, all designed to prevent obesity, heart disease, diabetes, and mental health problems. Interestingly, the Centers for Disease Control and Prevention, which acts as a national clearinghouse of health information, expanded the scope of their activities beyond communicable diseases by adding "and Prevention" in 1992. Prevention is also the norm in a number of other areas, including:

- Preventing tooth decay and periodontal (gum) disease through brushing, flossing, and professional hygienic cleaning.
- Preventing problems in our homes by having inspections to ensure adequate attic insulation and sealing windows and doors to prevent cooling and heating loss.
- Preventing major forest fires by conducting periodic controlled burns in many forested areas.
- Preventing skin cancer through the use of sunscreen.
- Preventing teen substance abuse and pregnancy through educational programs.

These messages and many others are a significant and noticeable part of daily life, so why is it that preventing problem behaviors in the classroom is not an explicit and central part of what all teachers learn in their preparation programs and in their professional development?

THE IMPORTANCE OF CLASSROOM MANAGEMENT FOR PREVENTING BEHAVIOR PROBLEMS

Student behavior problems have been a long-standing concern of educators. Consider that one of the earliest textbooks on teaching and classroom management, *Classroom Management: Its Principles and Techniques*, by William Bagley, was published in 1907. The purpose of the textbook was to provide a coherent and comprehensive set of principles and techniques that would allow the prospective teacher to effectively manage student behavior in the classroom. Almost 100 years later, in 2006, a seminal textbook in classroom management, the *Handbook of Classroom Management: Research, Practice, and Contemporary Issues*, edited by Carolyn Evertson and Carol Weinstein, was published. In between the Bagley and the Evertson and Weinstein publications, there have been countless textbooks, presentations, and journal articles on the subject of classroom and behavior management. Classroom management has always been, and always will be, a vital concern of educators.

For decades, issues about student behavior have routinely been at the top of national surveys focused on the concerns that professional educators and the general public have with America's schools (cf. Bushaw & Gallup, 2008; Gallup, 1983; Johnson, 2004; Johnson, Rochkind, & Ott, 2010). According to Johnson (2004), 97 percent of teachers and 78 percent of parents who responded to a survey believed that good discipline and appropriate student behavior are needed for successful schools. Interestingly, 78 percent of the teachers reported that there are students in their school who should be removed from regular classrooms because of persistent troublemaking, and 35 percent of teachers reported that they have considered leaving the profession, or know a colleague who has left, because of issues related to student discipline and behavior. In 2010, Johnson and colleagues found that 74 percent of respondents listed bullying and harassment in their schools as a serious concern, with 47 percent indicating these behaviors as very serious. Moreover, 76 percent of the public identified illegal drugs and students treating teachers with a lack of respect as serious problems, with 50 percent noting disrespect for teachers as very serious.

Concerns about students who exhibit behavior problems are understandable, because well-managed classrooms are a necessary prerequisite to effective teaching and learning in both the academic and the social/emotional areas. That is, teachers and other school personnel must create and maintain learning environments that allow efficient and effective learning to take place with a minimum of distractions, interruptions, and significant student behavioral incidents. Moreover, when student disruptions do occur, teachers must be able to react in an appropriate, effective, and consistent manner.

Effective management is even more important today, because teachers have to deal with ever-increasing numbers of students who are difficult to manage and teach (Evertson & Weinstein, 2006). Additionally, the increasing demands for educational accountability, which have focused on providing evidence of academic achievement through high-stakes, statewide testing mandated in federal laws such as the Elementary and Secondary Education Act of 2001 (No Child Left Behind) and the Individuals with Disabilities Education Improvement Act of 2004 as well as in state laws, require school personnel to maximize academic instruction to improve student achievement and to demonstrate satisfactory student progress (Yell, 2006). Student misbehavior can disrupt academic instruction, which has a negative effect on student achievement. Moreover, teachers may become frustrated by the loss of instructional time caused by attending to behavior problems. When teachers become frustrated with student behavior, they may react in ways that are less than effective and may actually exacerbate the very behaviors that caused the classroom problems in the first place.

NEGATIVE OUTCOMES ASSOCIATED WITH INEFFECTIVE CLASSROOM MANAGEMENT

Many negative outcomes are associated with ineffective classroom management. For example, in classrooms like Ms. Jansen's, where there is excessive off-task and disruptive behavior, students do not learn as much as they would in successfully managed classrooms, because disruptive behaviors take time away from teaching and learning. Conversely, when there is effective classroom management that minimizes student disruption and increases instructional time, academic achievement is increased.

Additionally, ineffective classroom management is a major cause of teacher burnout and dissatisfaction (Billingsley, 2003; Kilgore, Griffin, Otis-Wilborn, & Winn, 2003). In fact, stress related to inappropriate classroom management is one of the most frequently cited reasons for why novice teachers leave the profession early (Ingersoll, 2001). It is often the case that ineffective classroom management practices result in principals and supervisors giving low ratings to teachers who demonstrate poor management of their classrooms (Evertson & Emmer, 2009; Ladd, 2000). Moreover, school district administrators have described providing extensive supervision and support, as well as conducting comprehensive retraining, to beginning teachers because of their poor preparation in classroom management (Brock & Grady, 1997; Jones, 2006; Lytle, 2000). Many administrators are also faced with the problem of having to replace beginning teachers who have not been adequately prepared to manage classrooms (Jones, 2006).

Fortunately, with proper preparation, teachers can manage student behaviors in a proactive manner, thus preventing student disruptions and distractions and increasing instructional time and academic achievement. On the other hand, teachers often report that when they enter the teaching profession, they do not believe they are adequately prepared to manage student behavior in their classrooms (Jacques, 2000; Jones, 2006; McCormack, 2001; Meister & Jenks, 2000). Beginning teachers often describe their anxiety and apprehension about their ability to manage a classroom, and they fear losing control of their students (Fideler & Haskelhorn, 1999; Ingersoll & Smith, 2003). Beginning teachers often report that neither their teacher training programs nor their school-based inservice training prepared them to be skillful managers who can prevent problem behaviors in their classrooms (Herbert & Worthy, 2001; Jones, 2006). In fact, many beginning teachers blame their lack of classroom management skills on inadequate teacher preparation programs in the colleges and universities they attended (Jones, 2006; Ladd, 2000). Pilarsky (1994) quoted a beginning teacher who expressed these frustrations:

> I felt bewildered and more than a bit betrayed by my own teacher preparation program: all the learning theories and stages of development that I studied helped little when I was faced with managing a classroom of real children. . . . On the few occasions when my courses did deal with management issues, the lessons were so far removed from actual classroom situations that the benefits proved minimal. (pp. 78–79)

With the abundance of evidence showing that effective teachers can prevent student misbehavior, why are so many teachers not adequately prepared to manage their classroom using proactive, preventive approaches? Although there are many possible reasons why teachers may be inadequately prepared, a primary reason seems to lie at the feet of teacher education programs. Jones (2006) examined the problems with the content and instruction of classrooms in teacher education programs and identified a number of crucial areas:

- Many teacher education programs lack an integrated and comprehensive curriculum in classroom management.
- The approach of many teacher education programs is too theoretical and not specific.
- Beginning teachers do not leave their programs with the skills to work with students who present serious problem behavior or to manage crisis situations in the classroom when they occur.
- Many teacher education programs lack a connection between coursework and field experiences.

- There is often a serious disconnect between what many beginning teachers are taught in their programs and what they will actually encounter in their classrooms.

Clearly, beginning teachers need knowledge and skills in classroom management to prepare them for what they will encounter in their classrooms. Unfortunately, in many teacher education programs, this is not happening.

ADDRESSING THE CLASSROOM MANAGEMENT PROBLEM

The purpose of this book is to assist teachers in developing and maintaining proactive classroom management systems. By a proactive management approach, we mean that teachers create and maintain a classroom environment that promotes on-task and academically engaged behavior and prevents misbehavior. Such environments are conducive to student academic learning and, thus, can improve academic achievement.

In this introductory chapter, we provide a rationale for the overall importance of developing proactive, preventive behavior management systems in classrooms and discuss how preventive approaches are effective in reducing problematic student behaviors. When teachers embrace approaching behavior problems in the classroom by thinking prevention first, like Ms. Johnson in the scenario described at the beginning of the chapter, there can be an increase in appropriate student behavior, in time for teachers to teach content areas, and in positive opportunities for students to learn. Since it is often the case that the word "discipline" is used to denote a way to handle student behavior problems, we also describe how preventing behavior problems and disciplining students are similar in many ways. Finally, we present a model of effective classroom management that will be the basis for the strategies and procedures that we present throughout the remainder of this text.

When we teach our courses at our respective universities and work with teachers in their classrooms, discussions almost always center on difficult-to-manage students who create challenges for keeping classrooms as efficient learning environments. We often start our discussions with school professionals with a question: *What kind of things do you do to prevent problem behaviors from happening in the first place?* More often than not, however, we find that well-thought-out and systematic preventive strategies are not used. Classroom environments will not be efficient and effective places to learn unless they are built upon a firm foundation of prevention. Simply put, preventing student behavior problems is logical, and it is an investment with measurable payoffs for teachers and other education professionals along with students and their parents.

RESEARCH ON CLASSROOM MANAGEMENT

We have been addressing the importance of preventing student misbehavior through proactive classroom management, yet how do we know that prevention is such an important component? One answer is found in the foundational research of Jacob Kounin (1970) in a series of studies he conducted almost 40 years ago supporting the notion that preventing student behavior problems is a critical teacher activity. Additional research by Evertson and colleagues (2006) have confirmed and extended Kounin's findings and subsequent research on classroom management has continued to support their foundational findings.

Jacob Kounin's Research

Before the 1970s, approaches to classroom management were often based on procedures for disciplining students who misbehaved. In other words, the emphasis of these programs was on the reactions of teachers after students had behaved inappropriately. Such a view of managing student behavior began to change in the early 1970s, and a major impetus to this change was Jacob Kounin's book *Discipline and Group Management in Classrooms*, published in 1970.

Kounin was a professor of educational psychology at Columbia University who had an interest in the behaviors of teachers and students in classrooms. One day, he was lecturing to his psychology of human behavior class when he noticed one of his students in the back row reading a newspaper. He reprimanded the student (used a desist), and the young man put the paper away. At the same time, Kounin noticed that his reprimand had an observable effect on other class members. Students began to pay more attention to his lecture and write in their notebooks. While he had expected the desist to affect the behavior of the young man with the newspaper, he was surprised by the reaction of the other members of the class.

Kounin referred to the phenomena that he observed as "the ripple effect," which he defined as a teacher's method of handling the misbehavior of one student while, at the same time, influencing other students who were not the primary targets. The effects of the desist had rippled out among other students in the class, much like a stone thrown into pool causes waves to flow outward. From this experience, he conducted a series of studies to determine how teachers handled misbehavior.

In one of his research projects, Kounin videotaped many hours of classroom instruction in over 100 general education classrooms. Kounin focused his observation on students who exhibited problem behavior, but he was also interested in the disciplinary procedures used by teachers who had well-managed classrooms and those of teachers whose classrooms were characterized by serious management problems. Kounin hypothesized that differences in the disciplinary techniques used by teachers would account for differences in their ability to successfully manage and influence student behavior in their classrooms. What Kounin believed at the time, as most everyone did, was that teachers who had well-run classrooms were the more effective behavior managers. What he found, however, astonished him.

What amazed Kounin was that the techniques teachers used to manage student misbehavior resulted in no systematic differences in how students behaved. In fact, teachers who were successful classroom managers, whose classrooms were characterized by order and on-task behavior, and those teachers who were inept managers, whose classrooms were often out of control, were responding to student problem behavior in similar ways. Apparently, the management approaches in the classrooms that Kounin observed were similar for good and poor managers. That is, how teachers responded generally to the disruptive behavior of students seemed to have little or nothing to do with how effective teachers were at managing their classrooms.

Still believing that there must be some systematic differences between those teachers who were considered to be effective classroom managers and those who were not, Kounin reanalyzed the videotapes. He wanted to find out what it was teachers did that made a difference in how their students behaved, because seemingly, it had little to do with how teachers reacted to student problem behavior. His reanalysis of the videotapes showed clear differences in the ways the successful managers approached their teaching and structured their classrooms, but these teacher behaviors did not occur *after* students misbehaved. Rather, these teacher behaviors prevented student misbehavior from occurring in the first place. In other words, the effective managers were not reacting to student misbehavior. Instead, they were preventing it from occurring. In his 1970 book, Kounin wrote:

> The unexpected fact (that successful teachers prevent misbehavior) required unlearning on my part, in the sense of having to replace the original question by other questions. Questions about disciplinary techniques were eliminated and replaced by questions about classroom management; preventing misbehavior was given investigative priority. (p. 143)

The answer to Kounin's new research was that effective teachers prevent student misbehavior by eliciting high levels of student academic engagement that result in low levels of problem behaviors. Kounin also found that a number of key behaviors distinguished effective from less effective classroom managers. Interestingly, Kounin found that the teacher behaviors that led to high rates of work involvement and low rates of misbehavior among the students in the classes he observed were equally effective for students with serious problem behavior. From his investigative work, Kounin identified a number of effective teacher behaviors. He described these teacher behaviors as withitness, overlapping, and instruction.

WITHITNESS   Withitness was Kounin's term (Kounin, 1970) for the manner in which the most effective classroom managers monitor their students. He defined withitness as "a teacher's communicating to the children by her actual behavior (rather than by simple verbal announcing: *I know what is going on*) that she knows what the children are doing, or has the proverbial eyes in the back of her head" (pp. 80–81). Teachers exhibit withitness when their behavior communicates to their students that they are aware of all events going on within the classroom. According to Kounin, teachers need to constantly watch their students to ensure that students are (a) staying on task, (b) participating in learning activities, (c) behaving appropriately, and (d) complying with classroom rules and procedures. When teachers do not monitor student behavior, inattention and misbehavior among their students may increase, and students may not get assistance on learning activities when they need it (Yell, Meadows, Drasgow, & Shriner, 2009). Moreover, Kounin found that teachers who displayed withitness had high rates of student involvement and lower rates of student misbehavior in their classrooms.

Kounin found that teachers demonstrate withitness in their classrooms when they deliver behavioral desists or commands (reprimands) for their students to stop misbehavior (see Chapter 7 for a discussion about turning reprimands into redirects). When inappropriate behaviors occur, teachers should stop the misbehavior before it becomes more serious or spreads to other students. Additionally, withitness is communicated when the teacher chooses to correct the student (or students) exhibiting the misbehavior. When two students are engaged in separate but simultaneous problematic behavior, withitness is communicated when the teacher stops the most serious problem first. Thus, communicating withitness involves addressing misbehavior quickly and accurately (i.e., targets the correct student or students). In Kounin's studies, withitness was significantly related to increased student engagement in academic activities and reduced inappropriate student behavior.

OVERLAPPING   Kounin identified another teacher behavior that the most effective classroom managers exhibited, which he called overlapping (Kounin, 1970). Overlapping was also significantly related to student engagement and reduced problem behavior. According to Kounin, teachers engage in overlapping when they are able to manage two or more matters at the same time. For example, a teacher may be working with a small group at a table while other students are working independently. A teacher would be exhibiting overlapping when, while continuing the small group work, he or she delivers a desist to a student working independently who might be off task or bothering other students.

Kounin found in his research that many situations occurred every day in which a teacher was confronted with situations that called for overlapping. He also found that teachers who frequently displayed overlapping behavior were more successful classroom managers. Thus, effective classroom managers can manage more than one thing at a time and address misbehavior without disrupting ongoing activities.

According to Kounin (1970), teachers who communicated withitness and overlapping seem to have "eyes in the back of their head" (p. 81). The most effective classroom managers, therefore, monitored their classrooms and were aware of what was going on at all times. Students of a withit teacher know that the teacher is able to detect misbehavior quickly and accurately.

INSTRUCTION   Kounin also found that the most effective classroom managers engaged in certain behaviors during instructional activities. These behaviors were highly correlated with high rates of student engagement and low rates of student misbehavior. First, effective managers were those who taught lessons smoothly. That is, teachers did not interrupt instruction with irrelevant information or allow themselves to be drawn off task, and they kept their lessons moving briskly. Kounin called these characteristics smoothness and momentum. Second, effective managers ensured their students were attending during lessons by holding the students accountable for what was being taught. Teachers did this by frequently asking questions, randomly asking students to recite, using choral responding, and circulating among students and checking on their progress and understanding during independent work. Third, group lessons and independent seatwork were varied, challenging, and interesting. Kounin referred to these behaviors as group alerting and accountability. (For elaborations on instruction and classroom management, see Chapter 6.)

Over the years, others have confirmed and added to Kounin's findings about what effective teachers do in their classrooms. Researchers such as Carolyn Evertson, Edmund Emmer, and Linda Anderson have also shown that teachers who approach classroom management as a systematic process of establishing and maintaining an effective learning environment can be successful teachers who can prevent many problematic student behaviors.

Evertson, Emmer, and Anderson's Research

In the late 1970s and early 1980s, Evertson and colleagues conducted a series of seminal studies in classroom management (cf. Anderson, Evertson, & Emmer, 1980; Emmer, Evertson, & Anderson, 1980; Evertson & Emmer, 1982; Sanford & Evertson, 1981). In these descriptive–correlational studies (not true experimental studies), the researchers observed teachers from the beginning of the school year until the third week of school. The purpose of their studies was to examine and describe how effective classroom managers begin the school year and to determine what behaviors and skills characterized their teaching. The results from their studies were informative and strongly supported the findings of Kounin. One investigation involved 27 teachers in eight elementary schools, and a second investigation involved 51 teachers in 11 junior high schools. These studies resulted in the identification of a number of effective teacher behaviors and skills in areas such as:

1. Being a classroom leader.
2. Beginning the school year right.
3. Establishing rules and procedures.
4. Monitoring student behavior.
5. Stopping inappropriate behavior.
6. Delivering effective instructional activities.

BEING A CLASSROOM LEADER   According to Emmer, Evertson, and Anderson (1980), "the more effective classroom managers clearly established themselves as the classroom leaders" (p. 225). This did not mean, however, that the more effective managers were more authoritarian than the less effective managers (see Chapter 2 for a comparison of teacher management styles). To the contrary, the researchers described them as having better affective skills and being better listeners. According to Brophy (2006), teachers should be friendly and personable rather than austere and authoritarian. They should, however, also be businesslike with their leadership and convey purposefulness so that students know clearly what is expected of them.

BEGINNING THE SCHOOL YEAR RIGHT   The most effective teachers paid careful attention to classroom management and described their system to the students as soon as they arrived on the first day of school. The effective managers used a variety of procedures to teach their classroom management system, including explanations, rehearsal, modeling, and signaling. Moreover, the effective managers spent considerable time during the first week in school reviewing and reminding students about how the class would operate.

ESTABLISHING RULES AND PROCEDURES   Both the effective and the less effective managers developed rules and procedures for their classrooms. The more effective managers, however, integrated their rules and procedures by actively and thoroughly teaching them to their students. The effective managers clearly informed students about what was expected of them through their rules and procedures. The less effective managers also had rules and some procedures, but these were vague, not well thought out, not well integrated into their overall classroom system, and not taught to students in a systematic manner.

MONITORING STUDENT BEHAVIOR   The more effective managers kept the students engaged and closely monitored their academic performance and behavior. Seating arrangements allowed the teachers to see their students at all times. The less effective managers did not monitor student behavior closely and, as a result, had higher incidences of problem behavior and lower rates of student academic engagement. In less effective classrooms, inappropriate behaviors were sometimes stopped but just as likely to be ignored.

Effective managers also paid careful attention to their students' academic progress by circulating among their students during seatwork activities and monitoring their work. According to Evertson and Emmer (1982), "the more effective teachers . . . effectively communicated the attitude or expectation that their class time was for work-relevant activity, that they were aware of what students were doing, and that students were accountable for their work" (p. 495).

STOPPING INAPPROPRIATE BEHAVIOR   When students engaged in problem behavior, effective managers stopped it promptly and efficiently. They did not ignore inappropriate behavior; rather, they intervened quickly and consistently to correct it. Effective classroom managers were also more likely to mention to students the rule that was violated and describe the more desirable behavior they expected.

In contrast, the less effective teachers failed to deliver consequences for inappropriate behavior. Often, they delivered a warning to misbehaving students but failed to follow through if the misbehavior continued, and they most often did not acknowledge appropriate student behavior. Evertson and Emmer (1982) noted that students of the less effective teachers would often push the limits and engage in problem behavior because of the lack of consistency and follow-through. The researchers stated that the classroom organization and management of less effective teachers was inadequate and, thus, ineffective because of deficiencies in their rules and procedures and that they did not closely monitor student behavior. Less effective teachers were not vigilant and did not follow through consistently with misbehavior; thus, the unwanted behavior occurred with greater and greater frequency. In addition, difficulties in classroom management by less effective managers also resulted in instructional problems.

DELIVERING EFFECTIVE INSTRUCTIONAL ACTIVITIES   The more effective managers were judged to have better-organized instructional activities and to have effective time management. Transitions into new activities were smoother and shorter than those in the classrooms of less effective managers, and when students finished an academic task, effective teachers had other tasks to keep their students actively engaged. The effective managers also held students accountable for their work, monitoring frequently their progress on assignments. Essentially, little time was lost in the classrooms of the more effective managers.

Interestingly, the researchers found that effective classroom organization and management during the year could be predicted from the first several weeks of school. They stated further that the characteristics and behaviors that discriminated best between the most and the least effective managers were:

1. Quality of leadership, including credibility and predictability.
2. A workable set of rules and procedures taught to students during the first weeks of school.
3. Careful and consistent monitoring of student behavior.
4. Quick detection of misbehavior, and stopping it quickly.
5. Clear and consistently enforced consequences for appropriate and inappropriate behavior.

While Evertson and colleagues extended their research to provide professional development of teachers on becoming effective classroom managers, other researchers investigated various aspects of management, such as effective instruction and transitions.

Still More Prevention Research

The findings of these early classroom studies by Evertson, Emmer, and Anderson were a prelude to other investigations of classroom management. Doyle (1984) investigated how the most effective classroom managers planned and delivered academic instruction. He observed and described instruction in seven English classes in several junior high schools. Doyle found that the most effective classroom managers:

1. Taught lessons that filled the entire instructional period or went beyond it, and if not finished, students took work home to complete.
2. Gave clear directions so that students knew exactly what was expected of them.
3. Orchestrated smooth and efficient transitions between activities.
4. Demonstrated situational awareness by attending closely to the class (i.e., withitness).
5. Taught routines and were careful not to disrupt the rhythm and flow of events in the classroom.

Doyle's work confirmed that of Evertson and colleagues finding that the most effective managers established an effective classroom management system within the first month of the school year. Less effective managers often overestimated the amount of time a lesson or activity would take, thus making some class time unproductive. What is clear from these studies is that good planning, brisk pacing, smooth lessons, and interesting and worthwhile activities will prevent many behavior problems.

Evertson and colleagues (e.g., Evertson, 1985; Evertson, Emmer, Sanford, & Clements, 1983) used what they found from their classroom management studies to inform their professional development activities. What Evertson and others believed was that effective classroom management could be taught. Thus, they developed a program that prepared teachers to plan an effective classroom management system before the beginning of the school year by:

1. Arranging classroom space and supplies.
2. Choosing rules and procedures and teaching them to students.
3. Developing procedures for managing student work.
4. Establishing consequences and incentives.
5. Choosing activities for the beginning of the school year.
6. Establishing a focus for instruction and communicating expectations.
7. Maintaining the management system throughout the school year by monitoring student behavior and academic work, modeling and reinforcing appropriate behavior, and intervening to stop student misbehavior.

Their investigations revealed that teachers could learn and implement these strategies and procedures, thereby increasing student engagement and preventing student misbehaviors in their classrooms.

THE U.S. DEPARTMENT OF EDUCATION'S FOCUS ON PREVENTIVE CLASSROOM MANAGEMENT

In the Education Sciences Reform Act of 2002, the U.S. Congress created the Institute of Education Sciences (IES) in the U.S. Department of Education. The mission of the IES is to produce rigorous and relevant evidence to provide a foundation for educational practice and policy and to disseminate this information to the field. Specifically, the IES provides information on what works in education and what does not. The ultimate goal of the IES is to improve educational outcomes for all students. (For more information on the IES, see http://ies.ed.gov.)

One method that the IES uses to disseminate information on evidence-based educational interventions and strategies is the What Works Clearinghouse (WWC). The purpose of the WWC is to provide educators, researchers, policy makers, and the public with a central database of scientific evidence of what works in education. The WWC publishes practice guides to inform educators on the best evidence in a variety of instructional and behavioral areas. In 2008, the WWC released a practice guide on reducing behavior problems in the elementary classroom (Epstein, Atkins, Cullinan, Kutash, & Weaver, 2008). (For more information on the WWC, visit http://ies.ed.gov/ncee/wwc/. The WWC practice guides can be downloaded from http://ies.ed.gov/ncee/wwc/publications/practiceguides/.)

According to Epstein and colleagues (2008), the guide was intended to "help elementary school educators as well as school and district administrators to develop and implement effective prevention and intervention strategies that promote positive student behavior" (p. 1). Epstein and colleagues offered five specific recommendations and ways in which each recommendation could be implemented:

Recommendation 1: Identify the specifics of the problem behavior and the conditions that prompt and reinforce it.

Recommendation 2: Modify the classroom learning environment to decrease problem behavior.

Recommendation 3: Teach and reinforce new skills to increase appropriate behavior and preserve a positive classroom climate.

Recommendation 4: Draw on relationships with professional colleagues and students' families for continued guidance and support.

Recommendation 5: Assess whether schoolwide behavior problems warrant adopting schoolwide strategies or programs and, if so, implement ones shown to reduce negative and foster positive interactions.

Epstein and colleagues noted that recommendations 2 and 3 have strong research support, such as several well-designed, randomized control trials that supported the efficacy of these measures, and that recommendations 1, 4, and 5 have moderate support through correlational research.

In this, book we concentrate on recommendations 2 (modify the classroom learning environment) and 3 (teach and reinforce new skills). Many of the studies reviewed by Epstein and colleagues demonstrated the prevention of problem behaviors by altering or removing the factors that triggered their occurrence. According to the researchers, teachers can reduce the occurrence of problem behaviors by teaching and reinforcing classroom behavior expectations; rearranging the classroom environment, class schedule, and activities to meet students' needs; and promoting high rates of student engagement and on-task behavior. Moreover, the research studies showed that successful teachers implemented classroom management approaches in which they (a) establish an orderly and positive classroom environment, (b) teach rules and routines, and (c) provide a variety of interesting materials and activities at the appropriate level of difficulty.

Epstein and colleagues recommended that teachers actively instruct students in socially acceptable and appropriate behaviors. Further, teachers should maintain a classroom climate in which appropriate behaviors are acknowledged and reinforced. It is apparent from the work of Epstein and colleagues for the WWC that proactive classroom management as a means of preventing student problem behavior has strong research support. Thus, classroom management can be implemented as an evidence-based practice.

SUMMARY OF PREVENTION RESEARCH

The major goal of classroom management is to establish a climate that can prevent student behavior problems and be conducive to learning (Good & Brophy, 2008). Teachers can use the principles derived from the classroom research of investigators such as Kounin, Evertson, Emmer, and Anderson to set up an effective classroom management system that prevents student misbehavior, thus allowing more academic instruction. Ineffective classroom management often leads to student disruption and misbehavior, which impedes learning. Thus, the key to effective classroom management lies in preventing misbehavior and increasing student involvement and engagement in learning activities (Brophy, 1982). Teachers can incorporate a number of strategies from the classroom management research to prevent problem behaviors in the classroom.

CREATING AND MAINTAINING PROACTIVE CLASSROOMS

Teachers who use proactive classroom management strategies have fewer disruptions and management problems, more time for teaching, and high student achievement (Good & Brophy, 2008). The research of Kounin, Brophy, Evertson, Emmer, and others demonstrates that teachers can become competent classroom managers by systematically using certain principles in setting up their classrooms and interacting with their students. Evertson and colleagues extended their research to training teachers to become effective classroom managers (Evertson, 1985; Evertson et al., 1983). These researchers developed manuals that taught teachers effective classroom management procedures derived from their research findings and the findings of others. The results of their research showed clearly that teachers could learn effective management procedures and, when applied in their classrooms, that effective management could prevent disruptions and increase student engagement in academic activities (Brophy, 2006; Evertson & Harris, 1999).

Unfortunately, many teachers do not use the long list of what is known to create and maintain conducive learning environments. Often, a teacher's approach to classroom management is neither systematic nor based on what is known to be effective but, rather, is based more on untested theories or personal advice about "what works best for me" (Yell et al., 2009). Most of these untested theories and advice are not based on empirical evidence but on idiosyncratic personal experience. Effective classroom management, however, is not achieved through adherence to simple bromides, gimmicks, or a bag of tricks. There is no cookbook of techniques, special formulas, or management packages that fit all circumstances and situations. Rather, teachers become effective managers by understanding and developing personal management systems based on sound principles and guidelines supported by empirical evidence and information.

We believe, and researchers have confirmed, that three important prerequisites are needed to establish successful classroom management systems. These prerequisites involve behaviors and skills that teachers must exhibit in classrooms to create climates characterized by high rates of student engagement and low rates of student disruption. Specifically, these are the ability to:

1. Prevent problem behavior through creating a positive and structured classroom environment, maintaining positive student–teacher relationships, and being an effective teacher.
2. Respond to problem behaviors when they occur in a fair, consistent, and calm manner.
3. Intervene with students using both group and individual interventions, with the ultimate goal of teaching students to manage their own behavior, to be problem solvers, and to make wise behavioral choices.

The first prerequisite to a successful classroom management system is setting up a positive and structured classroom environment. As Kounin pointed out, teachers who are successful classroom managers prevent problem behaviors from occurring rather than merely reacting to problems that have already occurred. In a positive and structured classroom, teachers collaborate with their students to develop rules and procedures that everyone understands and follows. Moreover, teachers work to establish positive student–teacher relationships, which include modeling appropriate behavior, communicating positive expectations, and praising appropriate student behavior. Finally, because academics and behaviors are intertwined, the teacher must understand and follow the principles of effective teaching. For example, if a teacher does not develop lessons at an appropriate level of difficulty or wastes instructional time in transitioning between activities, the teacher may expect that problem behaviors will occur.

Successful classroom management systems also allow teachers to intervene with students who consistently exhibit problem behavior. These may include interventions with an entire group of students, such as a group contingency, or an intervention with an individual student, such as a behavioral contract (see Chapter 7). The ultimate goal of such interventions is to teach students to manage their own behavior, make wise behavioral choices, and solve their own problems.

Effective classroom management is not a mysterious art that some teachers possess and other teachers do not. Teachers are not born with the ability to control student behavior, and effective classroom management is not an accident. To be an effective classroom manager requires that teachers understand and practice a specific set of strategies and procedures that result in high rates of student engagement and learning and low rates of student misbehavior. Successful classroom management requires that teachers be able to (a) prevent problem behaviors, (b) respond appropriately to problems behaviors, and (c) intervene to reduce problem behaviors and teach socially appropriate behaviors. In the following chapters, we examine systematically the procedures necessary to become an effective classroom manager who understands how to prevent student behavior problems and be a great teacher.

Summary

The ability to manage student behavior in the classroom is not an art, possessed only by the fortunate few. Rather, it is a set of skills that can be learned and, if implemented with consistency, will result in an organized and efficient learning environment. Research by Kounin, Evertson, Emmer, and others have provided the teaching profession with clear principles to follow in organizing classrooms and preventing misbehavior. If applied systematically, these principles will enable teachers to establish their classrooms as effective learning environments with high rates of student engagement and low rates of student misbehavior (Brophy 2006). Brophy (1982) aptly summarized the principles of preventive classroom management derived from the research:

1. Teachers must be the authority figure and instructional leader in their classroom.
2. Good classroom management implies good instruction.
3. In addition to being effective, good classroom management strategies are cost-effective, because they allow the teacher to teach and students to learn.

Teachers and their students benefit greatly from the well-organized and managed classrooms that adhere to these principles.

Our purpose in this book is to help teachers develop philosophies, behaviors, and systematic classroom management plans based on the foundation of prevention. In Chapters 2 and 3, we explore how to create a positive classroom environment and provide classroom structure and organization to prevent behavior problems. In Chapter 4, we discuss the importance of teacher–student relationships in the classroom and how quality relationships can prevent behavior problems. In Chapters 5 and 6, we examine how morning meetings and effective instruction can minimize and prevent unwanted and inappropriate student behavior. In Chapter 7, we describe a number of prevention and intervention techniques aimed at problematic behaviors. Despite having an excellent preventive classroom management system, however, students will still exhibit problem behaviors; thus, in Chapter 8, we describe how best to respond to problem behaviors, including specific techniques to help teachers address appropriately and intervene effectively when those inevitable problem behaviors occur. In Chapter 9, we examine how teachers can help students learn to make wise behavioral choices. Finally, in Chapter 10, we put all the research-based classroom management information together to assist teachers in developing a coherent and systematic approach to prevent inappropriate student behavior in today's classrooms, and we describe potential future directions in education and behavior management.

References

Anderson, L. M., Evertson, C. M., & Emmer, E. T. (1980). Dimensions in classroom management derived from recent research. *Journal of Curriculum Studies, 12*, 343–356.

Bagley, W. C. (1907). *Classroom management: Its principles and techniques.* New York: Macmillan.

Billingsley, B. (2003). *Special education teacher retention and attrition: A critical analysis of the literature* (COPSSE Document RS-2). Gainesville: University of Florida, Center on Personnel Studies in Special Education.

Bohn, C. M., Roehrig, A. D., & Pressley, M. (2004). The first days of school in effective and less effective primary-grades classrooms. *Elementary School Journal, 104,* 269–287.

Brock, B., & Grady, M. (1997). *From first-year to first-rate: Principals guiding teachers.* Thousand Oaks, CA: Corwin Press.

Brophy, J. E. (1982). Classroom organization and management. *The Elementary School Journal 83,* 264–285.

Brophy, J. E. (2006). History of research on classroom management. In C. Evertson & C. Weinstein (Eds.), *Handbook of classroom management: Research, practice, and contemporary issues* (pp. 17–46). Mahwah, NJ: Lawrence Erlbaum.

Bushaw, W. J., & Gallup, A. M. (2008). *The 40th annual Phi Delta Kappa/Gallup Poll of the public's attitudes toward the public schools.* Bloomington, IN: Phi Delta Kappa International.

Cameron, C. E., Connor, C. M., & Morrison, F. J. (2005). Effects of variation in teacher organization on classroom functioning. *Journal of School Psychology, 43,* 61–85.

Doyle, W. (1984). How order is achieved in classrooms: An interim report. *Journal of Curriculum Studies, 16,* 259–277.

Education Sciences Reform Act, 20 U.S.C § 9510 *et seq.*

Elementary and Secondary Education Act, 20 U.S.C. § 16301 *et seq.*

Emmer, E. T., Evertson, C., & Anderson, L. (1980). Effective classroom management at the beginning of the school year. *Elementary School Journal, 80,* 219–231.

Emmer, E. T., & Stough, L. M. (2001). Classroom management: A critical part of educational psychology, with implications for teacher education. *Educational Psychologist, 36,* 103–112.

Epstein, M., Atkins, M., Cullinan, D., Kutash, K., & Weaver, R. (2008). *Reducing behavior problems in the elementary school classroom: A practice guide* (NCEE #2008-012). Washington, DC: National Center for Education Evaluation and Regional Assistance, Institute of Education Sciences, U.S. Department of Education.

Evertson, C. (1985). Training teachers in classroom management: An experimental study in secondary classrooms. *Journal of Education Research, 79,* 51–58.

Evertson, C., & Emmer, E. (1982). Effective classroom management at the beginning of the school year in junior high classes. *Journal of Educational Psychology, 74,* 485–498.

Evertson, C., & Emmer, E. (2009). *Classroom management for elementary teachers.* Upper Saddle River, NJ: Pearson/Merrill Education.

Evertson, C. M., Emmer, E. T., Sanford, J. P., & Clements, B. S. (1983). Improving classroom management: An experiment in elementary classrooms. *Elementary School Journal, 84,* 173–188.

Evertson, C., & Harris, S. (1999). Support for managing learning-centered classrooms: The classroom organization and management program. In H. J. Frieberg (Ed.), *Beyond behaviorism: Changing the classroom management paradigm* (pp. 59–74). Boston: Allyn & Bacon.

Evertson, C., & Weinstein, C. (Eds.) (2006). *Handbook of classroom management: Research, practice, and contemporary issues.* Mahwah, NJ: Lawrence Erlbaum.

Fideler, E., & Haskelhorn, D. (1999). *Learning the ropes: Urban teacher induction programs and practices in the United States.* Belmont, MA: Recruiting New Teachers.

Gallup, G. H. (1983). The 15th annual Phi Delta Kappa/Gallup Poll of the public's attitude toward the public schools. *Phi Delta Kappan, 65,* 33–47.

Good, T. L., & Brophy, J. E. (2008). *Looking in classrooms* (10th ed.). Upper Saddle River, NJ: Pearson/Merrill Education.

Herbert, E., & Worthy, T. (2001). Does the first year of teaching have to be a bad one? A case study of success. *Teaching and Teacher Education, 17,* 897–911.

Individuals with Disabilities Education Improvement Act, 20 U.S.C. § 1400 *et seq.*

Ingersoll, R. M. (2001). *Teacher turnover, teacher shortages, and the organization of schools* (Document R-01-1). Seattle: University of Washington, Center for the Study of Teaching and Policy.

Ingersoll, R., & Smith, T. (2003). The wrong solution to the teacher shortage. *Educational Leadership, 60,* 30–33.

Jacques, K. (2000). Solicitous tenderness: Discipline and responsibility in the classroom. In H. Cooper & R. Hyland (Eds.), *Children's perceptions of learning with trainee teachers* (pp. 166–177). London: Routledge.

Johnson, J. (2004). *Teaching interrupted: Do discipline policies in today's public schools foster the common good?* New York: Public Agenda.

Johnson, J., Rochkind, J., & Ott, A. (2010). *Bullying omnibus survey: Nearly three in four Americans say bullying is a serious problem in their local schools.* New York: Public Agenda.

Jones, V. (2006). How do teachers learn to be effective classroom managers? In C. Evertson & C. Weinstein (Eds.), *Handbook of classroom management: Research, practice, and contemporary issues* (pp. 887–907). Mahwah, NJ: Lawrence Erlbaum.

Kilgore, K. L., Griffin, C. C., Otis-Wilborn, A., & Winn, J. (2003). The problems of beginning special education teachers: Exploring the contextual factors influencing their work. *Action in Teacher Education, 25*(1), 38–47.

Kounin, J. S. (1970). *Discipline and group management in classrooms.* Austin, TX: Holt, Rinehart, & Winston.

Ladd, K. (2000). A comparison of teacher education programs and graduate's perceptions of experiences. *Dissertation Abstracts International, 61*(12A), 4695.

Lytle, J. (2000). Teacher education at the millennium: A view from the cafeteria. *Journal of Teacher Education, 51,* 174–179.

Marzano, R. J., Marzano, J. S., & Pickering. D. J. (2003). *Classroom management that works: Research-based strategies for every teacher.* Alexandria, VA: Association for Supervision & Curriculum Development.

McCormack, A. (2001). Investigating the impact of internship on the classroom management beliefs of preservice teachers. *The Professional Educator, 23,* 11–22.

Meister, D., & Jenks, C. (2000). Making the transition from preservice to inservice teaching: Beginning teachers' reflections. *Action in Teacher Education, 23*(3), 1–11.

Pilarsky, M. J. (1994). Student teachers: Unprepared for classroom management? *Teaching Education, 6,* 77–80.

Sanford, J. P., & Evertson, C. M. (1981). Classroom management in a low SES junior high: Three case studies. *Journal of Teacher Education, 32,* 34–38.

Yell, M. L. (2006). *The law and special education* (2nd ed.). Upper Saddle River, NJ: Pearson/Merrill Education.

Yell, M. L., Meadows, N. B., Drasgow, E., & Shriner, J. G. (2009). *Evidence-based practices for educating students with emotional and behavioral disorders.* Upper Saddle River, NJ: Pearson/Merrill Education.

Creating a Positive Classroom Environment

with T. Rowand Robinson

GOALS

- Explain the purpose for developing a positive classroom environment, including associated benefits.

- Differentiate between a positive classroom approach and one designed using a culture of punishment.

- Compare and contrast discipline of students in the classroom and punishment for aberrant behavior.

- Compare and contrast management styles that inhibit or promote the prevention of behavior problems.

- Describe the teaching philosophy that supports proactive approaches.

SCENARIO
Lower Elementary

A "tight ship" is one way to describe how Ms. Gonzalez runs her third-grade classroom. After the bell rings, students are to put away their belongings, grab their chairs, and sit in a circle in the back of the classroom. Most days, however, the students do not comply as fast as Ms. Gonzalez would like. On one particular day, instead of moving their chairs to the back of the room, Samuel and Juan were chasing each other around the classroom. Maria, Colleen, and Chanel were sitting at a table together trading items from their lunchboxes, and only three students actually followed the directions and made it to the back of the classroom. In her usual fashion, Ms. Gonzalez yells, *Samuel and Juan, next door to Mr. Riley's class NOW. We will have this meeting during recess for the rest of the week until you can get it right!* Once everyone was in a circle, Colleen talked about her project idea, and James said, *That sounds like someone stupid came up with that idea.* Colleen and her friends yelled back at James, and Ms. Gonzalez said sternly, *That is enough! James, put your name on the board, and if you do it again, I am calling your mother.* Later on, Ms. Gonzalez kept a student in the room to eat his lunch so that he could write sentences for not walking in line correctly, and Rebecca had to stand in front of the class and apologize to everyone for kicking Nesha under the table and wasting time.

Upper Elementary

Mr. Wordsworth has been teaching fifth-grade art for seven years. He is feared by all the fifth graders, who think he is mean, and they make fun of him outside of class. On many occasions throughout the semester, Mr. Wordsworth allows his students to work on their projects while he reads the newspaper at his desk. After a couple minutes on one such afternoon, his students were not engaged, and most were talking to one another. Martha was brushing her hair, Ahmad was rummaging through his backpack, and Jelani was even making a paper airplane at his seat. Mr. Wordsworth picked up his ruler and slammed it on his desk. Then he got out of his seat and picked up Martha's hairbrush, zipped up Ahmad's backpack, and finally ripped Jelani's airplane into little pieces in front of the whole class. Using a stern face, Mr. Wordsworth said, *Jelani, you're no aeronautical engineer—not by a long shot, and Martha, what are you, a beauty queen? The three of you can now make your way to the front office since you don't know how to stay busy.* Turning around to the rest of the class, he said, *Don't mess with me today. I am not in the mood. Let's get started.* Ten minutes into class, Mr. Wordsworth noticed that his students were all staring off into space. *Okay,* he said, *I've had it with this class. I'm sick of wasting my time!*

POSITIVE CLASSROOM ENVIRONMENT

Ms. Gonzalez and Mr. Wordsworth are not good examples of teachers who know how to manage their classroom environment in a positive manner. Approaching the management of student behavior using punitive and reactionary measures such as yelling, taking away recess, intimidation, threatening, and using humiliation do not ensure a well-run classroom. In fact, the behaviors they want to reduce, including noncompliance, disrespect, and general inattention, likely are going to continue throughout the year. Without some change, both teachers will continue to think they need to be more stern, intimidating, and loud and to use even more punishment to manage their students' behavior. That change could happen, but not without pointing out some fundamental ingredients they would need to recreate their classroom environments to result in a more positive community of students and a more positive approach to teaching.

In Chapter 5, we explore class meetings as a way to create and promote classroom community, and we describe how building a true community of learners is foundational to creating a positive classroom environment and for effective classroom management. Part of creating a positive classroom environment is the use of meetings, such as a morning meeting in the elementary setting, but there is much more. As with building a community of learners, a positive teaching environment is created when there is an obvious attempt to create well-designed learning activities and the prominent promotion of positive interaction among students and teachers (see also Chapter 4). The prominent promotion of positivity in a classroom should be a deliberate effort by everyone. Cooperation, collaboration, and learned independence in a classroom can lead to a student's intellectual, social, and moral/ethical development.

In almost all ways, the classroom is truly a teacher's territory and sphere of influence. Teachers, through thoughtful and deliberate planning, can organize, maintain, and monitor their classroom environment to facilitate learning. What is more difficult, and what can consume the instructional time available, as well as a teacher's emotional capacity, is managing aberrant student behavior. For any teacher, managing problematic student behavior, while at the same time maintaining a positive classroom environment, can be one of the most difficult tasks in education.

Our operating assumption in this book is that all teachers want to be positive in their relationships with their students and to have a classroom environment described by others as a positive classroom culture. We presume that all teachers, even ones like Ms. Gonzalez and Mr. Wordsworth, want to promote respect and fairness and to make their students feel welcomed every morning when they arrive in the classroom and valued and successful when they leave each day. Yet creating and maintaining a positive classroom environment as a way to prevent problem behaviors is complex, because students, perhaps more now than in times past, bring a host of complicated issues to school. Students can come from home environments where the necessary social skills for interacting appropriately in school are not taught or supported. Over time, they are increasingly exposed to violence through the media and have to successfully navigate through an ever-evolving society which, without adequate adult supervision, is increasingly difficult. In schools, there are the problems of teasing and bullying, and the advent of social media has expanded these negative situations beyond school borders. Negative issues and situations that students sometimes face can create stress and interfere with a teacher's ability to create a positive classroom environment. Even with these challenges, however, the number-one priority for teachers should be to create a positive classroom environment where they ground their actions within a solid foundation of care and concern. When students see that their teachers treat them with kindness and respect, they will perceive their teachers' action in response to their behavior as fair and in the best interest of the entire class. Students will view their teachers as working with them to be successful rather than as opponents and working against them.

Without a thoughtful, deliberate, and conscious plan for organizing, maintaining, and monitoring the classroom climate to promote a positive environment, it can become easy for teachers to fall back on negative techniques for managing behavior, such as:

1. Yelling at and arguing with students.
2. Creating power struggles, with winners and losers as the outcome.
3. Using confrontation and punishing students as the sole means of managing behavior.
4. Making disapproving comments to students for everyone in the class to hear.
5. Asking students why they act out.
6. Comparing the behavior of some students to the behavior of others.
7. Making unrealistic threats and publicly humiliating students through ridicule and sarcasm.

Obviously, these negative techniques are counterproductive to creating a positive classroom environment.

According to Childre, Sands, and Pope (2009), creating a positive classroom environment that addresses numerous student needs leads to (a) increased student learning, (b) lower levels of teacher stress and burnout, (c) increased interest in the material, and (d) fewer behavior problems. Strategies to create positive classroom environments should include proactive approaches that are designed to allow students the ability to take on much of the responsibility associated with controlling their own behavior.

Numerous specific techniques and strategies are presented throughout this book, and when put together as a philosophy of practice, they can create the positive classroom where preventing behavior problems becomes a teacher's primary focus. In this chapter on creating a positive environment to prevent behavior problems in the classroom, we describe a number of essential ingredients that, in combination with the practical ideas presented in other chapters, can and will prevent many behavior problems from happening.

First, we explore the culture of punishment that seems, even today, to permeate classroom behavior management systems. By examining the culture of punishment, we can demonstrate how a more positive approach to managing student behavior is in stark contrast to being retaliatory, unpleasant, hostile, and punitive when students behave in negative ways. Second, because discipline and punishment are sometimes considered to be synonymous, we explore what discipline really is and how the approach to disciplining students fits with creating a positive classroom environment. Third, we compare and contrast a number of classroom management styles, and finally, we explain how developing a teaching philosophy that supports proactive approaches can become a way of putting positive teaching approaches into action in the classroom.

CULTURE OF PUNISHMENT

Unfortunately, many informal approaches to behavior management are predicated on punishing students for their misbehavior (Vought, 1984). As we explain in Chapter 8, this type of approach to behavior management is reactionary and can actually have a reinforcing property for teachers and, sometimes, students. History is replete with examples that indicate the ineffectiveness of a punitive approach, such as the reform school movement in the late 1800s and early 1900s. In the 1970 book *Children and Youth in America: A Documentary History*, Robert Bremner provides a detailed account of the reform school movement for youth, mostly boys, who were incarcerated for being involved in a criminal act. During that period, Bremner explains, there was a slow transformation from boys being sent to reformatories "ragged, filthy, and in irons" (p. 467) to believing that kindness is a more effective means of reforming boys than punishment, that "no boy can be reformed without winning his confidence, and that [confidence] cannot be won by harsh treatment of force" (p. 468). It was the case, however, that in some institutions, this transformation was stubbornly slow, because there was a sense that punishment had to be "well known to the inmates. The law of punishment is a terror to evil-doers, and, properly used, is an accepted element of power in the discipline of the institution" (p. 468).

In schools, punishing student behavior as a way to maintain order in the classroom (often referred to as disciplining students or maintaining discipline) started when the first schools were established in the United States. As early as the 1600s, Massachusetts established a school system and included the ability for schoolmasters to punish students as necessary. Thus, many students were subjected to harsh punishments for a variety of infractions. Bremner (1970) provides an account from that time centered on a male student who disrupted class so much that it negatively affected his classmates' opportunity to learn. The schoolmaster told the student that he would be severely disciplined (i.e., beaten) every time a peer failed to respond or complete a lesson because of his disrupting behavior. Unfortunately, one classmate refused to open his book, because he wanted to see his disruptive peer receive a beating. After the first "drubbing," the student never appeared in school again.

Practices such as subjecting students to ridicule by forcing a child to wear a dunce cap, having a child sit alone in the corner away from instruction, or even beating a child with a cane for some infraction (i.e., corporal punishment) were not unusual during early schooling in America. Having a student remain after school to write sentence after sentence for some rule-breaking behavior was another common method. Bremner (1970) includes an account of a high school classroom that writer Randolph Bourne observed in 1914. Bourne remarked about the sterile environment and described the student's attitude as a "delightful one of all making the best of a bad bargain, and cooperating loyally with him [the teacher] in slowly putting the hour out of its misery" (p. 1120). Bourne went on to describe the "good" students and the "bad" students, with one account of a bad student whose behavior was "assertion against a stupid authority, a sort of blind resistance against the attempt of the schoolroom to impersonalize him" (p. 1120). Finally, Bourne concluded:

> But has there ever been devised a more ingenious enemy . . . than the modern classroom, catching as it does, the child in his most impressionable years? The two great enemies of [social learning] are bumptiousness and diffidence, and the classroom is perhaps the most successful instrument yet devised for cultivating both of them. (p. 1120)

As the viewpoint evolved that education served an important public role, laws were enacted that mandated attendance. For example, in the 1830s, truancy from school in the Boston area was identified as a criminal offense, and students who were detained for not being in school were often removed from their parents and placed in institutional settings. In Boston, officials established the School of Reformation, which according to Holloran (1989) ultimately led to the development of juvenile detention centers for thieves, pickpockets, and truants (i.e., street urchins). Of course, such settings often failed to adequately educate the youth of the day and resulted in the acquisition of unsavory behaviors that communities sought to avoid.

It would be unfair to portray the history of American education and its approach to managing behavior as all reactionary, punitive, and austere. Bremner (1970), for example, also provides accounts showing great awareness of how to prevent and intervene, when needed, with a moral and benevolent approach, which were steps toward "good teaching" rather than mere "school keeping" (p. 1133).

Even in current times, however, a variety of punishment procedures are used in schools in an attempt to stop problem behavior. Such procedures range from verbal reprimands (e.g., *I told you to stop talking, now sit and pay attention*) to corporal punishment (e.g., spanking, slapping) to expulsion from the school. Despite the belief that corporal punishment is no longer used in American public schools, only 30 states, Washington DC, and Puerto Rico have actually abolished it. In fact, according to Farrell (2009), corporal punishment continues to be a common practice in some states (e.g., Alabama, Arkansas, Mississippi) and is still used sporadically in others (e.g., Georgia, Louisiana, Oklahoma, Tennessee, Texas). Thus, in spite of mounting evidence that corporal punishments fail to teach appropriate behaviors and may actually provide models of inappropriate behavior, the practice is still used in many areas of the United States.

For some serious behavioral infractions, especially in special education programs for students who exhibit emotional or behavioral disorders, national legislation is being considered to prevent restraint and seclusion of students in schools that trend toward abuse. Surprisingly, this is the first national effort to ensure the safety of students and those professionals who work with them. The legislation would prevent and reduce inappropriate restraint and seclusion by establishing minimum safety standards in schools. Needless to say, the types of punishment used in schools on a day-to-day basis are more benign than restraint and seclusion.

What this section on the culture of punishment shows is that in education, and with society in general, there is and has been, for a long time, a tension between using positive approaches (e.g., kindness, caring, prevention, reinforcement) and punishing aberrant student behavior, creating sometimes negative and unwelcoming classroom environments. For some teachers and administrators, disciplining students is often used synonymously with punishing students or getting strict to obtain the types of behaviors that they want students to exhibit.

In our experience visiting schools and conducting professional workshops, we often hear teachers and administrators talk about the need to set up a "good discipline" system in their classrooms and school. As the conversations sometimes unfold, they are often thinking about implementing a hierarchy of reactions to behavior, with an emphasis in the hierarchy on punishments designed to get the students' attention. We hear, too, that they want to make sure positive approaches are incorporated, but it is interesting to think carefully about "discipline" as an approach to preventing behavior problems. In our teaching of classroom and behavior management to undergraduate and graduate students at our respective universities, we talk about prevention of behavior problems first but, at the same time, describe how discipline and prevention go together when creating a positive classroom environment.

HOW PREVENTION AND DISCIPLINE IN THE CLASSROOM ARE RELATED

Prevention as a foundation for effectively managing behavior in the classroom and creating a positive classroom environment is intertwined with a teacher's attempt to discipline students during the school day. Unfortunately, discipline has taken on such a negative connotation that it evokes visions of adults who react to student behavior by yelling and scolding, writing names on the board, taking away privileges, and sending them to time out. It is our belief that, because of the long-standing culture of punishment, discipline *can* mean punishing, reprimanding, or penalizing a student but *actually* means much more.

According to the *New Oxford American Dictionary* (Lindberg, 2008), "discipline" is the practice of training people to obey rules or a code of behavior, and the *Oxford American Writer's Thesaurus* (Stevenson & Lindberg, 2010) uses words such as "training," "teaching," "instruction," "regulation," and "direction" as synonyms for discipline. According to these definitions, discipline does not necessarily refer to reactive methods to punish students for inappropriate behavior.

To show how teachers sometimes misunderstand the true meaning of discipline, one elementary teacher, in response to questions about her definition of discipline, wrote:

> I think discipline requires a firm stance and authority. If students recognize you are in charge, they will listen. Sometimes it takes some yelling for students to listen but discipline doesn't have to be used on every student.

Another teacher wrote:

> *You have to be firm, and stay on top of them or they will walk all over you. Tough but fair.*
> *They are all sweet in their own way.*

Still another teacher, in her response, started out describing discipline as something positive and necessary, then proceeded to describe a more negative portrayal of punishing students if their behavior becomes unacceptable:

> *Discipline is an atmosphere of respect in the classroom. It is indescribably vital in a learn-*
> *ing environment, because it is discipline that ensures that all my students are focused*
> *and distractions are minimal. One part of my discipline routine is our color system. The*
> *students start out the day with their names on green and if they have exceptional behavior,*
> *they will move to blue. If their behavior is unacceptable, they will move to yellow and then*
> *to red. Once they get to red, they receive a consequence, such as a note sent home to their*
> *parents or they have to walk the track at recess. The severity of the punishment is based on*
> *the severity of the action.*

One teacher described her card system being her definition of discipline:

> *Well, students have a green, yellow, orange, and red card. They begin on green each day*
> *and have to move their card if they do not follow directions. Red requires a call home; that*
> *does not happen very often. This system seems to work very well for me.*

Yet some teachers felt differently and talked in terms of how we have defined discipline as opportunities to learn and grow:

> *Discipline is setting limits, encouraging self-control, establishing a positive tone and cre-*
> *ating a comfortable working/learning environment.*

> *Discipline is something hard to do, but well worth getting in place, especially at the begin-*
> *ning of the school year. I don't mean being mean and making my students hate going to*
> *school. I mean setting up my room so that my students can learn from their mistakes without*
> *getting punished all the time, giving them skills and opportunities to learn how to control*
> *their own behavior. That is hard because I have to take time to teach "how to get along skills."*
> *I eventually want my kids to learn how to manage their own behavior, or at least get better*
> *at it, so I really try to think about discipline being a positive rather than a negative thing.*

Punishing students for unwanted behavior is often associated with discipline in schools, but views about discipline can vary. Ideas about discipline in the classroom and executing a discipline plan can differ based on the teacher, classroom, and age level. Teachers often view discipline, however, as being a classroom feature that limits how their students act and as a reactive approach to managing student actions. As shown in Table 2.1, however, discipline should encourage and permit behaviors and provide instruction and support for learning appropriate ways to interact with others. Providing discipline in the classroom should be a way to prevent problem behavior, and discipline should be a positive framework to allow students to learn and grow.

TABLE 2.1	Comparing Discipline and Punishment
Discipline	**Punishment**
Is teaching students to control their own behavior to maximize their learning opportunities.	Is a hierarchy of penalties from verbal reprimands to corporal punishment and expulsion to an alternative educational placement.
Includes proactive strategies to prevent inappropriate behavior in the classroom.	Includes reactive strategies when students exhibit inappropriate behavior.
Should encourage and permit behaviors while providing instruction and support to learn appropriate ways of interacting with others.	Limits student behavior through actions such as yelling, scolding, writing names on the board, taking away privileges, and time out.
Is intended to actively teach students to make good decisions about how to act in and out of the classroom.	Is intended to reduce the likelihood that maladaptive behavior will occur in the future.

Reacting to misbehaviors by using time out, scolding, taking away privileges, office referrals, and in-school/out-of-school suspension can have punishing effects if they reduce the future occurrence of maladaptive behavior, yet these actions may not line up automatically with what is really meant by disciplining students. Rather, discipline is instructive in nature, more interactive between the adult and the learner than merely punishing behaviors. There was certainly more punishment than true discipline in the two classroom examples of Ms. Gonzalez and Mr. Wordsworth at the beginning of this chapter.

The true purpose of discipline is to actively teach students to make good decisions about how to act in complex social environments, such as classrooms and schools. Accomplishing this can include the use of punishing behaviors, but it will also require other positive teacher actions. Active teaching to equip students with the skills to make reflective decisions about their actions is part of an environment where discipline is approached from a learning perspective. Throughout this book, we provide a number of practical and evidence-based strategies that teachers can use to help their students make good and thoughtful decisions about their behavior. Succinctly, and in its broadest interpretation, discipline is teaching students to control their own behavior to maximize their learning opportunities.

When teachers use appropriate disciplinary procedures, they should (a) model positive character traits, (b) actively and explicitly teach students self-respect and self-control, and (c) allow students to learn from their mistakes rather than always being punished for them. Appropriate discipline provides students with an opportunity to learn through instruction in much the same way as a teacher instructs students in academic areas. For example, for struggling academic learners, effective teachers would show patience in their planned instruction, present students with multiple opportunities to master essential learning constructs, and provide guidance in a safe and caring way. Similarly, disciplinary procedures should be designed using a positive approach to managing students' behavior that instructs them to approach situations in a deliberative way and teaches students to ultimately manage their own behavior.

> **Q:** *I must admit, I was one who thought discipline was getting tough on kids. I was one to think that kids would run all over you unless you had "discipline" in the classroom. You know, I subscribed to the "Don't smile till Halloween!" mantra. I am thinking differently about discipline now, but where do I start? How can I turn my attitude about disciplining students upside down?*
>
> **A:** First, effective and positive discipline in the classroom starts with having empathy and compassion for our students and providing an efficient and effective classroom structure. As educators, we need to develop genuine empathy and compassion for students to know about their struggles, understand their perspectives and their concerns, listen to what they are trying to say, and meet their needs. Structure is setting up guidelines and limits and being positive toward managing student behavior. With these ideas in mind, you will be well on your way to providing appropriate "discipline" for your students. Everything in this book can help you turn your idea about discipline of students "upside down" and prevent problem behavior in the classroom. If you put all the ingredients in this book together into a philosophy of practice, you will have achieved a broad perspective about discipline in that it helps, rather than hinders, a student's ability to learn and become successful.

CLASSROOM MANAGEMENT STYLES

There has been a long history of punishment in schools, along with efforts to reform schools to make them more humane, with caring teachers who considered "good teaching" as opposed to just "school keeping." We have explored how approaching discipline from a learning perspective relates to prevention of behavior problems in the classroom, but understanding a teacher's leadership style and how it contributes to group climate is an additional fundamental ingredient for a positive classroom environment.

As early as the 1940s, researchers such as Anderson and colleagues (Anderson & Brewer, 1945; Anderson, Brewer, & Reed, 1946) studied, through classroom observations, what they considered to be "dominating" and "leading" teachers and how those teachers affected group climate in the classroom. Anderson and colleagues believed that dominating teachers were unilateral decision makers and forceful, while leading teachers invited input and worked with, not against, students, resulting in positive social integration. They described this socially integrative behavior among teachers and students as being spontaneous, flexible, adaptive, objective, scientific, and cooperative. Dominating teacher behavior, in contrast, was viewed as stifling students, facilitating teacher dependency and rote conformity, promoting resistance to change, and consistent with bigotry and autocracy (Anderson & Brewer, 1945).

Other researchers over the years have identified specific leadership styles. These include laissez-faire, authoritarian, and authoritative. These teacher management styles are summarized in Table 2.2.

Laissez-Faire

A laissez-faire management style may be referred to as permissive, nondirective, or lenient (Hersey, Blanchard, & Johnson, 1996). For example, the students determine the rules (if there are rules that govern the classroom setting), the consequences associated

TABLE 2.2	Types of Management Styles		
Laissez-Faire	**Authoritarian**	**Authoritative**	
Is permissive, nondirective, or lenient.	Incorporates little input from students in the classroom.	Is a balanced approach.	
Is often thought of as "hands-off" management.	Reserves all the power and decision making for the teacher.	Incorporates a student-centered approach.	
Is characterized by:	Is characterized by:	Is characterized by:	
1. Students determining rules/consequences.	1. Students taking a passive role in making decisions in the classroom.	1. High expectations for maturity.	
2. Nonexistent standards or expectations for behavior.	2. Expected conformity to and compliance with rules/directions.	2. Open dialogue about behavioral issues.	
3. Lack of student responsibility for student actions.	3. A punitive environment in which little reasoning or explanation is given for rules or boundaries.	3. An encouraging environment for student independence with an equal amount of limits/controls on student actions.	

with infractions, and the changes that are made to the ecology of the learning atmosphere. This management style may be characterized as having few behavioral expectations for students. Teachers are involved with students, but they put in place few demands or controls to structure the classroom. Teachers who operate with a laissez-faire approach may not require their students to regulate themselves or behave appropriately. In a classic study, the results of which are still considered to be valid, Lewin, Lippitt, and White (1939) found that students in a laissez-faire classroom were confused, frustrated, and not productive and experienced difficulty negotiating tasks.

A laissez-faire approach would make some sense if the students were highly skilled, experienced, trustworthy, and had excellent motivation to do their school-related work successfully on their own. Under most circumstances, however, students are developmentally emerging learners, not necessarily highly skilled at their craft or highly experienced. Some students, but certainly not all, are highly motivated and trustworthy, but trustworthiness is not universal. Students in a laissez-faire environment may exhibit impulsive behaviors and experience lower levels of school achievement. Further, students in such an environment will probably avoid taking responsibility for their own actions and, when in trouble, may blame someone else, even if it was their own fault. A laissez-faire type of management system can impact peer relationships, because inadequate emotional regulation in the school setting makes students immature and impedes friendships. If the students fail to learn to control their own behavior and always expect to get their way, they are less likely to treat others with respect and only rarely will engage in the give-and-take required for healthy relationships and a positive classroom environment.

Authoritarian

An authoritarian management style incorporates little input from the students in the classroom, and the teacher has all the power and makes all the decisions. The students learn little from this management style, because they are not given the opportunity to actively participate in the process of making decisions in the classroom. Hersey and colleagues (1996) found this approach to classroom management as being strict and characterized by high expectations of conformity and compliance to rules and directions. Lewin and colleagues (1939) found that students in an authoritarian classroom were apathetic, frequently frustrated, and likely to be in conflict with others if the teacher was not present. Such an approach does not allow open dialogue between teacher and student.

An authoritarian approach is a restrictive, punitive style in which teachers exhort students to follow their directions and to respect them because of their position of authority. Authoritarian teachers expect much of their students in the classroom, but they fail to explain their reasoning for the rules or boundaries. They expect students to comply with their demands without question. This approach fails to increase student social competence, because the teacher generally dictates what students should do instead of allowing them to choose for themselves. A student from this environment is more likely to look to others to decide what is right and, thus, to lack social independence.

An authoritarian approach to structuring a classroom management system produces students who rely on others to make decisions for them. In authoritarian settings, students fail to acquire the skills to act independently on a regular basis. Over time, students need to learn the skills to guide their lives without outside assistance and to identify situations in which they need to turn to others for help. A collaborative approach to decision making is accomplished by structuring an authoritative, not an authoritarian, classroom, one that incorporates the opinions and desires of all the stakeholders associated with that specific environment.

Authoritative

An authoritative classroom management style may be referred to as balanced. It is characterized by a student-centered approach that holds high expectations of maturity and compliance to classroom rules and directions while allowing an open dialogue about behavioral issues (Hersey et al., 1996).

An authoritative classroom environment encourages students to be independent but still places limits and controls on their actions. A teacher who embraces this approach is rarely as controlling as a teacher in the authoritarian setting, allowing students to explore more freely and, thus, having them make their own decisions based upon their own reasoning. They set limits and demand maturity, but in terms of enforcing consequences, the teacher explains the reasons underlying specific outcomes so that students are aware of those consequences prior to their actions. Consequences in an authoritative environment are measured and consistent, not harsh or arbitrary.

This type of classroom environment sets clear standards for the students, monitors limits that are set, and allows students to develop autonomy. The setting is designed to elicit mature, independent, and age-appropriate behavior of children. Lewin and colleagues (1939) found that students in an authoritative classroom were more spontaneous in initiating and persisting in task completion. An authoritative classroom results in students having higher self-esteem and independence because of its democratic, give-and-take nature. This environment is conducive to academic achievement, and it fosters positive teacher-to-student and student-to-student relationships. This management style is most favorable for preparing students to become independent and contributing members of the classroom community.

As one teacher explained in reaction to a question about the types of management styles that teachers have:

> *In my school, we have teachers who are "old school" when it comes to student discipline . . . they yell, they scream, and they haul out the paddle (we still paddle at my school). Then we have the teachers who do not want to deal with it . . . they automatically send the student to the principal or assistant principal at the first sign of disobedience. Then there are those who just let their room run crazy and either (1) don't care or (2) don't have a clue what to do. If people knew about some better management styles, I bet they would think twice about what they do. Me, I would like to think that I fall into the authoritative type or maybe more democratic. I want my students to be independent but I still have to have limits, and they should know those. I try, as much as I can, to allow my students to make their own decisions, and I support them in that. I try also to have a positive approach to my teaching. Knowing this kind of information would be especially helpful for new teachers who are relatively unprepared and untrained for behavioral issues.*

Hopefully, it is apparent that the authoritative management style matches the goal of preventing problem behaviors in the classroom that we focus on in this book. A management system that is overly lenient and permissive and does not provide enough direction for student behavior, or one that positions students toward compliance with rigid rules and expectations of conformity through punitive means, weakens attempts to achieve the following goals:

- To ensure open dialogue with students.
- To establish clear standards for students.
- To set limits in the classroom that are reasonable and understood by all stakeholders.
- To create an environment for students to develop ever-increasing autonomy in their day-to-day activities.

As we have explored, a management style is the general approach a teacher uses to be a leader in the classroom. Like business managers, teachers are responsible for maximizing the output of the students in their classroom. Yet teachers are also responsible for individual students' academic, social, and emotional output, with an end product of success in school and life in general. From our examination of management styles, it seems that Ms. Gonzalez and Mr. Wordsworth each have a combination of laissez-faire and authoritarian, with neither management style facilitating the maximum student academic, social, or emotional output. For those teachers, understanding the types of management styles and what student behaviors they can produce might help them approach differently the way they manage their students in their classroom. Without also examining carefully their philosophical orientation to teaching, teachers cannot maximize an effective and efficient management style that will prevent behavior problems in the classroom.

> **Q:** *Is it the case that teachers exhibit one management style all the time, every day? Even knowing that an authoritative style would prevent problem behaviors the best, wouldn't teachers sometimes be a little laissez-faire and a little authoritarian?*
>
> **A:** In the business world, effective managers have different approaches based on their circumstances and opportunities to be proactive in response to unfolding events or demands. In a way, the same holds true for teachers and how they lead a classroom of learners. Purely authoritarian teachers are not good leaders, and students often react negatively to this type of approach. Because students are just learning to be adults, however, there are times when authority trumps collaboration, autonomy, and open dialogue, especially in situations where safety is an issue. In some situations, things in the classroom just have to be done, and there is little time for questioning the teacher's authority. And yes, teachers can be a little laissez-faire every once in a while!

TEACHING PHILOSOPHY

It seems that every teacher has a philosophy of teaching, but few are able to clearly and emphatically articulate what they believe. This is not surprising, because who has had the structured opportunity to think substantively and, perhaps, write down what he or she believes about their teaching? One university professor in education shares his teaching philosophy with his students during a conversation about teaching goals and values. His teaching philosophy is centered on a philosophical stance from a state teacher many years ago who reportedly said, *Formal teaching is a very small and inconsequential part of learning. In truth, people teach themselves.* This university professor goes on to say that he provides his students with content, expectations, guidance when needed, timelines, opportunities for discourse in class, formative and summative evaluations, and ongoing support, and that while he provides structure, he believes, or it is his philosophy, that his adult students really teach themselves. While this may apply to adults more than to younger learners, especially those in elementary school, it is an example of someone who is clear about what he believes in terms of teaching and learning. With a clearly understood teaching philosophy as a guiding foundation, teaching behaviors will most likely follow.

Understanding the importance of developing an explicit teaching philosophy is one of the foundational aspects of teaching and providing a positive learning environment. Being explicit about a teaching philosophy means:

- Understanding that teachers have an underlying theory, belief, or core value(s) about what engaging in the act of teaching is all about.
- Being open and unambiguous about what a teaching philosophy is.
- Articulating a set of ideas or beliefs about teaching.

In the above example of the university professor, there is most certainly an understanding of a core value or belief, and this professor has articulated a position about teaching in an open and unambiguous way.

In one of the undergraduate classes that we teach, there is an assignment for students to interview a teacher in their practicum setting about their teaching philosophy. This is an open-ended question, with no intent to define what a teaching philosophy may consist of, so the responses are varied. Interestingly, most teachers talk about their belief that all children can learn and be successful. For instance, one teacher wrote:

> My *teaching philosophy has always been that every student, regardless of where they come from, can learn. It is true that some have to work harder or receive more support because of their individual backgrounds, but they can still do it. They can still be great achievers. Because of the poverty level here at my school, there is a high mobility rate (students in and out of the school system frequently) among the students. As a consequence of this, I feel the constant need to adapt and modify the curriculum to fit all of my students' needs. It takes a lot of extra time and work on my end, but the results prove that it is working, so I keep doing it.*

Another teacher wrote:

> *All kids are capable of learning; we just have to look more at their progress. Kids learn at various paces, they don't all catch on at the same time. We should have high expectations for all of them. We should figure out which way they learn best and use it.*

Finally, another teacher wrote:

> *All students are unique individuals and in spite of the state and national legislative world we live in, I need to remember that. I think every one of my students can and will be successful. They all come into my classroom with strengths and weaknesses in both their academic knowledge and their character development. They will never all fit in the same mold and will never all make the same gains. I want to have expectations that are reasonable for each individual child. I try to maintain a sense of humor and be warm without losing sight of the fact that they need for my expectations and boundaries to be clear.*

Writing a teaching philosophy is important for new K-12 teachers who are looking for positions, because these statements of philosophy are often required as part of the application process. Colleges and universities most often request teaching statements or philosophies from applicants for faculty positions, and they are often required for permanent status or tenure decisions in K-12 settings. Being open and unambiguous about a teaching philosophy by writing it down can help teachers compare the philosophical underpinnings to their actual teaching practice and management styles. Answers to several questions can be a starting point:

1. What do you believe about teaching and learning by students?
2. Why do you think that way?
3. What do you think about the social and emotional learning of students? Are they intertwined with the academic instruction and management of the classroom? Why, or why not?
4. Do your beliefs about teaching match what you do in the classroom?
5. What do you see other teachers do that you do not like? How would your approach be different?

Writing a teaching philosophy can also allow for discovering if your behavior management in the classroom matches what you believe about student learning.

Remember that learning, in this case, is not just in the academic area, but includes a student's social and emotional learning as well.

Q: *I wrote a teaching philosophy years ago as part of a graduate course assignment, but I never connected it to my actual teaching. Now I see it may help uncover some of my core beliefs and how I can better manage my classroom. I know I didn't consider anything specific in the area of managing my students' behavior. What should I do next?*

A: You have taken the first step, and now you are on your way. Developing a set of questions like those in the chapter text can be a start, but remember, broad philosophical statements will not be of much help unless you are able to provide examples that you can see happening in your room. For example, if you believe that collaboration is important to your teaching and your management style, give concrete examples of how you would do that. If you believe in hands-on learning and student self-discovery, provide examples of how you would facilitate that type of learning. Given that this chapter includes ideas about how a teaching philosophy can illuminate an approach to classroom management, how would your beliefs and values help prevent behavior problems and create a positive classroom environment?

Summary

A positive classroom environment is created when a teacher promotes appropriate interaction among students and teachers. The classrooms of Ms. Gonzalez and Mr. Wordsworth, described at the beginning of the chapter, are not examples of positive classroom environments. Using punitive and reactionary measures, such as yelling, taking away recess, intimidation, and humiliation, does not ensure a well-managed classroom. The behaviors that both Ms. Gonzalez and Mr. Wordsworth want to reduce, such as inattention, noncompliance, and disrespect, will most likely continue unless some significant changes are made in a number of areas.

In this chapter, we explored the history of using punishment in American public education, how that tradition continues today, and how some teachers and administrators continue to use punishment and discipline synonymously. We investigated what discipline really is and how approaching discipline as an opportunity for student learning can promote a positive approach to managing a classroom of learners. What we tried to do in this chapter is provide a more general way of thinking about discipline and how discipline provides students with learning experiences that are not necessarily negative, punitive, or reactionary.

We also looked critically at three management styles—laissez-faire, authoritarian, and authoritative—and found that Ms. Gonzalez and Mr. Wordsworth were more authoritarian in their management, resulting in the negative behaviors that their students exhibited. In some ways, however, each teacher also was a little laissez-faire in the way that he or she provided leadership in the classroom, resulting in behaviors that they did not want. If they were more cognizant of an authoritative or democratic approach to the way that they managed their classroom, their students' behaviors might be different.

Finally, we provided information about writing a teaching philosophy as a way to explore formally how it should match what a teacher believes about a student's academic, social, and emotional learning. Being open and unambiguous about a teaching philosophy by writing it down can help teachers compare their philosophical underpinnings to their actual teaching practice and management styles.

Overall, this chapter explored some foundational aspects of creating a positive classroom environment. It was not our intent here to provide specific strategies and proven, day-to-day practices and techniques. More specific approaches are found in other chapters, but when the ideas of this chapter are combined with those specific strategies, preventing problem behaviors in the classroom can become a reality. By comparing the culture of punishment and discipline for positive student learning, understanding management styles, and writing a teaching philosophy, we can begin to orient teaching toward promoting a positive and creative classroom environment.

Additional Resources

On the Web

Page Title	Annotations	Web Address
Discipline vs Punishment	Questions to ask before assuming a child is misbehaving	http://www.boostforkids.org/LearnWithBoost/BoostforParents/DisciplinevsPunishment/tabid/163/Default.aspx
Discipline vs Punishment	Discussion of the difference between discipline and punishment and how the two work together	http://www.hevanet.com/kort/2007/HARRIS1.HTM
Laying the Foundation for Positive Classroom Behavior	Tips for creating a positive classroom environment	http://www.teachervision.fen.com/classroom-management/teaching-methods/6400.html
What is your classroom management profile?	Classroom management style quiz	http://www.cbv.ns.ca/sstudies/gen3.html

In the Literature

Gillen, A., Wright, A., & Spink, L. (2011). Student perceptions of a positive climate for learning: A case study. *Educational Psychology in Practice, 27*(1), 65–82.
This article discusses students' perceptions of what creates a positive classroom climate for learning. It investigates preferred learning environments and explores the elements identified by students as contributing to a positive classroom.

Walker, J. T. (2009). Authoritative classroom management: How control and nurturance work together. *Theory Into Practice, 48*(2), 122–129.
This article discusses the interplay between the academic and social aspects of the classroom. It parallels the classroom and parenting styles necessary for igniting students' interaction and understanding in the classroom.

References

Anderson, H. H., & Brewer, H. M. (1945). Studies in teachers' classroom personalities I: Dominative and socially integrative behavior of kindergarten teachers. *Applied Psychological Monograph* (no. 6). Stanford, CA: Stanford University Press.

Anderson, H. H., Brewer, J. E., & Reed M. F. (1946). Studies of teachers' classroom personalities III: Follow-up studies of the effects of dominative and integrative contacts on children's behavior. *Applied Psychological Monograph* (no. 8). Stanford, CA: Stanford University Press.

Bremner, R. H. (1970). *Children and youth in America: A documentary history.* Cambridge, MA: Harvard University Press.

Childre, A., Sands, J. R., & Pope, S. T. (2009). Backward design: Targeting depth of understanding for all learners. *Teaching Exceptional Children, 41*(5), 6–14.

Farrell, C. (2012). *Corporal punishment in US schools.* Retrieved February 12, 2012, from http://www.corpun.com/counuss.htm

Hersey, P., Blanchard, K. H., & Johnson, D. E. (1996). *Management of organizational behavior* (7th ed.). Upper Saddle River, NJ: Prentice-Hall.

Holloran, P. C. (1989). *Boston's wayward children: Social services for homeless children, 1830–1930.* Cranbury, NJ: Associated University Presses.

Lewin, K., Leppitt, R., & White R. K. (1939). Patterns of aggressive behavior in experimentally created social climates. *Journal of Social Psychology, 10,* 271–299.

Lindberg, C. A. (Ed.). (2008). *Oxford American Writer's Thesaurus.* New York: Oxford University Press.

Stevenson, A., & Lindberg, C. A. (Eds.). (2010). *The New Oxford American Dictionary.* New York: Oxford University Press.

Vought, J. J. (1984). Punishment and alternative strategies for decreasing a behavior. *Personnel & Guidance Journal, 62*(10), 588–591.

Structuring and Organizing the Classroom

GOALS

- Explain effective arrangement of the classroom as a way to prevent behavior problems.

- Present strategies for establishing classroom procedures.

- Describe strategies for developing rules and consequences for managing behavior.

- Explain effective methods to transition from one classroom task or activity to another.

SCENARIO

Ms. Zeibert is a first-year, second-grade teacher who has little experience with structuring and organizing a classroom. She began her student teaching experience after the start of the school year, so she missed the opportunity to use most of the strategies for setting up a classroom, including establishing rules and procedures and structuring transitions. Ms. Zeibert set the rules for her classroom in advance of the arrival of her students, failed to word the rules in positive terms (e.g., keep hands and feet to yourself), and created too many rules to be effective. When students did not follow the rules, the consequences often escalated to levels that were too harsh. For example, Ms. Zeibert created a check system that focused on students' inappropriate behaviors. Each time a student broke a classroom rule, Ms. Zeibert placed a check mark next to their name on the board. With the third check mark, a call home was made, and with the fourth, children were sent to the office or parents were asked to pick up their child. At the end of the first month of school, Ms. Zeibert's principal starting receiving phone calls from frustrated parents complaining about their child being sent to the office and missing class time or about having to leave work to pick their child up from school. The principal noted that the Ms. Zeibert's management system must be changed to maintain students in the educational setting and suggested identifying consequences that were more appropriate.

Ms. Zeibert did not plan or anticipate the need for structured procedures or transitions. The first few days of school resulted in large blocks of time lost due to students becoming sidetracked, because the procedures to start and end each class period were unclear. During the first few weeks of school, Ms. Zeibert slowly realized that she must develop classroom procedures and teach her students how to follow them. This realization also led to identifying procedures related to miscellaneous unanticipated events to facilitate smooth classroom flow and to increase the time in which students were academically engaged.

The research we reviewed in Chapter 1 resulted in the development of a knowledge base on classroom management and a set of principles that teachers can use to guide them in making important decisions about how to set up their classrooms. According to Good and Brophy (2008), these findings converge on the conclusion that "teachers who approach classroom management as a process of establishing and maintaining effective learning environments tend to be more successful than teachers who place more emphasis on their roles as . . . disciplinarians" (p. 110). Ms. Zeibert learned through experience that effective rules and procedures in the classroom can lead to increased student engagement.

In Chapter 1, we also discussed how effective classroom management systems are preventive or proactive rather than reactive. The essence of proactive classroom management is establishing and maintaining order in the classroom. When teachers have orderly classrooms, it does not mean that teachers must act in a rigid manner or that students must maintain absolute silence; instead, the students follow the procedures required by a particular classroom situation. In proactive classrooms, teachers maintain order by acting before a problem takes place rather than waiting and reacting after the problem has occurred.

The scenario about Ms. Zeibert depicts ineffective learning environments where order is not maintained. Effective teachers devote time at the beginning of the school year to address how everyone in the classroom will get along with each other and the procedures to ensure that there is order and activities flow smoothly. Of course, what constitutes order will vary across the situations that occur during the school day. For example, order during silent reading will be different from order during physical education class. Nonetheless, the purpose of establishing order in the classroom is to create an environment in which teaching and learning can take place whatever the situation.

In this chapter, we examine an important component of proactive management: the way in which teachers structure the environments in their classrooms to prevent problem behavior and maintain order. We will discuss (a) setting up the physical environment; (b) developing and teaching classroom procedures, rules, and consequences; and (c) managing transitions. Addressing these important proactive components will help to ensure that teachers structure and organize their classroom in ways that enhance learning and minimize disruption.

SETTING UP THE PHYSICAL ENVIRONMENT

One of the first decisions that all teachers face at the beginning of a school year is how to set up the physical classroom environment. Teachers have many choices to make about how their classrooms will be arranged, such as where the teacher's desk will be placed or how the students' desks will be arranged. These decisions are important, because the way that teachers choose to arrange the physical environment in their classroom can affect student behavior and learning.

When setting up their classroom, teachers should follow three important principles:

1. Arrange the classroom so that the teacher can see all the students at all times and students can see the teacher.
2. Ensure that high-traffic areas are free from congestion and allow easy movement.
3. Arrange student seating in ways that facilitate student involvement.

Whether a teacher is in an elementary, middle, or high school setting, or in a self-contained special education classroom, these principles remain the same. Moreover, these principles apply to the many different activities that occur during a typical school day, such as small group activities, teacher presentation, guided practice, and transitions.

Principle #1: Arrange the classroom so that the teacher can see all the students at all times and students can see the teacher.

Supervising students is a major classroom management task (Emmer & Evertson, 2009; Evertson & Emmer, 2009). In Chapter 1, we presented the research findings of Jacob Kounin (1970). Recall that Kounin demonstrated the importance of actively supervising students at all times, an attribute he termed "withitness." According to Kounin, teachers exhibit withitness when their behavior communicates to students that they are aware of all the events going on in their classroom. Withitness, or active supervision, involves teachers (a) moving among their students and scanning the environment, (b) interacting with students, (c) giving positive feedback for appropriate behavior, and (d) correcting inappropriate behavior.

Because supervision of students is a critical task, teachers must position themselves where they can see all their students and can scan and monitor the entire room at all times. In addition to monitoring, teachers should also move about the room and interact with students. Marzano, Marzano, and Pickering (2009) suggested that teachers spend equal amounts of time in all sections of their classrooms. Thus, teachers should systematically walk to all areas of their classroom and pay particular attention to those places that are not easily seen. Marzano and his colleagues further suggested that teachers develop patterns of moving about their classrooms (e.g., walking up one row and down another, briefly moving to and standing in each quadrant of the room) and, when teachers are standing still at the front of the room, that they attempt to make eye contact with all their students to show that they are "withit."

Clearly, to ensure that teachers can see all their students at all times and that their students can see them, teachers must adopt room arrangements with clear lines of sight between their position in the classroom and their students. The specific type of arrangement (e.g., teacher's desk in the front of the class, teacher's desk in the back of the room) is not as important as having a clear and unobstructed view of the students. When arranging classroom furniture, it is important to consider carefully the placement of filing cabinets, bookcases, and other objects so that the line of sight is not obstructed. To ensure clear lines of sight, Evertson and Emmer (2009) suggested that after arranging their classroom, teachers should stand in different parts of the room and check for blind spots.

> **Principle #2:** Ensure that high-traffic areas are free from congestion and allow for easy movement.

The physical design of classrooms, along with the flow of classroom traffic, is an especially important factor in managing distractions, decreasing problem behavior, and increasing student attention. And this is certainly an area in which a teacher has control. For example, in a typical classroom, there are many areas in which students tend to gather (e.g., sinks, pencil sharpeners, water fountains, group work areas, computer stations). What is important here is that some areas will be used frequently by students, and these areas should be (a) separated from each other, (b) open and accessible, and (c) easy to get to and from. This will minimize congestion and increase the smooth flow of traffic.

Similarly, teaching materials and supplies should be placed in areas where the teacher and the students can locate and access them easily. Because such areas may be used frequently, it is important that they be set apart from other high-traffic areas. In this way, teachers can minimize the likelihood of overcrowding and student bottlenecks. Evertson and Emmer (2009) also pointed out that having supplies and materials in a well-defined space with easy access by students will reduce the time needed to ready activities, thus avoiding distracting slowdowns and breaks in the flow of lessons.

> **Principle #3:** Arrange student seating in ways that facilitate student involvement.

There are many different ways in which teachers may arrange student seating. Seating arrangements are important considerations, because they can increase attention and student participation. Teachers should let the lessons or activities influence the students' seating arrangements. For example, students can be sitting at individual desks in rows and columns for whole-class presentation and individual work, and then students could move to a small table for group work. A few general rules, however, will ensure that seating arrangements encourage student involvement and increase student attention.

First, where a student sits in relation to a teacher can increase the likelihood of student involvement in a teacher's lesson. Students who sit in what is called the action zone are more involved in what was being taught (Savage & Savage, 2010). The action zone is in the front and center rows of traditionally structured classrooms, with the teacher at the front of the class and the students in desks directly in front. Student rates of participation and appropriate behavior are typically greater for students who are seated in the action zone than for students who are not. The action zone concept also seems to exert a similar effect in semicircular and clustered seating arrangements. The implications of research on the action zone are that (a) students who have problems with attention, behavior, and participation in class should be seated in the zone and (b) teachers should carefully and systematically monitor and interact with students who are seated outside the action zone. Students who tend to be off task and disruptive should be placed nearest the teacher, who can then more easily monitor these students and immediately and easily reinforce appropriate behavior. It is also important that teachers do not place potentially disruptive students in close proximity to each other.

In fact, the potentially troublesome students should be seated next to students who are more likely to behave appropriately.

Second, for large group presentations, students should be seated in an arrangement where all students face the teacher. If arrangements in such situations have students seated with their backs to the teacher, these students are more likely to have their attention wander and to engage in misbehavior. For example, many teachers use projection devices for presentations and other large group activities. Good and Brophy (2008) suggest placing students' desks in an area where students can see the presentation without moving their desks or having to turn around. Further, the areas around students' desks should also be open and allow free movement among the various sections of the classroom.

Third, students' desks should be arranged in a way that leaves open spaces between rows or clusters of desks to allow the teacher to move effortlessly around the classroom. When teachers move freely about the classroom, they can easily monitor student behavior, interact with students, and check student progress. Additionally, students are more likely to perceive that the teacher is withit. A number of researchers have also reported that the closer teachers are in relation their students, often referred to as proximity control, then (a) the greater the control of a teacher's interactions with students, (b) the higher the rates of academic engagement, and (c) the lower the rates of student disruption. Additionally, proximity control seems to be most effective when a teacher is within about three feet of a student. Teachers therefore should move about their classrooms and make frequent individual contacts with their students.

In summary, setting up an efficient and effective classroom environment is a simple way to begin establishing a proactive classroom and, thus, to prevent behavior problems. The ways in which teachers arrange students' desks can facilitate teacher–student interactions and minimize problem behaviors. Three important principles to keep in mind when arranging the classroom are (a) arrange the classroom so that the teacher and students can all see each other, (b) ensure that high-traffic areas are free from congestion and allow easy movement, and (c) arrange student seating in ways that facilitate student involvement.

Q: *I am noticing that the behavior of three students who sit close to the supply cabinet is continuing to deteriorate. They bother the students who go to the cabinet to pass out supplies and cause disruption, lose focus during instruction, and cause mild disturbances throughout the day. What changes can I make to ensure these three students stay on task?*

A: When you have a classroom management problem, use the principle of parsimony. That is, when you have competing theories about why a problem may exist and want to choose an appropriate action, choose the simplest one first. In this case, the first and simplest theory about your problem is that the students will reduce their behavior problems when the teacher is close by, so increase your proximity control. If that proves difficult to do all day, every day, the second theory may be that the students are acting out because they feel they are hidden from your view. Can you see the students at all times? If not, perhaps you should change the arrangement of the seating in the classroom so that you can keep eye contact with them, and move one or more of the students into the action zone. In your planning of where in the action zone to place these students, remember to seat them next to students who are more likely to behave appropriately.

DEVELOPING AND TEACHING CLASSROOM PROCEDURES, RULES, AND CONSEQUENCES

Proactive classroom management begins with the way that teachers structure and organize the classroom at the beginning of the school year (Good & Brophy, 2008). The beginning of the school year is of critical importance for establishing order in the classroom, because it is an opportunity to define the procedures, rules, and consequences for behavior. Classrooms are comprised of diverse students, assembled in crowded conditions for long periods of time, with specific tasks to accomplish. And for these tasks to be accomplished, it is crucial that teachers have explicit, specific rules and procedures. Rules define general expectations or standards for student conduct, and procedures consist of the prescribed ways of managing various activities and duties that recur frequently in the classroom (Good & Brophy, 2008). In a meta-analysis of classroom management studies, Marzano, Marzano, and Pickering (2009) found classrooms that effectively enacted classroom rules and procedures had 28 percent less student disruptions than classrooms in which rules and procedures were not in place. In this section, we address developing and teaching classroom procedures and then developing and teaching classroom rules and defining consequences.

Developing and Teaching Classroom Procedures

Procedures, or routines, are actions that students engage in at particular times or during particular activities that are directed at accomplishing specific tasks. Typically teachers set up procedures for certain events that occur day in and day out. Procedures, therefore, are established for how students will accomplish these tasks in the most efficient manner. Procedures and routines are certainly an important part of proactive classrooms, because they prescribe the student behaviors that are necessary for the smooth operation of the classroom. Thus, in proactive classrooms, teachers instruct their students how to accomplish these classroom procedures and routines quickly and quietly.

When students follow effective classroom procedures correctly, there is little or no confusion about what needs to be done and when, student down time is minimized, and time available for learning is maximized. In the scenario that opened this chapter, Ms. Zeibert realized that she needed to establish procedures for everyday tasks in the classroom, because without these, she was losing valuable instructional time. When teachers plan classroom procedures, they need to consider what types of activities will be a part of the students' daily classroom life and determine what methods are appropriate for implementation. As shown in Table 3.1, a multitude of classroom tasks or activities can recur throughout the school day that may need well-defined procedures for proactive and efficient classroom management.

When students are aware of and follow classroom procedures with minimal assistance from their teacher, their on-task behavior and engagement is increased, because they are not asking for directions and teachers are not giving instructions for everyday activities. In classrooms without well-defined procedures, time is lost in managing routine chores rather than being spent on more productive activities (Savage & Savage, 2010). Thus, procedures are important components of efficient and effective proactive

TABLE 3.1	Examples of Classroom Tasks and Activities	
Entering the classroom	Small group activities
Asking for help from the teacher	Getting classroom materials
Handing in assignments	Storing classroom materials
Going to the restroom	Using computers, iPads, etc.
Preparing to end class	Safety procedures (e.g., fire alarm, problems in the classroom, intruders on campus)
Obtaining teacher permission to talk, leave desk, etc.	What to do when a student is finished with an assignment
Using the trash can	
Having materials ready for class	Dealing with classroom interruptions or delays
Leaving the classroom	Working independently
Completing seatwork	

classroom management systems. Teachers can follow three major principles for developing and teaching classroom procedures:

1. Identify those predictable events that occur every day.
2. Determine how students can most efficiently complete each classroom task or activity.
3. Teach the procedures, provide practice opportunities, and check for understanding.

Principle #1: Identify those predictable events that occur every day.

Every elementary class has certain times in which students must stop one activity and begin another. These activities can be related to nonacademic events (e.g., entering class, sharpening pencils, gathering materials), academic work and lessons (e.g., asking for teacher assistance, beginning independent work, distributing materials), and interactions with and among students (e.g., contributing to small group discussions, getting the attention of the class). These activities tend to go much more smoothly when procedures have been developed for the activities. To identify these activities, teachers should think about a typical school day and what types of events occur regularly and then determine what steps are needed to complete the procedure correctly and efficiently.

Principle #2: Determine how students can most efficiently complete each classroom task or activity.

Teachers should decide what outcomes they desire as a result of the procedures and routines and then outline the steps necessary to reach those outcomes. Additionally, teachers should think about what errors students might possibly make when performing the procedure. Essentially, teachers should do a task analysis of the procedure. Thus, teachers must design instruction in how to follow procedures much like they design academic instruction. The key to this principle is determining how each classroom task or activity can be completed in the most efficient and effective manner possible.

> **Principle #3:** Teach the procedures, provide practice opportunities, and check for understanding.

After teachers have identified the events that occur every day and determined procedures that allow efficient completion of classroom tasks or activities, they must teach those procedures to students. Ms. Zeibert's students were unable to successfully use any classroom procedures due to lack of instruction that should have taken place during the first week of school. Procedures, like academic subjects, should be planned and then taught directly to students using presentation, modeling, practice, feedback, and reinforcement (Savage & Savage, 2010). It is also important that students practice the procedures. Cue cards can be made for young students that list the steps they must follow to accomplish the procedures and routines. Because students may forget a particular procedure or not perform it correctly, occasional reteaching of the procedures may be needed throughout the school year. When students learn the classroom procedures and routines, they will be able to follow them without wasting classroom time.

According to Colvin and Lazar (1997), when instructing students in classroom procedures, teachers should adhere to the following five teaching steps:

Step 1: **Explain.**   Tell students the rationale for following the particular procedure. Invite discussion and student contributions, and then monitor student understanding by asking questions.

Step 2: **Specify student behaviors.**   Teach students how to correctly follow the particular procedure. Tell students what signal will indicate that the procedure is to be followed.

Step 3: **Practice.**   Ask students to specify the behavior they are to engage in during the procedure. Then, have students take turns modeling the steps of the procedure. Repeat until all students can demonstrate the procedure correctly.

Step 4: **Monitor.**   Observe students during the particular procedure. Acknowledge and praise students who complete the procedure correctly. Provide reminders, prompts, and corrections to students who do not complete the procedures accurately.

Step 5: **Review.**   Conduct a brief review two to three weeks after the procedure has been established. If problems have occurred, conduct a practice session. Continue to monitor the procedure, and occasionally provide an acknowledgment for accurately completing the procedure.

In summary, teachers should plan procedures for recurring events, teach the routine to the class, require compliance, and monitor students as they perform the routines. Teachers who take such actions early in the school year can expect that their classroom management systems will run much more smoothly and efficiently.

Developing and Teaching Classroom Rules and Consequences

In their classroom management studies, Evertson and Emmer (Emmer & Evertson, 2009; Evertson & Emmer, 2009) found that a fundamental way in which effective teachers established and maintained an orderly learning environment was by having rules and consequences. Classrooms are crowded and busy places, so some type of regulatory mechanism is necessary to achieve important classroom goals.

Classroom rules define the expectations for appropriate classroom conduct and provide the foundation for expected behavior. Clearly stated rules describe what is, and what is not, acceptable in the classroom, and they provide students with guidelines for appropriate classroom behavior that, if followed, allow teaching and learning to take place in an efficient manner. Additionally, classroom rules that are taught and enforced decrease the likelihood of problem behaviors occurring. Developing, monitoring, and enforcing rules are a critical element in maintaining orderly and productive classrooms.

When planning classroom rules, teachers should determine what student behaviors are most important for ensuring an environment conducive to teaching and learning. Because of the importance of rules in the overall functioning of the classroom, teachers, when they develop classroom rules, should be mindful of their classroom management styles and teaching philosophy, as we talked about in Chapter 2. Having knowledge about the most effective management style along with articulating a personal teaching philosophy will guide teachers in monitoring and enforcing their classroom rules. Teachers can follow six principles for effective development and use of classroom rules:

1. Determine the behaviors that are important for teaching and learning to occur in the classroom. If there are school rules, the classroom rules should correspond to them.
2. Develop a few, positively stated rules that are clearly defined and objectively written.
3. Include a "catch-all" rule.
4. Teach, practice, and post classroom rules.
5. Monitor student behavior and acknowledge students when they follow the rules.
6. Enforce compliance with the classroom rules.

Principle #1: Determine the behaviors that are important for teaching and learning to occur in the classroom. If there are school rules, the classroom rules should correspond to them.

There are three issues that teachers should consider before creating their rules: What are the schoolwide rules or code of conduct? Should general or specific rules be developed? And to what level should students be involved in planning the rules?

First, teachers should examine the schoolwide discipline plan or code of conduct. It is increasingly common for schools to have whole-school discipline plans that encourage and reward certain behaviors while prohibiting and correcting others. This will certainly be the case in schools that have adopted the schoolwide positive behavior supports (PBS) model developed by Sugai and Horner (Sugai & Horner, 2006, 2008) (for excellent resources on schoolwide PBS, readers are directed to the website of the Technical Assistance Center on PBS at http://www.pbis.org/). Schools where PBS has been adopted have defined procedures for teachers to incorporate school rules into their classrooms. As Evertson and Emmer (2009) point out, it is to the teachers' advantage to apply rules consistently across all classes and the entire school, because this will make the rules easier for students to learn and for teachers to monitor, acknowledge, and enforce. Additionally, it is more likely that the rules will acquire legitimacy in the eyes of the students when they are applied throughout the school (Emmer & Evertson, 2009; Evertson & Emmer, 2009).

Rules can be developed in general or specific terms. As shown in Table 3.2, general rules cover numerous behaviors, while specific rules address discrete behaviors.

Although general rules cover more behavioral situations, they are often ambiguous and must be explained so that students clearly understand the expected behaviors. They also necessitate identifying what the rules cover. For instance, *Be polite* may include raising your hand and waiting to speak after being called on, talking with an inside voice in the classroom, and not interrupting conversations.

General rules have great appeal, because they communicate goals that all students should strive to achieve. Unfortunately, general rules often fail to detail the precise behaviors that students should exhibit and fall short of conveying specific behavioral expectations. Moreover, they are often ambiguous and difficult to monitor and enforce.

On the other hand, specific rules clearly delineate the classroom expectations. When teachers develop specific rules, students are more likely to understand them. Moreover, specific rules are easier to monitor and enforce. When teachers develop specific rules, they must identify the behaviors that they consider to be the most important to address, monitor, and enforce.

Savage and Savage (2010) contend that students should be included in the rule development process, because this supports ownership by the students. They believe that teachers and students should negotiate the rules, because when students feel that their input is valued and they are included in the management of the classroom, they are more likely to behave appropriately. According to other authors (e.g., Morgan & Jenson, 1988), however, teachers need to ensure that certain rules that are of importance to them and the school are included in the final list of classroom rules, even if students disagree with them. There is no clear evidence that including students in rule making makes any difference in establishing effective classroom rules (Doyle, 2006). Nonetheless, discussion of classroom rules and a common understanding of the purposes and content of the rules are important. An approach to rule development that

TABLE 3.2	Examples of General and Specific Rules
General Rules	**Specific Rules**
Respect others	Arrive to class on time
Be polite	Keep hands, feet, and objects to self
Be helpful	Have materials out at the beginning of the class
Take care of the classroom	Follow teacher directions the first time given
Behave at all times	Raise your hand and wait to be called on to talk

supports students' contributions toward the development of classroom rules can be useful as long as the rules that the teacher deems to be essential are included in the final list. Additionally, teachers must be flexible and open to adjusting the rules if the environment or situation calls for it.

Principle #2: Develop a few, positively stated rules that are clearly defined and objectively written.

After determining what the classroom rules will cover, the teacher develops the actual rules by following three basic guidelines:

1. *Rules should be written in positive terms.* It is preferable that rules should inform students of the appropriate behaviors they are expected to exhibit rather than the behaviors in which students should not engage (e.g., *Raise your hand for permission to talk* rather than *Do not talk in class*). Ms. Zeibert did not know this important principle and the two reasons for writing positive rules: (a) negative rules only identify one prohibited behavior, and (b) negative rules do not teach appropriate behavior.

2. *The number of classroom rules should be kept to a minimum.* Only the most important rules should be chosen for the final list; this will keep rules simple to learn and understand. Too many rules may make it too complex for the teacher to monitor them effectively and to provide consistent enforcement. Simply put, if the rules are not enforced, they will lose their effectiveness. Additionally, too many rules make it more likely that the students and teacher will have difficulty remembering them. Morgan and Jenson (1988) recommended that teachers have no more than five or six rules.

3. *Rules should be clear and written objectively.* When rules are clear, teachers and students will know if they have been followed or violated. On the other hand, when rules are ambiguous, students may be unsure if they are following them, and teachers may be unsure when they are broken. Such uncertainty or ambiguity may lead to problem behavior and, most certainly, will result in the rules becoming ineffective. Moreover, when a student disagrees about violating a rule that may be unclear, an argument or power struggle between the student and teacher may ensue.

Principle #3: Include a "catch-all" rule.

Because rules generally address only a limited number of important classroom behaviors, teachers should include a "catch-all" or compliance rule in the final list (e.g., "Follow teacher directions"). A catch-all rule should be general enough to address a number of situations. Of course, with a rule of this nature, it is especially important that teachers spend time clarifying the rule. That is, teachers need to tell students the rationale for including the rule, teach the rule to their students, and ensure student understanding.

Principle #4: Teach, practice, and post classroom rules.

After rules have been established, it is necessary for teachers to develop a plan to teach them to their students. Regardless of the age of students, teachers should not assume that just posting the rules or mentioning them briefly will ensure that their students understand them. Even with secondary students, teachers must not assume that students understand how to follow the rules until they have been explained and demonstrated. Of course, how the rules are taught will vary in accordance with the students' ages, yet the teaching process should include effective teaching strategies. Additionally, it may be important to occasionally reteach the rules during the course of the school year, especially with younger children and students who exhibit problem behaviors.

Students should have opportunities to discuss the rules, give examples of appropriate and inappropriate adherence to the rules, and to practice following the rules. Classroom rules should be posted in a conspicuous place where students can see them at all times and teachers can refer to them easily. Posting the rules serves as a constant reminder to students and the teacher. Posting also allows other staff, substitute teachers, and visitors to see what is expected of students.

Principle #5: Monitor student behavior, and acknowledge students when they follow the rules.

The end goal of having classroom rules is not that students merely know the rules, but that they follow them. Unfortunately, simply telling students classroom rules will not always result in complete compliance. Teachers should monitor students' compliance with classroom rules and acknowledge and reinforce rule-following behavior. Evertson and Emmer (2009) found that the more effective classroom managers monitored consistently their students' compliance with the classroom rules.

Teacher attention, acknowledgment, and praise can be useful tools for increasing students' rule-following behavior. Teachers should frequently provide acknowledgments or positive consequences, like those in Table 3.3, when students follow the rules. In other words, catch students being good, and let them know they have done well. Additionally, a teacher should tell students why they are being praised (e.g., *Nick, raising your hand is following our rules, great*).

Using a positive consequence for a student who follows rules has the following advantages:

1. It is easy to do and takes little teacher effort.
2. It is natural and frequently reinforcing to a student.
3. It helps to build a positive relationship with the student.
4. It shows the other students what behavior is expected and acknowledged.

Principle #6: Enforce compliance with the classroom rules.

TABLE 3.3 Positive Consequences for Rule-Following Behavior	
Specific teacher praise	Nonverbal approval (e.g., smile, touch)
Student of the day	Structured free time
Tokens, points, check marks, stars	Student choice of activity
Lunch with teacher or friend	Free reading time
Positive note or e-mail home	Positive referral to the office
Line leader	Free homework pass
Teacher assistant	Special seat
Extra computer time	Name on board

Teachers should always emphasize positive approaches in teaching and encouraging appropriate student behavior. Occasionally, however, students will violate classroom rules. When this happens, teachers must demonstrate a willingness to act by correcting the offending students quickly, efficiently, and consistently. When correcting a rule violation, teachers should give corrective feedback by describing the rule that was broken and the appropriate behavior that the student should have exhibited. When students persist in breaking rules, teachers should implement clear and consistent consequences. (Recall that according to Kounin [1970], one of the hallmarks of teachers who exhibited "withitness" was that they corrected misbehaving students quickly and efficiently.)

Negative, or reductive, consequences should be implemented when students break classroom rules. The types of negative consequences that teachers' use and the way in which they use them can determine whether certain students will follow the classroom rules and whether they respect the teacher. Colvin and Lazar (1997) noted that whereas positive consequences should be a teacher's primary response toward student behavior, negative consequences play an important role in effective classroom management. Negative consequences are procedures that teachers use to stop or suppress an inappropriate behavior when students choose to break classroom rules. Morgan and Jenson (1988) noted that a student is more likely to accept negative consequences when teachers apply consistently the consequences without publicly criticizing them.

Whenever possible, negative consequences should be logically related to the misbehavior. Students must see the connection between a given action and the subsequent result (Sugai & Horner, 2008). For a student who fights with another student at recess, for example, a logical consequence may be that recess privileges are removed for a certain amount of time. Ms. Zeibert, in our scenario that opened this chapter, routinely used illogical and harsh consequences in response to students' behaviors.

Teachers often have difficulty identifying negative consequences. As a result, teachers often attempt to come up with negative consequences shortly after a student misbehaves. Such approaches may lead to the inconsistent and irrational use of consequences, which students will perceive as unfair and unreasonable, and this may undermine the teacher's authority and effectiveness as a classroom manager. Thus, it is important that negative consequences (see Table 3.4), like rules, be planned in advance. When teachers know what consequences they will use, and how they will use them,

TABLE 3.4	Negative Consequences for Rule-Violating Behavior	
Stay after class	Restitution (e.g., if you break it, you have to fix it)	
Loss of privileges: recess (for misbehavior at recess), class job, going on the field trip (for chronic behavior problems)	Missed opportunity to earn points, stickers, stars, tangible rewards	
Notice to parent	Parent conference	
Office referral	Time out	

before serious problem behavior occurs, they will become more confident and competent when addressing such behavior. Consequences, like rules, should be clear, specific, and whenever possible, logically related to the rule infraction.

As with teaching classroom rules, direct instruction of classroom consequences, both positive and negative, is one of the most important tasks a teacher needs to accomplish during the first few days and weeks of the school year. The teacher should first explain the consequences. Students should have opportunities to discuss the consequences and be given examples of the consequences as well as when and how they will be administered. The consequences should be posted in a prominent place within the classroom. The posting will be a constant reminder of the consequences to students and the teacher.

It is also important that teachers deliver such consequences appropriately. Delivering positive consequences should be conducted in a way that emphasizes the appropriate behavior and be delivered at the earliest opportunity. When a teacher delivers a negative consequence, it should be done privately, in a calm manner, and in a way that preserves the student's dignity. Teachers should never administer a negative consequence when they are angry, because there might be a temptation to use a consequence that is too severe for the behavior.

Morgan and Jenson (1988) suggested that teachers use a preplanned "What if?" chart, in which they list the negative consequences on the right side of the chart and how much or how long the consequence will be used on the left side. The negative consequences are also listed in terms of severity. If teachers have preplanned their consequences in this way, they will be less likely to deliver consequences that do not match the misbehavior in severity.

When administering a consequence it is very important that the teacher:

1. Remind the student of the rule being broken.
2. Provide a warning that if the behavior does not stop, the consequence will be administered.
3. State what the consequence will be in a matter-of-fact manner.
4. Implement the consequence if the behavior does not stop.
5. Return to whatever he or she is doing (e.g., teaching a lesson).

Additionally, Colvin and Lazar (1997) suggested that after a negative consequence is administered to a student, the teacher should look for the first opportunity to recognize that student's positive behavior. Of course, it is crucial that consequences be delivered in a consistent manner.

In summary, researchers have shown the importance of proactive classroom management. Perhaps no area is more under a teacher's control than how classroom procedures, rules, and consequences are arranged. Teachers should approach developing and teaching procedures and rules in the same way that they approach teaching an academic skill. We suggest that teachers follow Colvin and Lazar's (1997) instructional format of (a) explaining the rationale, (b) specifying student behaviors, (c) providing practice activities, (d) monitoring student performance, and (e) conducting occasional reviews. Both rules and consequences are an important part of a proactive classroom management strategy because they define the relationship between student behavior and consequences as well as guide and direct both teacher and student behavior (Morgan & Jenson, 1988). In fact, Savage and Savage (2010) believe that teachers who complain that their students are constantly testing their authority are often those teachers who do not have a clear set of classroom rules or enforce them consistently.

Q: *I worked with my students to develop rules in my classrooms, but it just doesn't seem to make any difference. We went over the rules several times during the first week of class, and there continue to be numerous rule violations. We are now in the third month of school, and it's like my rules don't exist. How can I get my students to follow the rules?*

A: Unfortunately, if students have been ignoring the rules for three months, their behaviors will likely be ingrained and difficult to address. It would have been best to take action to address the rule violations as soon as they began to occur. Remember the principle of parsimony, and ask yourself the following questions.

First, do the students know the rules? Did you teach the rules, post them, and have the students practice the rules? If they don't know the rules, then you need to teach them.

Second, do you monitor the students, acknowledge them when they do follow the rules, and privately administer consequences when they violate the rules? Kounin (1970) observed that the best classroom managers display "withitness." These teachers monitored their students, recognized them for appropriate behavior, and never ignored inappropriate behavior. When inappropriate behavior occurred, it was addressed quickly and efficiently. When students misbehave and the teacher does nothing, this tells the students that either the teacher does not notice the misbehavior (is not withit) or the teacher does notice the misbehavior but won't do anything about it. In either case, some students will quickly learn they can do whatever they want, whenever they want. If you haven't been withit, concentrate on improving your observation skills and delivering appropriate positive and negative consequences.

Third, if your students know the rules, you exhibit withitness, and you deliver positive and negative consequences quickly and efficiently, you may need to have someone come and observe your classroom. A second set of impartial eyes observing your teaching and the students' behavior may often see things that you have missed and can give you helpful suggestions.

MANAGING TRANSITIONS

Transitions are teacher-directed shifts in activities designed to guide students toward stopping one activity and beginning another. While relatively little attention is given to transitions when teachers plan their schedules, transitions often claim inordinate amounts of instructional time each day (Evertson & Emmer, 2009). Transitions between lessons, classes, or activities, if not managed effectively, are opportunities for students to become disengaged from instructional activities and for disruptive behavior to occur (Good & Brophy, 2008). Moreover, when transitions are not conducted efficiently, the resulting disruptive or off-task behavior may spill over into the next activity. That is, when students become disengaged because a transition to another activity is lengthy, it often is difficult to get them reengaged.

Teachers can minimize wasted time during transitions, and lessen the likelihood of disruptive behavior, if they develop routines to make transitions run smoothly. Managing routines, however, requires that teachers thoughtfully plan transitions in advance and constantly monitor them. A teacher's goal in transitions is to bring one activity to a successful conclusion and begin the next one without undue delay and disruption (Emmer & Evertson, 2009).

Researchers have investigated the effect of transitions on instructional time and disruptive behavior. For instance, Evertson and Emmer (2009) reported that teachers were faced with increased disruptions during transition times as compared to instructional time, and Gettinger and Kohler (2006) reported that in elementary classrooms, more than 30 transitions from one activity to another take place each day, accounting for more than 15 percent of classroom time. As mentioned, ineffective transitions can disrupt the flow of instruction and contribute to disruptive behaviors. Thus, it is important to incorporate strategies purposefully to decrease time spent during transitions. The techniques that seem to facilitate such effective transitions include (a) providing transition directions to students a few minutes before the end of task or activity, (b) preparing tasks and activities in advance of a new activity to reduce wait time, and (c) ensuring that the communication is clear and that students follow the provided guidance.

Teachers need to facilitate the development of in-class transition skills much like other skill sets. Efficient transitions are important to the proactive classroom, because well-organized and quick transitions between activities result in increased academic learning opportunities, which can positively affect student achievement and prevent problematic behavior. Thus, compliance with a teacher's directions during transitional periods is important to a successful flow in the classroom setting. Teachers can follow four principles to ensure that transitions are accomplished quickly and with minimal student down time during the transition period:

1. Plan for transition times.
2. Teach the transition procedure.
3. Prepare the materials for the next activity before the transition time.
4. Signal the beginning of transition times, and give clear directions to students during the transition period.

Principle #1: Plan for transition times.

Teachers should plan classroom transitions thoughtfully. This means that the steps of the transition process should be outlined and explained to the students. Additionally, students should practice the transition and be reinforced for following the procedures quickly and efficiently. For example, a particularly difficult transition time occurs when students return from lunch. Often, they enter the classroom individually and mill about until the next class begins. An effective practice is to have a predetermined activity for the students to engage in immediately upon returning to the classroom. Before lunch, the teacher can provide instructions about the activity they will begin on returning from lunch and have the students prepare for this activity before they leave. For example, *When we return from lunch, we will begin our science lesson. Please put your science book and notebook on top of your desk, and when you return, open your books to page 24 and raise your hand. I will be looking for students who are ready as soon as I walk into the room.* Upon entering the room after lunch, the teacher immediately scans the room for students who have followed directions and reinforces their appropriate behavior. For example, *I see that Nick, Eric, and Alex have their books open to page 24. Thank you for following directions!* This practice will be even more successful if the activity is the same every day, allowing a consistent routine to be established. The important factor is to minimize unstructured time and prepare children in advance for completing transitions successfully.

A teacher's task, therefore, becomes identifying strategies that increase the likelihood that students will comply with directions targeting transitions. Potential steps include (a) teaching students at the beginning of the school year to complete transition routines and (b) establishing a signal for the beginning and end of the transition.

Principle #2: Teach the transition procedure.

In proactive classrooms, teachers approach transitions as an instructional issue. That is, teach the students how to complete transitions quickly and efficiently rather than waiting for students to waste time and become disruptive and then reacting to the problem. Earlier in this chapter, we suggested that teachers adapt Colvin and Lazar's (1997) model for teaching procedures. Colvin and Lazar also used this model to teach students how to transition from one activity to another:

Step 1: Explain.   Tell students the rationale for making quick and disruption-free transitions. Invite discussion and student contributions, and then monitor student understanding by asking questions.

Step 2: Specify student behaviors.   Teach the students how to quickly and quietly transition from one activity to another. Tell students what signal will indicate that the transition is about to begin.

Step 3: Practice.   Ask students to specify the behavior they are to engage in during the transition. Then, have students take turns modeling the quick and quiet transitions. Repeat until all students can demonstrate the procedure correctly.

Step 4: Monitor.   Observe students during the particular transition. Acknowledge and praise students who complete the transition correctly. Provide reminders, prompts, and corrections to students who do not complete the transitions accurately.

Step 5: Review.   Conduct a brief review two to three weeks after the transition has been established. If problems have occurred, conduct a practice session. Continue to monitor the transition, and occasionally provide an acknowledgment for accurately completing the transition.

Principle #3: Prepare the materials for the next activity before the transition time.

Teachers should have all materials ready before a lesson begins so that they do not have to spend time locating them. Instead of having students wait while the teacher is finding the materials for the next activity, the teacher or students distribute materials to the class immediately after the first activity finishes. Implementing a transition procedure such as this is an important part of proactive classroom management, because it leads to increased time spent on academic activities and less time on transitioning from one activity to the next.

Establishing procedures that students know and follow makes for a more efficient classroom. Less instructional time is wasted, and the opportunity for disruption is decreased. Moreover, the amount of dead time, or time when students are waiting for a change of activity and have nothing to do, is minimized. Management problems are often the result of students being idle, bored, or distracted (Good & Brophy, 2008). By developing and teaching classroom rules and procedures, teachers can minimize delays, down time, and distractions, thus preventing problem behaviors.

Principle #4: Signal the beginning of transition times, and give clear directions to students during the transition period.

Doyle (2006) states that teachers can effectively use signals to begin transition times and that teachers should instruct their students in the purpose of the signal and in how students should move through the transition period. When students are transitioning from one activity to another, teachers should give clear directions to students and monitor events. Marzano, Gaddy, Foseid, Foseid, and Marzano (2009) suggested that a way to reduce transition times is to appoint a student leader for each transition.

Teachers should acknowledge students who efficiently manage the transition and correct those who do not. Doyle (2006) reported that less effective classroom managers did not prepare or monitor their students during transition periods. As a result, students spent longer times in transition periods, and disruptions increased.

To summarize, students are required to transition from one activity to another many times during a typical school day. The more efficient the transition, the less instructional time is wasted. If transitions are poorly planned and executed, however, instructional time will be lost, and the likelihood of behavior problems and disruptions will increase. The goal of the transition, therefore, is to end one activity successfully and move the students quickly into the next. Effective classroom managers decrease the amount of time that students spend transitioning and monitor transitions to ensure that they are accomplished efficiently. Teachers can do this by:

1. Planning for transitions.
2. Teaching the transition procedure.
3. Preparing materials for the next activity before the transition time.
4. Signaling the beginning of transition times, and giving clear directions to students.

Additionally, students who efficiently complete transitions should be acknowledged, and students who have difficulties should be corrected.

Q: *I am aware of how important transitions are for preventing behavior problems in the classroom, but it seems like sometimes we have efficient transitions and other times we have problems. I do many of the things that you suggest, but is there anything I am missing or need to think about to have better consistency and efficiency?*

A: Clearly, you understand the importance of teaching students how to make efficient transitions. Moreover, because your students sometimes successfully transition from one activity to another, they know that is an expectation in your classroom and understand how to transition quietly and quickly. Are there any particular times when your students have problems with transitions? For example, is there is a change in the daily schedule when the transition problems occur? Do problems occur when the students transition from active to quiet activities? In these situations, you may want to briefly remind the students, shortly before the transition occurs, how they are supposed to move from one activity to the next. This is a procedure called precorrection, which we address in Chapter 8. Then, a few minutes before the transition begins, give the students a verbal prompt to begin getting ready to move to the next activity. As always, acknowledge the students who transition quickly and quietly.

Summary

This chapter provided information on the ways in which teachers should structure and organize their classrooms to prevent problem behavior and maintain order. We discussed (a) setting up the physical environment, (b) establishing and teaching procedures, (c) developing and teaching rules and consequences, and (d) managing transitions. Through structuring the learning environment, teachers attempt to make their classrooms as predictable as possible.

As shown in Figure 3.1, teachers who want structured and organized classrooms must develop and implement classroom procedures and rules and then instruct students on how to correctly follow these procedures and rules. Be withit, and know what is going on in your classroom at all times. Acknowledge and provide positive consequences when students follow procedures and rules correctly, and provide corrective feedback when students do not. When students follow the procedures and rules, teachers will have orderly classrooms where it is more likely that they can teach and that students will learn.

Teach students how to transition between activities. If students are able to end a task or activity and begin another efficiently, quietly, and quickly, disruptions will be minimized, and time available for classroom activities will be increased.

Yes	No	Action
❏	❏	The teacher directly teaches and posts typical classroom procedures and routines.
❏	❏	The teacher directly teaches and posts efficient transition routines.
❏	❏	The teacher directly teaches and posts classroom rules.
❏	❏	The teacher monitors student behavior and has a system for acknowledging students who follow classroom procedures, routines, and rules.
❏	❏	The teacher directly teaches and posts classroom consequences (positive and negative).
❏	❏	The teacher knows what all students are doing all of the time (i.e., the teacher exhibits withitness).

FIGURE 3.1 Checklist of important actions in structuring the classroom.

Additional Resources

On the Web

Page Title	Annotations	Web Address
Classroom Architect	Interactive tool used to set up and manipulate classroom layout	http://classroom.4teachers.org/
Classroom Rule Ideas	Ideas for rules in the classroom, with an emphasis on building a classroom community	http://www.ehow.com/info_7842392_classroom-rule-ideas.html
Head Off Behavior Problems with Classroom Procedures	Suggestions for tasks in the classroom for which procedures are necessary	http://www2.scholastic.com/browse/article.jsp?id=3749726
Sponge and Transition Activities	Fast-paced activities to make transitions more effective and fun	http://atozteacherstuff.com/Tips/Sponge_and_Transition_Activities/

In the Literature

Evertson, C., Poole, I., & the IRIS Center. (2002). *Effective room arrangement.* Retrieved January 11, 2012, from http://iris.peabody.vanderbilt.edu/case_studies/ICS-001.pdf

This case study investigates ways to arrange a classroom based on the function and availability of space. The authors provide numerous images of possible arrangements and plans for implementation in the classroom.

McIntosh, K., Herman, K., Sanford, A., McGraw, K., & Florence, K. (2004). Teaching transitions. *Teaching Exceptional Children, 37*(1), 32–38.

This article details how to teach transition behaviors to students in a sequential and logical manner. The authors emphasize the use of rationales and positive reinforcement during the teaching process.

References

Colvin, G., & Lazar, M. (1997). *The effective classroom manager: Managing for success.* Longmont, CO: Sopris West.

Doyle, W. (2006). Ecological approaches to classroom management. In C. M. Evertson & C. D. Weinstein (Eds.), *Handbook of classroom management: Research, practice, and contemporary issues* (pp.97–125). New York: Lawrence Erlbaum.

Emmer, E. T., & Evertson, C. M. (2009). *Classroom management for middle and high school teachers* (8th ed.). Upper Saddle River, NJ: Pearson/Merrill Education.

Evertson, C. M., & Emmer, E. T. (2009). *Classroom management for elementary teachers* (8th ed.). Upper Saddle River, NJ: Pearson/Merrill Education.

Gettinger, M., & Kohler, K. M. (2006). Process-oriented approaches to classroom management and effective teaching. In C. M. Evertson & C. D. Weinstein (Eds.), *Handbook of classroom management: Research, practice, and contemporary issues* (pp. 73–95). New York: Lawrence Erlbaum.

Good, T. L., & Brophy, J. (2008). *Looking in classrooms* (10th ed.). Upper Saddle River, NJ: Pearson/ Merrill Education.

Kounin, J. S. (1970). *Discipline and group management in classrooms.* New York: Holt, Rinehart, & Winston.

Marzano, R. J., Gaddy, B. B., Foseid, M. C., Foseid, M. P., & Marzano, J. S. (2009). *A handbook for classroom management that works.* Alexandria, VA: Association for Supervision & Curriculum Development.

Marzano, R. J., Marzano, J. S., & Pickering, D. J. (2009). *Classroom management that works: Research-based strategies for every teacher.* Alexandria, VA: Association for Supervision & Curriculum Development.

Morgan, D. P., & Jenson, W. R. (1988). *Teaching behaviorally disordered students: Preferred practices.* Upper Saddle River, NJ: Pearson/Merrill Education.

Savage, T. V., & Savage, M. K. (2010). *Successful classroom management and discipline: Teaching self-control and responsibility* (3rd ed.). Thousand Oaks, CA: Sage.

Sugai, G., & Horner, R. (2006). A promising approach for expanding and sustaining the implementation of schoolwide positive behavior support. *School Psychology Review, 35,* 245–259.

Sugai, G., & Horner, R. H. (2008). What we know and need to know about preventing problem behavior in schools. *Exceptionality, 16,* 67–77.

CHAPTER

4

Understanding and Fostering Teacher–Student Relationships to Prevent Behavior Problems

Christopher L. Van Loan and Mike Marlowe

GOALS

- Explain the importance of developing healthy teacher–student relationships.
- Describe what influences teacher–student relationships.

- Provide strategies for gauging, maintaining, and improving relationships.
- Design a relationship-driven classroom.

SCENARIO

Terrence is a 10-year-old, fourth-grade boy who lives with his aunt, uncle, and younger brother while attending the neighborhood school. Terrence lived with his mother until age six but was removed from the home because of her drug and alcohol addiction. The teachers at his school believe that Terrence's aunt may have a significant alcohol addiction as well. Terrence's father has been in and out of jail on various drug charges and is currently working as a dishwasher at a golf and country club. Although he is an irregular presence in his son's life, Terrence still looks up to his dad and wishes to please him by one day being a pro golfer. At school, Terrence is viewed by most of the teachers as untrusting, withdrawn, angry, and resistant.

Ms. Brenner, Terrence's teacher, prides herself on being a "no-nonsense" teacher. She believes her role is to deliver curriculum in an efficient and methodical manner. Believing that "distance" is necessary to maintain authority and respect, she stays detached from students like Terrence. One day, during a science lesson on inertia, Terrence is sullen, withdrawn, and as usual, has difficulty paying attention to the lesson. As before, Ms. Brenner tries to correct his off-task behavior mostly by punishment, and as before, she has little success. Ms. Brenner often tells Terrence that if he does not pay attention, do his assignments, and act like school is his job, he will probably end up in jail. Terrence typically responds by rolling his eyes, mumbling under his breath, and sometimes, even pushing paper off his desk. Ms. Brenner does not know that Terrence's father has spent time in jail.

Ms. Brenner views Terrence as an angry, resistant boy who needs to learn to follow the rules and obey directions. By mid-November, Ms. Brenner has given up trying new things to get Terrence to act appropriately. It is her belief that Terrence takes too much time away from the other children. As a result, Terrence is often left on his own, and his negative view of adults is confirmed once more.

Everyone has memories of their school days and, perhaps, a fond memory of one teacher who was special and who you would do anything for. The question is, why was that teacher so special? What was it that made this teacher so unique? The answer may lie in the fact that the student and the teacher had a high-quality teacher–student relationship, one that was a powerful determinant of academic and social outcomes.

For challenging students like Terrence, the quality of the teacher–student relationship is a salient variable in preventing behavior problems. Moreover, initiating and sustaining a meaningful relationship with a troubled student is the only context that allows successful intervention (Brendtro, Brokenleg, & Van Bockern, 2002; Long, Morse, Fecser, & Newman, 2007). If education professionals are not successful in developing a meaningful interpersonal bond with students who have behavior problems, then a good portion of effective pedagogical techniques and behavioral interventions becomes mundane and ineffective. According to Long (2008), it is like a car engine without any oil. It is not going very far before it heats up and shuts down. Scholars like Gharabaghi (2008) argue that for troubled students, building a relationship is, in effect, the intervention, and from our point of view, building a quality teacher–student relationship can thus prevent problem behaviors and contribute to a student's academic, social, and emotional well-being.

In this chapter, we discuss what teachers can do to reduce problem behaviors through developing high-quality teacher–student relationships, the dimensions involved in relationships with students, and how these dimensions can be used to gauge relationship quality. We follow up by discussing the attributes of relationship-driven teachers and then present techniques for setting up a relationship-driven classroom.

HOW TEACHERS CAN INFLUENCE TEACHER–STUDENT RELATIONSHIPS

There is a basic assumption that adults want the very best for their children. Generally, society trusts that schools will create positive opportunities and success for the students they serve. One of the key factors within a school that contributes to a student's academic and social success is the interpersonal aspects of education. Yet for students like Terrence, many negative life events, such as maltreatment, poor child care, and divorce, can contribute to social and academic difficulties in school. Additionally, academic challenges caused by learning disabilities, physical disabilities, cognitive deficits, emotional disorders, and other health impairments, such as attention deficit/hyperactivity disorder, may also contribute to a student's social and academic difficulties. If not addressed, negative life events and learning challenges can result in a dual risk for more severe social and emotional problems for many students that may be lifelong (Erickson & Pianta, 1989; Pianta & Walsh, 1996).

For years, researchers have suggested that an early emphasis on high-quality teacher–student relationships may assuage the lifelong difficulties and problems of students at high risk for emotional or behavioral challenges (Meehan, Hughes, & Cavell, 2003). Early positive relationships with adults, defined as a low degree of conflict, an appropriate degree of dependency, and a high degree of closeness, have been found to buffer the negative trajectories forecasted for students who experience negative life events or demonstrate challenging behaviors. In fact, students at high risk for behavioral difficulties who experience positive relationships with their teacher have shown improved social and academic outcomes (Murray & Greenberg, 2001; Pianta, Belsky, Vandergrift, Houts, & Morrison, 2008). Because adult–child relationships are so crucial to social and emotional competence, any strained or coercive relationship may contribute to school-related difficulties. Hence, quality relationships between teachers and students are a viable intervention for reinforcing positive social, emotional, and academic development.

An emphasis on building relationships, however, is only part of the equation necessary for fostering the academic, social, and emotional needs of students. Teachers should consider their instructional and emotional practices along with what drives the classroom environment as being equally important techniques to best promote positive academic, social, and emotional development for their students. Moreover, it is important to remember that relationships are bidirectional. Although it takes "two to tango," teachers can consciously act in a manner to foster meaningful relationships with their students.

Consider Instructional Practices

For many teachers, a strong mastery of content knowledge *and* the ability to link that knowledge to a student's schema, or the way a student looks at the world, is a key component within a high-quality teacher–student relationship. Teachers who emphasize strategies for concept development or how all facts are interconnected will promote higher-order thinking rather than simple memorization of disparate facts. Such strategies give students greater success in promoting academic growth and improving relationships. Additionally, providing some structure to instruction by consciously linking and connecting facts and concepts provides students with usable knowledge that can generalize to standardized tests. Along with connecting facts to concepts, the provision of quality feedback and modeling also enhances the metacognitive skills needed for academic and social development (Pianta, La Paro, & Hamre, 2006). Whenever possible, making instruction relevant and interesting to students will increase student engagement and improve academic outcomes. This can be accomplished by considering the interest of the student and scaffolding the content to their next zone of proximal development (Van der Veer & Valsiner, 1994) or next level of understanding.

Ms. Brenner, the teacher in the scenario at the beginning of this chapter, has a strong mastery of her science content, but the fact that she did not link Terrence's interest in golf to the lesson on inertia reduced her chances of connecting concepts for him. Thus, she missed the chance to establish a meaningful relationship. At the time, Ms. Brenner did not know that Terrence's father worked at a local country club, had spent time in jail, or that Terrence is frequently disappointed with his dad, who often cancels scheduled visitations. When Terrence does visit with his father, he usually gets to "hang out" with other staff members at the country club, who do fun things like ride in the golf carts and pick up balls on the driving range. Unbeknownst to Ms. Brenner, Terrence often dreams of owning his own set of clubs, and unbeknownst to Terrence, Ms. Brenner enjoys playing golf on weekends and was even on her high school golf team. If Ms. Brenner considered Terrence's interests, linked his interest to her lesson so that he saw connections, and included teacher modeling and positive feedback, she would be better able to connect with Terrence (and other students like him) and build quality relationships.

Consider Emotional Practices

How a teacher's emotions are perceived by students has a direct influence on the quality of a teacher–student relationship. By consciously reflecting and considering affect or mood, a teacher has a better chance of improving teacher–student interactions. Improved interactions, over time, lead to higher-quality relationships. A teacher's warmth and sensitivity have been associated with achievement gains in first-grade students (Hamre & Pianta, 2005) and have been shown to mollify the disruptive behavior of some children (Rimm-Kaufman, La Paro, Pianta, & Downer, 2005). In the case of Terrence, had Ms. Brenner refrained from derogatory comments about that student's future, their interactions may have been more instructionally and emotionally supportive.

Teachers often find social situations in the classroom aversive when students display problem behavior, which can result in less instructional and emotional support. Teachers who are sensitive to the emotional environment tend to be more aware of their students' academic performance and social functioning. Students who experience emotional support from their teachers will have greater achievement gains, have fewer behavior problems, and be more willing and motivated to comply with classroom norms and teacher expectations (Wang, Haertel, & Walberg, 1997).

Q: *I have never thought carefully about my affect in the classroom or about providing emotional support for my students. What can I do to improve my emotional practices?*

A: To be emotionally resilient for your students, you must first take care of yourself. To be able to reflect consciously and consider how your affect and your emotions may affect your relationships with your students, try emotionally refreshing techniques like meditation, a monthly massage, an outlet to express your feelings without judgment, or a brisk walk. Seek out other empathetic teachers who work well with diverse student populations for advice on how to professionally keep negative emotions from taking over during the school day. We realize the stresses and complexity of working with a variety of students, but if you regularly take care of your mind, body, and spirit, you will be at your best for your students.

Consider What Drives the Classroom Environment

A teacher's emphasis on student productivity and effective classroom management has been associated with developing high-quality teacher–student relationships. Student productivity can be enhanced through established routines whereby students are engaged using high-interest activities with clear directions. Teachers who set these routines during the first days of the school year have a better chance of shaping student behavior to meet their expectations, and teachers who use strategies throughout the school year to help students self-regulate their learning and behavior to achieve goals have been shown to improve productivity (Pianta et al., 2006). From the start of the school year, teachers using a proactive approach to behavior management and use of immediacy behaviors, such as teacher "withitness" (Kounin, 1970) (see Chapter 3), can drastically reduce problematic student behavior and increase academic productivity.

Sometimes, students like Terrence zone out and are prodded by their peers. If Ms. Brenner were to respond to Terrence's *Hey, quit it!* and not to the student who prodded him, she would demonstrate a lack of withitness, potentially reinforce negative behaviors, and jeopardize opportunities to establish quality relationships. Selecting classroom rules and focusing on consistent enforcement helps with fairness in the classroom. Teachers who encourage democratic classroom practices and who allow and accept student feedback are more likely to promote desired behavior and improve student autonomy, which can improve teacher–student relationships.

The classroom environment, which is comprised of academic, social, and emotional dimensions, is directly linked to the quality of teacher–student relationships. Students with emotional and behavioral difficulties often negatively affect the classroom through exhibiting undesired externalizing behavior. The way a teacher decides to handle classroom interactions will positively or negatively influence the emotional and academic environment and directly impact the quality of relationships. Frequently, within conflict-oriented relationships, teachers who engage in a higher frequency of social commands often lead to student dependency or increasingly conflictive interactions. Conversely, teachers who create an environment that includes strong instructional and emotional supports improve the quality of teacher–student relationships.

For example, Hamre and Pianta (2005) found that at-risk, first-grade students who were placed in classrooms offering strong instructional and emotional supports achieved teacher-rated academic scores and student–teacher relationship scores similar to those of low-risk peers. Alternatively, similar students who were placed in less supportive classrooms were rated lower in achievement and higher in conflictive student–teacher relationship scores by their teacher. Hamre and Pianta concluded that the probability of future conflict-oriented relationships between students and teachers can be moderated by the quality of the classroom environment.

Q: *Okay, so a lot of evidence suggests that building relationships seems to work for younger elementary children, but what about students in the upper elementary grades?*

A: Older students state that they understand a teacher cares by the way in which that teacher challenges and guides them during social and academic situations. In a sense, the way you deliver the challenge or guidance, and how your students perceive or interpret any interaction, is key to a caring, close relationship. We suggest adding jokes and a bit of good-hearted or playful sarcasm to match an older student's sense of humor along with the serious purpose underlying the lesson. You may also want to frequently make a sincere comment about their appearance within academic and social contexts, as older students are becoming concerned with how they look.

Consider That Relationships Are Bidirectional

Quality social interactions that take place over time lead to meaningful relationships. In the classroom, it is important to remember that building relationships is bidirectional and requires reciprocity from teacher and student. Terrence, for example, did not make instruction or emotionally supportive interactions easy for Ms. Brenner.

Within the teacher–student relationship, reciprocity can be seen as an exchange of norms, beliefs, or values, where the teacher provides the student with student-recognized needs *and* the student reciprocates through fulfilling the expected classroom norms. How teachers and students decide to invest in, not invest in, or disengage from a relationship is based on both teacher and student behavior and the perception of how each person's needs are being met.

If teachers want to understand the quality of relationships in their classroom, it is essential to consider individual interactions with a student over time. For example, teacher praise, which is one type of teacher–student interaction, has positive effects on academic and behavioral outcomes (Walker, Colvin, & Ramsey, 1995). However, it is important to remember that not only what you say but also how you say it may improve or undermine the desired effects. In fact, praise and reward, which are often viewed as positive, may also be perceived by students as manipulative and impact the quality of future interactions. If teacher–student interactions are viewed as controlling or coercive, both the teacher and the student may see the classroom environment as punishing, which will lead to escape or avoidance behaviors. Instead, teachers should consider giving encouragement by commenting on specific behaviors. When teachers use behavior-specific praise, they avoid the coercive and controlling perceptions and actually increase the likelihood of similar behavior occurring in the future. For example, instead of telling a student *I like what you did, good job,* a teacher may say, *Terrence's hand is up, let's hear what he has to say!*

A student's behavior certainly contributes to the overall quality of the relationship. Researchers have shown that students with aggressive behaviors have significantly fewer interactions with their teachers than students without behavioral difficulties, resulting in less effective instruction and lower-quality relationships. Because Terrence and Ms. Brenner have increasingly low rates of interaction with each other, any situation where Ms. Brenner corrects Terrence's misbehavior can increase his aggression, prompting both of them to disengage from the relationship and, thus, yielding lower-quality instruction. Teachers who consider and adjust their negative interactions to more positive ones, over time, have a greater likelihood of promoting quality relationships within their classroom.

Q: *I believe firmly in a positive approach to behavior management, but how do I balance the need for effective control of my classroom and building quality relationships with my students?*

A: The key to any high-quality teacher–student relationship is a balance between good management of student behavior and cooperation. Effective classroom management and student–teacher cooperation are not mutually exclusive; rather, they can complement each other in the hands of a skilled teacher. Students rely on teachers for guidance and instruction more so than teachers rely on students. Thus, teachers should consider body language and tone of voice, and they should concentrate on the student's behavior, not the student. This should happen during each and every interaction to communicate that the teacher is, indeed, in control of the classroom and, at the same time, takes a personal and vested interest in each student.

DIMENSIONS INVOLVED IN TEACHER–STUDENT RELATIONSHIPS

Student relationships with teachers comprise many complex components and intersecting characteristics. Relationships unfold over time, and they evolve based on individual characteristics, such as basic personality, beliefs, history of interactions, intelligence, and gender. Predisposing student factors, both biological and developmental, also affect interactions with teachers; however, an examination of factors such as depression, bipolar disorders, and posttraumatic stress disorder are beyond the scope of this chapter. Instead, we emphasize variables that capture those dimensions of teacher–student relationships that a teacher can influence: (a) conflict, (b) closeness, and (c) dependency. Each of these dimensions can directly influence a student's academic and behavioral performance. Understanding these dimensions and how they can influence teachers and students can help with developing quality teacher–student relationships.

Consider the Degree of Conflict

Conflict is the degree to which a teacher perceives a relationship with a student as being negative and conflict-oriented (Pianta, 2001). A high degree of conflict in teacher–student relationships has been correlated with a teacher's willingness to provide academic and emotional support (Birch & Ladd, 1997). Because conflict-oriented relationships have been related to a variety of negative outcomes for many students (Pianta & Stuhlman, 2004), it is important that teachers act in a way that promotes warm, close interactions. In part, how a teacher interacts with a student is based on that teacher's perceptions of that student, and how teachers perceive the degree of conflict within a relationship with a student is correlated with their efforts to address problematic behavior (Hamre, Pianta, Downer, & Mashburn, 2007). Such a complex web of interactions requires techniques to reduce conflict and promote higher-quality relationships, such as the strategies we provide later in this chapter. Moreover, Hamre and colleagues found that teachers who reported greater depression, who had lower teacher efficacy, and who were also observed to provide less emotional support were associated with more conflict-oriented relationships with their students. No doubt, part of having low conflict with students requires self-evaluation, ongoing training, and time to take care of you.

Some researchers have explored the influence of conflictive relationships on behaviors such as aggression and conduct problems. Hughes, Cavell, and Jackson (1999) examined elementary children nominated as aggressive over a three-year period to determine the influence of teacher–student relationship quality on subsequent levels of aggression. These researchers found that initial teacher and student reports of poor relationship quality were associated with teacher-rated student aggression during succeeding years. An early high-quality relationship with students is of utmost importance for their future success in life.

A high level of conflict between teachers and students can be used to predict student academic and behavioral difficulties. For example, Hamre and Pianta (2001) found a relationship between academics and relational negativity such that a large percentage of students suspended during the longitudinal study had been identified during kindergarten as having conflictive teacher–student relationships. Related longitudinal investigations revealed that kindergarten children who were at risk for grade retention but who also had more open and less conflictive relationships were more likely to be promoted to first grade than those students with less open and more conflictive relationships (Pianta & Steinberg, 1992; Pianta, Steinberg, & Rollins, 1995).

Teachers can reduce conflicts with students by making a greater ratio of positive comments than negative or neutral comments in the classroom. For even the most challenging students, there are situations during the school day when they behave appropriately; thus, teachers should look carefully for opportunities to provide positive comments about their behavior and academic performance, even if the behavior is only a close approximation to what you really desire. Another way to reduce conflict with students is to use strategies for perspective taking during difficult moments. For example, acknowledging that you understand the feelings of a student who is angry with one of his classmates, and explaining to the student what you would do to manage your emotions, demonstrates your ability to understand his perspective. It is also important to consider your tone of voice, which when used correctly and with forethought can neutralize conflictive situations.

Other considerations for teachers regarding the relational dimension of conflict are:

- Be aware of frustrations, and try to compartmentalize them when dealing with a challenging interaction.
- Think about the end game before acting. Determine what outcome is desired from an encounter with students, and then choose the action most likely to encourage that outcome.
- Understand the function of students' behaviors. Why are they doing what they are doing? When they engage in problem behavior, what are they trying to get or avoid?
- Include clear descriptions of any approximation of desired behavior when providing behavioral feedback.
- Be aware of tone of voice. How would you sound to an outside observer? How will a student receive your message?

Q: *What can I do easily to start reducing the conflict that I have with a student in my class?*

A: Use the concepts of conflict as a lens through which to view your relationship with your student. Since you have noticed that you are engaging in a high level of conflict, try greeting the student in the morning with a handshake, saying his or her name, and making a compliment like *I noticed that you like those new type of sandals that just came out. I like them, too.* You might also mention that you heard the student likes baseball or has an extensive doll collection. You might even ask them to see the collection someday. Try these types of strategies for several weeks, take notes on the types of interactions you have, and see if the level of conflict subsides. If at first the student refuses to shake your hand, continue to reach out, and don't take it personally. It may be the case that it takes a while for the conflict to subside, but patience will help.

Consider the Degree of Closeness

Closeness is the degree to which a teacher and student experience affection, warmth, and open communication (Pianta, 2001). Ladd and Burgess (2001) investigated whether the degree of relational stressors and supports, which are indicators of close relationships, influences the trajectory of childhood aggression. They found that increased levels of teacher–student closeness and peer acceptance might improve aggressive children's problem-solving skills, levels of participation, and bonds to school. Similarly, Howes, Hamilton, and Matheson (1994) found that young children's security with teachers, as measured by teacher reports and observations, was negatively associated with conflict (i.e., aggression) and positively associated with companionable behaviors (i.e., closeness, warmth, empathy). Interestingly, African-American and Hispanic children at high risk for school failure were found to receive greater benefit from close teacher–student relationships than their Caucasian peers (Murray, Waas, & Murray, 2008).

In a related study, Hamre and Pianta (2001) demonstrated that children who trust their teachers are more motivated to succeed in school than children with lower-quality teacher–student relationships. In a similar way, teachers and students who exhibit warm feelings toward each other are also correlated with a student's positive attitude toward school (Birch & Ladd, 1998). That is, students who experience warm feelings for their teacher may feel safe in the classroom environment and, therefore, are more likely to exhibit desired academic and social behaviors than peers with poor teacher–student relationships.

The warmth or closeness that a teacher demonstrates can improve a student's engagement, academic achievement, and quality of relationships. Teachers who demonstrate empathy mediate a student's perception of a close relationship with his or her teacher, thus making the student more likely to engage in academic tasks. The use of well-timed, behaviorally descriptive praise statements, such as a telling a student about the good selection of words used in a sentence or *Way to be a gentleman and hold the door for us*, can also encourage warm, close interactions. A teacher's nonthreatening use of close proximity and eye contact can increase positive interactions, reduce undesired behavior, and promote academic achievement. Sometimes, it can be as simple as a gentle look in the eye, a smile, and a meaningful handshake. As a caution, some students may become too close and use their teachers as a shield to protect them from anxiety-producing situations (e.g., social or academic challenges). This may result in less initiative, and they may be more tentative in self-discovery during instruction.

Considering the relational dimension of closeness, teachers can:

- Greet each and every student at the door upon entry throughout the school year. If you miss some students while talking to another, that's okay; you'll get them tomorrow.
- Use students' names, and mention something personal about them.
- Connect academic content to something that interests the student.
- Look at each and every student, and listen to what he or she says. Use their comments sporadically throughout instruction.

Consider the Appropriate Degree of Dependency

Dependency describes the degree to which a teacher perceives students as being overly dependent or lacking age-appropriate levels of autonomy (Pianta, 2001). Conversely, due to the nature of teacher–student relationships, a degree of student dependency is needed to establish a secure base for academic and emotional growth (Pianta, 2000). Finding the right amount of academic and social dependency for your students should be considered on an individual basis. It is best to strive for a balance where students feel safe to explore academic and social challenges yet are willing to seek assistance when needed.

Researchers have linked students' overdependency on teachers to low self-concept and low social competence. Further, dependent teacher–student relationships may be more common in students with emotional and behavioral difficulties. For example, researchers have associated overly dependent preschool children with low social competence and aggression (Blankemeyer, Flannery, & Vazsonyi, 2002). Aggressive children who self-rated higher in social competence were more likely to perceive the teacher–student relationship as more favorable than aggressive students who self-rated lower in social competence. Blankemeyer and colleagues concluded that aggressive children who possessed more social competence are more likely to have improved academic and social outcomes, including more positive teacher–student relationships. Given the evidence that social competence requires independent management of social skills and that students with less social competence are frequently less bonded to teachers, those teachers who emphasize interventions that improve the quality of social competence may improve student bonds to teachers and decrease overdependency. Some techniques for improving interactions and increasing autonomous opportunities with your students are presented later in this chapter.

When considering the relational dimension of dependency, teachers should:

- Try to mix in lessons that are reaching toward each student's next proximal academic level. You don't have to address every student every time, but try!
- Construct your lessons so that students process the information with you. Students may still need teacher guidance, but make it so they do not overly depend on you to solve the task.
- Give parts of an answer, and allow students to process and make connections at their own thinking speed.

Q: *How do I know if my students are overdependent on me, and what can I do to improve their autonomy?*

A: Often, you know if you have overly dependent students when they seem to hang around you more than their peers. They wait for you to make decisions, frequently seek you out during free time, and seem to be afraid of exploring new experiences without you. Without proper guidance, these students may become targets for bullies, or even become bullies themselves. By talking openly about your feelings and how you control your own fears, you can act as an emotional coach and model self-control, with the goal of these students ultimately being able to soothe their anxieties.

GAUGING THE QUALITY OF YOUR RELATIONSHIP

As we have explored, conflict, closeness, and dependency, as mutually perceived by teachers and students, contribute to an overall relational quality. By understanding the degree of conflict, degree of closeness, and appropriate degree of dependency, a teacher can gauge the quality of the relationship. The degree of conflict, closeness, and dependency between teachers and students influences the classroom environment, particularly the related elements of emotional and instructional outcomes. Teachers who gauge their interactions by and consciously adjust their behavior toward their students using the appropriate degrees of low conflict, high perceptions of closeness, and appropriate degree of dependency contribute to an environment that is conducive for meaningful relationships. Although students contribute to the overall classroom environment through social and academic behaviors, a teacher can guide the quality of relationships by adjusting and structuring interactions and the classroom environment in a way that improves the likelihood for preserving and enhancing desired behaviors.

Q: *What tips will help me consider consciously the degree of conflict, closeness, and dependency that will also allow me to alter my own behavior?*

A: We all know we breathe, but think about your breathing—right now. Do you notice when you inhale and exhale? Now that you are thinking about it, you are probably changing your rate of breathing, or at least are more aware of your breaths. That means you are changing your behavior due to being consciously aware of your behavior. Now think carefully about the degree of conflict, closeness, and dependency when interacting with your students, and see if your behavior, over time, changes and if your relationships improve.

ATTRIBUTES OF RELATIONSHIP-DRIVEN TEACHERS

"Relationship-driven" is a term used to denote the high priority placed on preserving and enhancing the teacher–student relationship. The cornerstone of a relationship-driven approach to working with students having behavior problems is commitment (Marlowe, 1999, 2006; Hayden & Marlowe, in press). It is the unequivocal commitment of one individual to another that evokes positive change. Students who disrupt class or exhibit other behavior problems need to have a committed relationship for success in school. Students need to know that adults in school care about them and that they are valued. For students like Terrence, the significant adults in his life may have been unable to provide adequate commitment, but this does not mean he is unworthy of commitment from others. Many students who have behavior problems arrive at school with a history, perhaps, of dysfunctional relationships with adults, and as a result, they are often wary of adults. When this is the case, students can be, using Erikson's (1963) term, embodying basic mistrust. Thus, students need to experience a model of functionality in action before they can begin to trust.

A teacher's primary task is to model, among other things, how a functional adult behaves, relates to others, and handles negative situations, because humans learn best through observation (Bandura, 1995). When watching a functional adult, the student learns how to be part of a relationship in a healthy and appropriate way and what it feels like to be cared for by a functional adult. The question remains, however, what constitutes a functional adult? Torey Hayden, the author of eight books chronicling her day-to-day work as a special education teacher and child psychologist, outlined the attributes of a functional adult in a workshop on the relationship-driven classroom (Hayden & Marlowe, 2005). A functional adult, according to Hayden, should be able to do the following things with a student:

- Be fair, moral, and honest.
- Know his or her own strengths and weaknesses.
- Know how to deal safely and effectively with feelings.

- Take responsibility for actions.
- Show resilience.
- Maintain reasonable optimism, and behave consistently and predictably.
- Recognize and respect boundaries, and set boundaries that are fair and appropriate.
- Have realistic expectations of students.
- Know how to be firm, fair, and friendly, all at the same time.
- Take care of students, and not let them be put in dangerous situations.
- Help students realize their full potential.

Trust is probably the single biggest barrier to quality relationships with students in the classroom. Until students trust teachers, students will be unwilling to let their guard down and feel respected and appreciated. As far back as 1982, Hobbs wrote about the role of trust:

> Trust between student and staff is essential. It is the foundation on which all principles rest. Trust is the glue that holds teaching and learning together. Trust is the beginning of the re-education process. (pp. 22–23)

Trust, like self-esteem, is tricky, because it is not something you can teach. It is not something you can buy, and it is not something you can demand. For teachers, developing trust with students is a process, not a goal, and it is essentially the process of experiencing functionality in action. The most outstanding thing about trust is that it is earned, and by being a functional adult as we have described, you can gain student trust.

We recommend the following steps to build trust between teacher and student:

1. *Listen.* Listen to students when they talk. Stay in the moment, and pay attention. Hear what they are saying as opposed to what you think they are saying or what you want them to say. The moment you manage to communicate that you are genuinely listening to them, they will trust you.
2. *Be extra consistent.* When students are among new people and in a new environment, it is normal for them to feel anxious and disinclined to trust. Consistency eases these feelings more quickly.
3. *Respond positively to the student to show genuine regard.* Smile. Greet students when you see them. Try not to talk over them or ignore them when talking to someone else. Also, acknowledge the student's effort to forge a relationship, such as *Thank you for telling me that. It helps me understand what happened.*
4. *Articulate worries you perceive a student to have.* By the way you are sitting, I sense that you feel bad about that. Can I help? or You don't look very happy today.
5. *Articulate what you can be trusted not to do.* Many students from difficult backgrounds have a history with adults that include punishment, abuse, and abandonment. If this is the case, being open about the boundaries that you, as a functional adult, will never cross is often helpful in forming relationships. On the other hand, never promise what you know you cannot deliver.

When a teacher shares emotions, it can engender trust as well. Sharing emotions allows a teacher to model self-awareness. Students tend to form relationships most easily with people they believe are like them. Several tips can help a teacher share emotions:

1. *Acknowledge your feelings.* *I feel frustrated when I see everybody out of their seat* or *I feel excited when it's time for art.* Use appropriate talk by sharing your internal thoughts on how you are handling your feelings. *I feel overwhelmed after all that concentrating. Going outside in the fresh air will make me feel better.*

2. *Acknowledge your physical state, particularly tiredness and stress.* This not only enables students to see how a functional adult handles such physical states, it also helps them to better understand your behavior.

3. *Talk about your experiences as a student of the same age and how you did similar things.* Most students cannot conceive of their teacher ever having been a student, and most are intrigued by stories that show you had feelings and experiences similar to their own.

4. *Share personal items.* Such items can include photographs, particularly of yourself during your student years.

5. *Participate occasionally in ordinary events with students.* Join them for lunch, or play games that take place out of class.

Finally, while sharing your human side with your students is an important part of establishing and strengthening relationships, always keep clear and not cross the boundaries of a functional adult. These boundaries will vary from person to person, but remember, the objective is to be a warm, friendly person and a functional one as well.

Q: *I teach at a school where issues of poverty create student behaviors that are most difficult to handle and manage effectively. How can a teacher build relationships with students who are relationship-resistant?*

A: It is a paradox that the very students most in need of healthy relationships tend to resist them. Sometimes, difficult-to-manage students isolate themselves intentionally from others by making themselves as objectionable as possible. Two essential elements in establishing relationships with relationship-resistant students are differential acceptance and empathy. Differential acceptance is the ability of teachers to receive large doses of anger, aggression, and hostility from students without reacting in a similar way. These behaviors should be accepted for what they are—namely, expressions of pain and anguish from the many hurts inflicted upon them. Empathy requires teachers to actively search students' behaviors, symptoms, words, feelings, and silences for clues to their inner selves. Difficult-to-manage students need a teacher's best effort to appreciate and help them with what they are experiencing and feeling. A teacher also needs to exhibit a determined effort to understand their students' point of view.

SETTING UP A RELATIONSHIP-DRIVEN CLASSROOM

A teacher who understands the importance of using teacher–student relationships to positively affect student behavior spends ample time thinking about a classroom that is relationship-driven. Hayden and Marlowe (2005) discussed the parameters teachers should consider when setting up a relationship-driven classroom by describing strategies for (a) establishing boundaries, (b) what happens when rules are broken, and (c) creating a positive classroom environment.

Establishing Boundaries

The first and most important ingredient in a successful relationship-driven classroom is the clear articulation of ground rules or clear boundaries for student and teacher behavior. As an extension of the discussion in Chapter 3 about developing and teaching classroom rules, this means not only deciding on what rules and limits on behavior are necessary for order in the classroom but also how these rules will be enforced while balancing the goal of building and maintaining quality relationships.

The first reason why rules and clear boundaries are so important for a relationship-driven classroom is physical safety. Equally compelling, however, is the need for psychological safety. Some students, particularly those who exhibit emotional and behavioral difficulties, have issues with self-control; thus, they are in need of rules for behavior that can provide immediate safety. Rules for the relationship-driven classroom should communicate that the teacher is in control. This does not mean control as in *I'm bigger and stronger than you are, and that's why you have to follow my rules,* which can encourage conflict and power struggles. Rather, the rules and articulated boundaries should communicate *I know your situation at the moment might be out of control, but I am in control of myself. I am strong and safe and I will be able to successfully keep you safe.* For this to happen, a teacher in a relationship-driven classroom needs to keep students safe by providing clear and consistent limits on their behavior so that they do not hurt themselves or others.

The second reason for establishing rules is consistency. Most troubled students have experienced inconsistent adult behavior in response to their actions, and that can lead to anxiety and uncertainty when adult–student interactions occur. Clear ground rules communicate that teachers are predictable in how they respond when the student misbehaves, leading to the belief that teachers are trustworthy, because the student knows how they will respond.

Four guidelines are useful in developing ground rules for a relationship-driven classroom. Briefly, these are:

1. Make the rules simple and easily communicated.
2. Keep the rules open-ended and capable of being flexibly interpreted.
3. Add rules as you need them.
4. Display the rules prominently.

First, make the rules simple and easily communicated. In Torey Hayden's (1980) book *One Child*, she had only two rules: (a) "Do your best work," and (b) "You are not allowed to hurt anyone or anything." These rules were easily comprehended by all the students as well as easily remembered and repeated. In contrast to Hayden's second rule, however, be positive in stating the rules, because it is helpful for students to know what they are expected to do as opposed to what they are not to do.

Second, keep the rules open-ended and capable of being flexibly interpreted. "Do your best," for example, is an open-ended, flexible rule, which allows both the teacher and the student some wiggle room in interpreting and applying it. "Do your best" allows the teacher to acknowledge that on a particularly difficult day, half an assignment probably is the student's best, even though normally, the student would be expected to finish it. The second rule, "You are not allowed to hurt anyone or anything," is more specific to issues of safety, but it also allows flexible interpretation in instances of accidental behavior and in what constitutes "anything."

Third, add rules as you need them. While it is important to have ground rules at the beginning of the school year, they can be changed, amended, and added to, if necessary.

Finally, display the rules prominently. By displaying rules in the classroom, it gives them importance and legitimacy, and it makes them more objective. A conflictive classroom interaction can be diffused by stating *The rule says . . .* rather than *I say . . .* This removes you from any potential conflict.

What Happens When Rules Are Broken

Devising rules that are fair, flexible, and workable provides the framework of the relationship-driven classroom, but the engine that drives it is found in what happens when rules are broken. How should a teacher respond when rule-violating behavior happens? Chapter 3 provided tips for developing and enforcing classroom rules, but here, we extend this perspective by highlighting *how* you work with classroom rules while preserving relationships and preventing behavioral difficulties in the classroom.

In a relationship-driven classroom, consequences are not the only appropriate response to rule violation. Sometimes, consequences for rule violation are the appropriate response, but other times, they are not. When rules are violated, teachers must acknowledge their role as a teacher and not as a psychologist, social scientist, or prison guard. A teacher's job is to teach. Therefore, rule violation should be approached with an open mind to allow teachable moments, because students (a) may not know how to behave differently, (b) have misconceptions about how they should behave, or (c) have misconceptions about themselves. When students have a lack of knowledge or misconceptions about themselves, teachers are obligated to help students learn how to behave differently. Consequences, by themselves, may be inefficient and inadequate in teaching students how to engage in appropriate behavior.

While approaching misbehavior as a teachable moment can be an appropriate strategy to manage classroom behavior, there are times when consequences are the best response. As mentioned in Chapter 3, star charts and token economies can be efficient tools for managing intransigent behavior; however, the teacher–student relationship should be preserved.

When designing and implementing a relationship-driven classroom, knowing the array of available and relevant consequences from the outset is key. Teachers must determine what kind of consequences they are comfortable with and are able to implement efficiently. Is it the evil eye, stern reprimand, loud voice, time out, public apology, or loss of privileges? For some teachers, the basic belief is that educators should respond strongly to a misbehavior the first time that misbehavior occurs, with the intent of having an immediate effect, yet this seldom happens. Too strong of a response may produce a teacher–student conflict with emotional side effects. A student may react to a strong consequence with fear or anger, and these emotions may overwhelm the intent of the consequence, which is to alter the behavior. Too strong a response can easily lead to power struggles and the need for the student to "save face" or to have the last word. When responding strongly to misbehavior, it also is difficult to escalate to an even stronger response. Most often, using the least severe consequence is the better starting point.

Use logical consequences when feasible and safe to do so. Logical consequences are related clearly to the behavior being managed (e.g., the student who cuts in the lunch line has to go back to the end of the line). Logical consequences for inappropriate behavior may be more acceptable to students, because they are related to the unacceptable student action and they tend to be less harsh than consequences such as loss of points or tokens, time out, detention, and suspension (Fay & Funk, 1995). It is best practice to follow up the delivery of a consequence with a therapeutic conversation. With no intent to lecture the student, this conversation can ensure the connection between actions and consequences is established, and it is consistent with a relationship-driven classroom.

What should be avoided at all costs are vindictive consequences for student behavior, such as harsh and unrelated punishments, yelling, sarcasm, embarrassment, or exclusion. What is easy for any teacher to do is to react with consequences that are, ultimately, an expression of chronic frustration, anger, or even rage. Vindictive and emotion-laden consequences that breed resentment, anger, and disrespect may temporarily stabilize the behavior, but they generally do not lead to long-term change.

Creating a Positive Classroom Environment

In this section, we extend the discussion in Chapter 2 about the classroom environment being a key ingredient for proactively preventing behavior problems. In addition to teachers understanding their leadership style and how they define discipline, considering teacher–student relationships and how those relationships influence student learning is important. The ultimate goal of a relationship-driven classroom is internal change. Simple student obedience, while helpful, is of limited value, because it is externally governed. If the external authority (i.e., the teacher) is not present, the desired student behavior most often is not present. In structuring a relationship-driven classroom, it is important for the classroom to be a place that encourages student behavior change rather than obedience.

Student behavior change requires several components. Briefly, these are:

1. The teacher is open to approximation.
2. Students are allowed the freedom to fail.
3. Students have opportunities for successful positive social interaction.
4. Students have reasonable freedom from excessive or harsh punishment.

The first component, as we suggested earlier, is for the teacher to be open to approximation. Approximation happens as new behaviors are learned. For new behaviors to be learned, small increments, or approximations of the behavior, are sequentially put together over time and, eventually, become fully articulated and internalized. All behaviors require several steps in the right order along with practice. For change to take place, students need to try out new behaviors and be secure that their efforts are positively recognized and supported with ample reassurance that they are moving in the right direction. The following brief story by Nawrocki (2007) illustrates why classrooms should allow approximation to take place:

> I once heard the story of how whales are trained. Apparently a rope is laid across the bottom of the whale's tank. Every time the whale swims over it, it receives a reward. The rope is raised off the bottom of the tank, not high enough for the whale to go beneath it. Again, every time it swims over the rope, the whale gets

a treat. Eventually, the rope is raised high enough that the whale can go over or under. Every time the whale goes over, it gets a reward. Every time it goes under, it gets a scolding. Just kidding. Nothing happens. It can go over or under, but if it goes over, it gets a reward. Higher and higher the rope goes until it is at the surface of the pool, and then, out of the pool. Eventually, you get a two-ton whale to jump over a rope. Think about your most challenging student. Lay the rope on the bottom of the pool and start over. (p. 46)

The second component of student behavior change in a relationship-driven classroom is to allow students the freedom to fail. Not all student behavior change efforts will be successful. When students try but fail to change their behavior, it does not mean their efforts are invalid, wrong, or useless. In a relationship-driven classroom, there is an understanding between the teacher and students that individuals can learn from failure, but this only happens in a climate where failure is not a major source of humiliation, distress, or punishment.

The third component is that students need opportunities for successful positive social interaction. Every young person has a deep need to belong, to be held in high esteem, and to be loved. The famous psychologist Abraham Maslow (1954) described how most maladjustment in society could be traced to the failure to gratify the basic human need for belonging. More recently, Glasser (1998) argued that the need for belonging is one of the five basic needs written into the human genetic structure. Thus, the psychological sense that one belongs in a classroom and school community is a necessary antecedent to change. In a relationship-driven classroom, acceptance and belonging are fulfilled for each student, which is fundamental for student behavior change.

The last component for student behavior change is reasonable freedom from excessive or harsh punishment. Learning to do things differently involves a certain amount of trial-and-error behavior and approximation. Indeed, changing a behavior inevitably involves failure and backsliding as part of the natural learning process. Thus, any environment designed to encourage change, such as a classroom, requires a reasonable amount of freedom from harmful punishment. There are times, however, when punishment is appropriate and when it is a healthy part of the learning experience, but use of harsh or extreme punishment needs to be the exception, not the rule. For genuine change to take place, the student needs the opportunity to interact, approximate, experiment, and occasionally, fail without punishment as the only response.

When building a relationship-driven classroom, the obvious goal is to create a positive environment in which change can take place. Hayden and Marlowe (2005) suggested a number of practical steps to take when planning a relationship-driven classroom based on teacher–student relationships. These include (a) build in a structured routine, (b) plan for and embrace opportunities for joy and enthusiasm, (c) build in opportunities to communicate, and (d) build in opportunities to teach stress reduction and relaxation skills.

BUILD IN A STRUCTURED ROUTINE   A well-thought-out daily classroom routine is the backbone of a successful relationship-driven classroom. Structure is needed not to gain control but to provide predictability, to create a sense of safety, and to bring organization to thoughts and actions. As previously discussed, students with significant behavior problems may come from chaotic and erratic backgrounds that contribute significantly to their difficulties. The establishment of routines in the classroom can help students settle in more quickly and is often enough to calm many lesser behavior problems. A structured routine also creates order. Many students who exhibit difficult behavior are chaotic thinkers and have difficulty following directions, making changes, and focusing their attention, and a structured and orderly classroom helps to minimize their problems. Finally, a structured routine provides a level of inherent discipline in which boundaries are more clear and unpredictable triggers occur less commonly.

PLAN FOR AND EMBRACE OPPORTUNITIES FOR JOY AND ENTHUSIASM   Hobbs (1982) understood that students should know some joy each day and look forward to some joyous event the next day. By building opportunities for joy and enthusiasm into your curriculum, you encourage the students to feel joy and excitement about being in the classroom.

There is a difference, however, between planning opportunities for joy and excitement and rewards. In the classroom, a reward is conditional on a student behaving in a certain way. An opportunity for joy, excitement, and enthusiasm is unconditional. Think of the difference as being unconditional in the way that math instruction is unconditional as part of the curriculum. Whatever your behavior, math instruction still happens during the day.

VanderVen (2009) believes the idea that children and youth need to experience joy, whether they deserve it or not, is difficult to convey. There is, perhaps, a tendency for educators to believe that because opportunities for joy and enthusiasm are fun, they are to be withdrawn in response to inappropriate behavior or given out in response to appropriate behavior. As we heard one time from a practicing teacher who was enrolled in a university class on activity programming, *If I can't take fun activities away from kids, then what can I take away?* Interesting and engaging activities that can provide joy, excitement, and enthusiasm should not have to be earned as part of a rigid accounting process. In a relationship-driven classroom, there should be unconditional activities in the curriculum during which students can feel enthusiasm for being in the class and experience genuine joy.

Opportunities for building joy are endless, including art and musical activities, drama, imaginary journeys, outdoor science investigations, field trips, physical activities, games, and cooking, but the techniques cannot be prescribed. The techniques depend on the style, the *joie de vivre* or the joy of living, and the personal interests of the teacher. Joy should be reciprocal. Teachers must have fun to provide joy in the classroom; thus, they must feel enthusiastic about the activities. Enthusiasm is both contagious and powerful, and it is a vastly underrated individual and group motivator. Difficult students find an enthusiastic teacher hard to resist.

BUILD IN OPPORTUNITIES TO COMMUNICATE   Communication is the engine that drives all significant relationships. To forge helpful, meaningful relationships with students, teachers need to communicate effectively. At the same time, students need to communicate effectively with their teachers. The easiest way for teachers to ensure opportunities for reciprocal communication in the classroom structure is to pay attention. Notice students' behavior, their personal changes, their interests, and what they care about. Truly listen when they talk, look them in the eye, and use their name frequently during the conversation.

Journaling provides an ideal medium for students to communicate with their teachers. A journal can simply be a spiral-bound notebook in which students record their feelings, their ups and downs, and their hopes, wishes, and dreams. Students can also record things that happened to them and other important events in their lives. While some children have a difficult time expressing their emotions, providing a topic or a story starter, such as "Write about a time when you were really embarrassed," can give students a safe place to start. For some students, you may need to consider modeling how to write or write for them. Teachers can provide 20 to 30 minutes each day for students to write, and they can leave notes or comments about what their students have written.

Another opportunity to facilitate communication in the classroom is opening and closing a circle. Children gather in a circle to start and finish the day. Opening exercises include greeting everyone, show-and-tell activities, troubleshooting classroom problems, and discussing a general outline of the day. Closing exercises can include an assessment of how things have gone, positive feedback, and good-byes.

Still another opportunity to facilitate communication is using a suggestion box, in which students can leave notes, either anonymous or signed, and "suggestions" about issues and events that may need to be discussed. For example, students might disclose how family conditions do not allow them to complete their homework or that persistent bullying is happening on the playground or after school.

BUILD IN OPPORTUNITIES TO TEACH STRESS REDUCTION AND RELAXATION SKILLS When confronted with stress, the majority of students who exhibit difficult-to-manage behaviors are unable to successfully calm themselves. Methods that some students use to cope with stress are often inappropriate, haphazard, or unhealthy, such as verbal and physical aggression, drug and alcohol abuse, or inappropriate eating. With a constant focus on always accomplishing goals, students are not usually given the opportunity to "waste time doing nothing" or to engage in activities that do not have a clear outcome. Because most student instruction, schedules, and rewards are controlled externally by others, students sometimes turn to external means of stress control, such as drugs, alcohol, or food, and as a result, they do not develop an internalized ability to reduce stress for themselves.

According to Goleman (2008), students can profit markedly from being taught stress reduction and relaxation skills in a direct manner as part of the curriculum, so it is helpful to incorporate explicit instruction during stress reduction activities. Some considerations when planning stress instruction within the classroom include:

- Structure the day so that high-impact activities are interspersed with low-impact activities. If this is already being done, students may benefit from knowing about this strategy so that they can learn to structure themselves this way.
- Call attention to the need to relax and frequently model how you relax yourself. Many students do not recognize when they are reaching a critical stress point. It is important to label stress so that students can identify when they are experiencing high levels of it and how to engage in relaxing activities.

Numerous forms of simple stress-reducing activities can be implemented in the classroom where you can encourage your students to apply your instruction, such as:

Exercise. Teachers can send students outside for a run around the playground or have them do jumping jacks or stretch in class. Any activity that makes everyone inhale and exhale rapidly is generally helpful in reducing stress.

Spontaneous movement. This can be creative dance movement to music or even less formal than that. If there are long periods of sitting during the school day, teachers can choose a student to lead the movements of "head, shoulders, knees, and toes" while all the other students copy the movements.

Energizers. Teachers can use short activities, sometimes referred to as "energizers," that integrate physical activity with academic subjects. Gilbert (1977) provides hundreds of examples of energizers targeted to lessons in language arts, math, science, and social studies. You may wish to throw a ball to students while reciting basic facts from a lesson, play Simon-says games incorporating content from the lesson, or use body parts to measure objects within the room.

Laughter/humor. Never miss a chance to laugh. Nothing can be as relaxing and de-stressing as laughter. "One laugh banishes a thousand worries" is an ancient Chinese proverb. Help children see the funny side of things, and indulge in giggling with them. Include activities that will raise a laugh (see, e.g., Stephenson & Thibault, 2006). Try using comic clippings and having the class make a skit based on them, telling silly knock-knock jokes, or showing silly video clips related to the lesson.

Relaxation exercise/deep breathing. Relaxation exercises can calm the body and focus the mind, and they are widely available on CD. Deep breathing exercises are taught in conjunction with meditation and yoga, yet teachers do not need to practice meditation or yoga to use the helpful breathing exercises. Deep breathing has been shown to reduce overall stress, and it is a strategy to use when facing stressful situations.

Music. It has been said that music is your friend, so you should invite it in often. Classical and ambient music, and music specially designed for slowing brain waves, are all widely available. Consider playing it when students are engaged in independent work and at times when students can focus on it and not simply have it in the background. Listening to music gives space to calm down, and listening to calming music can lower respiration and heart rate as well as change our emotional mood.

Peace corner. A peace or calming corner is a place where students can go whenever they are feeling overwhelmed, stressed, angry, or otherwise out of control. Teachers can include the whole class in designing the space and decorating it with pictures or photos of the students' favorite peaceful places and elements from nature. This peace corner can be equipped with quiet instrumental music, coloring books, and art materials. The space may be large enough for students to lie down, with comfortable pillows and a device to play soothing music or recordings of the sounds of nature. It is always the case, however, that ground rules need to be developed to use the peace corner appropriately.

Reading aloud. Younger students enjoy being read to, and this tends to be an excellent way to slow down the day and give students a chance to relax and calm down.

Guided visualization. Guided visualization works well as a relaxation exercise. It can be a means of calming a group of students or reorienting them. Guided visualization is also a way of providing a break when students are unable to go outside or otherwise have some significant change in the daily routine. Through guided visualization, you can take students on a rocket trip to the moon, an African safari, or an underwater journey. What is important is to match the visualization to the audience, but even students who are highly distracted or have mild forms of disabilities such as autism can usually be drawn into guided visualization.

Q: *It seems that relationship building may take a long time. How long should it take, and what stages should I expect?*

A: Relationship building with challenging students has been referred to as an endurance event. True change in students who have difficult behavior takes a considerable amount of time. Under the best conditions, it may take eight weeks for a higher-quality teacher–student relationship to become established. Researchers who have studied troubled children suggest the process of relationship building proceeds through three predictable stages: (a) casing, or an initial period of orientation and becoming acquainted; (b) limit testing, or a period of trying out the relationship; and (c) integration, or a period of adapting to a predictable style or pattern of interaction.

Although the length of time in each stage varies with individual students, here is what you may encounter. Troubled children engage in casing when they meet a new teacher and are uncertain about what to expect. They will attempt to determine what power the teacher has in the classroom and within the organization, and they will attempt to diagnose the social power of their peers. After attempting to case the environment, students test out boundary limits directly through their actions. A student needs to know whether the teacher can be trusted with secrets, how the teacher will handle anger, and how the teacher will respond in a range of situations. Successfully managed, limit testing provides a foundation for integration, which is a more secure and predictable relationship between teacher and student.

Summary

Positive teacher–student relationships at school and in the classroom are powerful influences on students' academic, social, and emotional development and are key to managing undesired student behavior. Within the framework of preventing problem behavior, developing relationships with students can be a powerful ingredient for effective teaching, especially when working with students who have chronic behavioral issues that impede their school success. Teacher–student relationships are influential in student exploration and mastery, self-regulation, motivation, social and emotional skills, and resilience. To build positive, meaningful relationships with students, it is important to be conscious of three relationship dimensions: (a) the degree of conflict, (b) the degree of closeness, and (c) the appropriate degree of dependency. Although relationships are bidirectional, teachers are the adults, and they are more capable of change than the students they teach. As such, we have provided various techniques that will allow teachers to adjust and gauge the quality of their relationships and to promote a relationship-driven classroom to prevent unwanted and inappropriate student behavior. These include the skills and attributes needed to develop strong, healthy, trusting bonds with others as well as the laying of ground rules, how to respond to misbehavior, building in opportunities for joy and enthusiasm, stress reduction, and communication. By incorporating the suggestions in this chapter, teachers can prevent behavior problems by emphasizing higher-quality relationships that result in improved academic, social, and emotional outcomes and a better quality of life.

Additional Resources

	On the Web	
Page Title	**Annotations**	**Web Address**
Love and Logic	Tips for managing a classroom while preserving the teacher–student relationship	http://www.loveandlogic.com/
Getting to Know You	Tips, games, and activities teachers can use to learn about students	http://www.teachablemoment.org/images/knowyou.pdf
Reclaiming Youth International	Strategies for adults who work with children having emotional or behavioral difficulties	http://www.reclaiming.com/content/
The Official Torey Hayden Website	Website of Torey Hayden, a teacher of students with emotional and behavioral disorders	http://www.torey-hayden.com/
Teacher Student Relationships Are Really Important!	Strategies teachers can use to improve their relationships with students	http://www.priceless-teaching-strategies.com/teacher_student_relationships.html

In the Literature

Arnove, R. F. (2010). Extraordinary teachers, exceptional students. *Phi Delta Kappan, 92*(2), 46–50.

This article parallels the attributes of successful coaches to the qualities needed in a classroom teacher. The author discusses how teachers can build relationships with youth that allow them to become the best possible student.

References

Bandura, A. (1995). *Self-efficacy in changing societies*. Cambridge, UK: Cambridge University Press.

Birch, S. H., & Ladd, G. W. (1997). The teacher–child relationship and children's early school adjustment. *Journal of School Psychology, 35*, 61–79.

Birch, S. H., & Ladd, G. W. (1998). Children's interpersonal behaviors and the teacher–child relationship. *Developmental Psychology, 34*(5), 934–946.

Blankemeyer, M., Flannery, D. J., & Vazsonyi, A. T. (2002). The role of aggression and social competence in children's perceptions of the child–teacher relationship. *Psychology in the Schools, 39*(3), 293–304.

Brendtro, L. K., Brokenleg, M., & Van Bockern, S. (2002). *Reclaiming youth at risk. Our hope for the future*. Bloomington, IN: National Educational Service.

Erikson, E. (1963). *Childhood and society*. New York: W. W. Norton.

Erickson, M. F., & Pianta, R. C. (1989). New lunchbox, old feelings: What kids bring to school. *Early Education and Development, 1*, 15–23.

Fay, J., & Funk, D. (1995). *Teaching with love and logic*. Golden, CO: Love and Logic Press.

Gharabaghi, K. R. (2008). Reclaiming our toughest youth. *Reclaiming Children and Youth, 17*, 30–32.

Gilbert, A. (1977). *Teaching the 3Rs through movement experiences*. Minneapolis: Burgess Publishing Company.

Glasser, W. (1998). *The quality school*. New York: Harper & Row.

Goleman, D. (2008). Introduction. In L. Lantieri (Ed.), *Building emotional intelligence* (pp. 1–4). Boulder, CO: Sounds True.

Hamre, B. K., & Pianta, R. C. (2001). Early teacher–child relationships and the trajectory of children's school outcomes through eighth grade. *Child Development, 72*(2), 625–638.

Hamre, B. K., & Pianta, R. C. (2005). Can instructional and emotional support in the first-grade classroom make a difference for children at risk of school failure? *Child Development, 76*(5), 949–967.

Hamre, B., Pianta, R. C., Downer, J. T., & Mashburn, A. J. (2007). Teachers' perceptions of conflict with young students: Looking beyond problem behaviors. *Social Development, 17*(1), 115–136.

Hayden, T. (1980). *One child*. New York: Avon Press.

Hayden, T. (Producer), & Marlowe, M. (Director). (2005). DVD. Workshop on relationship-driven classroom management, Boone, NC, March 17–18.

Hayden, T. & Marlowe, M. (in press). *Teaching children who are hard to reach*. Thousand Oaks, CA: Corwin Press.

Hobbs, N. (1982). *The troubled and troubling child*. San Francisco: Jossey-Bass.

Howes, C., Hamilton, C. E., & Matheson, C. C. (1994). Children's relationships with peers: Differential associations with aspects of the teacher–child relationship. *Child Development, 65*, 253–263.

Hughes, J. N., Cavell, T. A., & Jackson, T. (1999). Influence of the teacher–student relationship on childhood conduct problems: A prospective study. *Journal of Clinical Child Psychology, 28*(2), 173–184.

Kounin, J. (1970). *Discipline and group management in classrooms*. New York: Holt, Rinehart, and Winston.

Ladd, G. W., & Burgess, K. B. (2001). Do relational risks and protective factors moderate the linkages between childhood aggression and early psychological and school adjustment? *Child Development, 72*(5), 1579–1601.

Long, N. (2008). Breaking the trust barrier. *Reclaiming Children and Youth, 17*, 56–58.

Long, N., Morse, W. C., Fecser, F. A., & Newman, R. G. (2007). *Conflict in the classroom* (6th ed.). Austin, TX: Pro-Ed.

Marlowe, M. (1999). Reaching reluctant students: Insights from Torey Hayden. *Reclaiming Children and Youth, 7*, 242–245, 254.

Marlowe, M. (2006). Torey Hayden's teacher lore: A pedagogy of caring. *Journal of Education for Teaching, 32*, 93–103.

Maslow, A. (1954). *Motivation and personality*. New York: Harper & Row.

Meehan, B. T., Hughes, J. N., & Cavell, T. A. (2003). Teacher–student relationships as compensatory resources for aggressive children. *Child Development, 74*(4), 1145–1157.

Murray, C., & Greenberg, M. T. (2001). Relationships with teachers and bonds with school: Social emotional adjustment correlates for children with and without disabilities. *Psychology in the Schools, 38*(1), 25–41.

Murray, C., Waas, G. A., & Murray, K. M. (2008). Child race and gender as moderators of the association between teacher–child relationships and school adjustment. *Psychology in Schools, 45*(6), 562–578.

Nawrocki, M. (2007). *Thanks for chucking that at the wall instead of me*. Toronto, ON: Chestnut Publishing Company.

Pianta, R. C. (2000). *Enhancing relationships between children and teachers*. Washington, DC: American Psychological Association.

Pianta, R. C. (2001). *Student teacher relationship scale. Professional manual*. Odessa, FL: Psychological Assessment Resources.

Pianta, R. C., Belsky, J., Vandergrift, N., Houts, R., & Morrison, F. J. (2008). Classroom effects on children's achievement trajectories in elementary school. *American Educational Research Journal, 45*(2), 365–397.

Pianta, R., La Paro, K., & Hamre, B. K. (2006). *Classroom assessment scoring system manual: (Pre-K) version*. Baltimore: Brookes Publishing.

Pianta, R. C., & Steinberg, M. S. (1992). Teacher–child relationships and the process of adjusting to school. In R. C. Pianta (Ed.), *Beyond the parent: The role of other adults in children's lives* (pp. 61–80). San Francisco: Jossey-Bass.

Pianta, R. C., Steinberg, M. S., & Rollins, K. B. (1995). The first two years of school: Teacher–child relationships and deflections in children's classroom adjustment. *Developmental and Psychopathology, 7*, 295–312.

Pianta, R. C., & Stuhlman, M. W. (2004). Teacher–child relationships and children's success in the first years of school. *School Psychology Review, 33*, 444–458.

Pianta, R. C., & Walsh, D. J. (1996). *High-risk children in schools: Constructing sustaining relationships*. New York: Routledge.

Rimm-Kaufman, S., La Paro, K., Pianta, R., & Downer, J. (2005). The contributions of classroom setting and quality of instruction to children's behavior in the kindergarten classroom. *Elementary School Journal, 105*(4), 377–394.

Stephenson, S., & Thibault, P. (2006). *Laughing matters: Strategies for building a joyful learning community*. Bloomington, IN: Solutions Tree.

Van der Veer, R., & Valsiner, J. (Eds.). (1994). *The Vygotsky reader*. Oxford, UK: Blackwell.

VanderVen, K. (2009). Why focusing on control back-fires: A systems approach. *Reclaiming Children and Youth, 17,* 8–12.

Walker, H. M., Colvin, G., & Ramsey, E. (1995). *Antisocial behavior in school: Strategies and best practices.* Pacific Grove, CA: Brookes Publishing.

Wang, M. C., Haertel, G. D., & Walberg, H. J. (1997). Learning influences. In H. J. Walbert & G. D. Haertel (Eds.), *Psychology and educational practice* (pp. 199–211). Berkeley, CA: McCatchan.

5

Conducting Meetings in the Classroom

GOALS

- Provide teachers with the rationale for conducting classroom meetings.

- Describe realistic strategies to build effective elementary classroom communities through morning meetings.

- Provide examples that support the classroom meeting approach for developing positive classroom communities.

SCENARIO

Ms. Shapiro starts her class on Monday morning like she normally does. Students are instructed when they come into the classroom to complete their brief morning assignment, sign up for a math problem to solve on the board, and then sit quietly in their seats to read. A few students comply, but most walk aimlessly about, bothering other students while they are putting up their backpacks and saying mean things to each other. Some students throw paper on the floor, and some go in and out of the room and into the hallway. Five minutes after the starting bell, Jason walks in late, and JaKerri yells across the room, *Ewwww! Why'd he have to come to school?!* Jason yells back, *Shut up, dog face!* The whole class laughs. Jason then walks quietly to his desk with his head low and pulls out his reading book. Once Jason sits down, Coco gets up out of her seat to sharpen a pencil and tugs on JaKerri's hair, then loudly whispers, *Yep, I think it's a wig!* Paul lets out a loud laugh, while DeShawn yells, *What are we doing today? Do we have PE or is that lady from the zoo coming today with some cool animals?* Ms. Shapiro tries desperately to respond to the disrespect for other people by her class in general and to the specific behaviors of JaKerri, Jason, Coco, Paul, and DeShawn and still get the school day started. Just when things start to settle down, however, a visitor walks in, and Jaylen shouts, *Hey, everybody, look out! It's Principal Jones!*

By definition, a community is a group of people who interact with each other and share a common space. For years, however, education professionals minimized, ignored, or did not understand, like Ms. Shapiro, the role that the classroom community could play in the education of children and youth. Teachers and other education professionals believed they needed to control student behavior through autocratic means, because the focus was an academic one that required passive listeners and learners. In that frame of reference, there was no recognition or reliance on interpersonal relationships, student beliefs or interests, or student need for power and just some plain, simple fun. Succinctly, teachers controlled the classroom to minimize distractions, unilaterally orchestrated learning activities, and demanded passive compliance to maximize student learning (Watson & Battistich, 2006). Through the years, however, professional educators have come to accept the classroom as a robust environment suitable for arranging activities that are more student-centered, with an emphasis on adult–student collaboration and positive peer-to-peer interactions built on the framework of a relational community (Pianta, 2006).

For any elementary classroom, an explicit and deliberate relational community of learners and school professionals is foundational for preventing problem behaviors and for effective classroom management (Smith, 2001). Creating a positive classroom community should be explicit, in that there are well-designed activities and prominent promotion of positive interaction among students and teachers. It should also be deliberate, in that there is a purposeful and conscious effort of all involved in a classroom to:

1. Share resources and beliefs.
2. Identify needs and take risks.
3. Cooperate, and at the same time, learn independence.
4. Develop a cohesiveness that can promote a student's intellectual, social, and moral/ethical development.

In an elementary setting, such as Ms. Shapiro's classroom, the community can be established through democratic meetings designed to change classroom dynamics so that students become partners with the teacher, thus expanding their role in the classroom to establish better relational bonds among their peers and adults. Through group meeting formats, the intellectual, social, and emotional needs of the group are met, as are the needs of each individual. When the group shares positive relational values and each individual in the learning environment shares it equally, the foundation is laid to prevent inappropriate behaviors that are damaging to the group and the classroom community.

Creating and sustaining a positive classroom community to prevent behavior problems in elementary school environments necessitates approaches that are situational and developmentally appropriate. Smith (2001) wrote, "Despite the challenges, teachers need to make creating a positive classroom community a daily priority" (p. 2). Typically, elementary classrooms are self-contained, with a teacher and students who, for the most part, spend their entire day engaged in instructional tasks together. Creating a safe and caring community may be more readily attainable in elementary than in secondary schools, where older students meet with a variety of teachers across the school day. In elementary settings, the teacher has some flexibility outside of the mandated academic instructional time to accomplish the goal of mutual caring and respect that will establish a positive classroom community. Because the secondary setting is structured around blocks of academic instruction, little, if any, time is allotted specifically for anything outside the core academic instruction. This does not preclude secondary teachers from building a classroom community, but there are differences in how education professionals in each setting may go about establishing a positive community. One way to build a caring and respectful community of learners in elementary classrooms is through a morning meeting.

MORNING MEETING

Ms. Shapiro is not alone in trying to start the school day with her class on a positive note. Starting class in an elementary room full of young learners is not an easy task, especially when there is no focal activity, daily procedure, or expectation on which the students can rely. What Ms. Shapiro needs is a positive and facilitative method for allowing her students to interact with each other, but to do it in a way that includes predictability of events, nurturing of mutual respect, trust, and a real sense of belonging. A formalized meeting each morning in the classroom can accommodate these goals and allow students a way to interact with positive outcomes in a trusting and safe environment. Thus, a morning meeting can help establish a sense of community in the classroom that, in turn, reduces the chances for problem behaviors like those described in Ms. Shapiro's classroom.

A morning meeting is part of an approach called the *Responsive Classroom®*, developed by the Northeast Foundation for Children (see Charney, 2002; Kriete & Bechtel, 2002), and in this approach is referred to as Morning Meeting. The *Responsive Classroom* includes numerous classroom techniques that are detailed in this book, such as working with students collaboratively to develop rules for classroom behavior; working with students who misbehave in a way that allows them to fix what they did and learn from their mistakes in a positive way; setting up the classroom to encourage student independence, cooperation, and productivity; and using collaborative problem solving through conferencing and role playing.

The Northeast Foundation for Children (2012), developer of the *Responsive Classroom* approach to teaching, believes that classroom and behavior management is much more than learning what to do when students break the rules or are noncompliant. The foundation delineates seven principles that are the underpinnings of the *Responsive Classroom* approach:

1. The social curriculum is as important as the academic curriculum.
2. How children learn is as important as what they learn: Process and content go hand in hand.
3. The greatest cognitive growth occurs through social interaction.
4. To be successful academically and socially, children need a set of social skills: cooperation, assertion, responsibility, empathy, and self-control.
5. Knowing the children we teach—individually, culturally, and developmentally—is as important as knowing the content we teach.
6. Knowing the families of the children we teach and working with them as partners is essential to children's education.
7. How the adults at school work together is as important as their individual competence: Lasting change begins with the adult community.*

---

*Seven principles reprinted by permission of Northeast Foundation for Children, Inc., www.responsiveclass room.org/sites/default/files/pdf_files/rc_fact_sheet.pdf

Research indicates that after implementing the *Responsive Classroom* approach, teachers collaborated with each other more, felt more effective and more positive about their teaching, and offered more high-quality instruction (Rimm-Kaufman & Sawyer, 2004). Students in a *Responsive Classroom* showed greater increases in reading and math test scores (Rimm-Kaufman, Fan, Chiu, & You, 2007), and they also had better social skills and felt more positive about school (Brock, Nishida, Chiong, Grimm, & Rimm-Kauffman, 2008; Rimm-Kauffman & Chiu, 2007). Although this emerging research is on the *Responsive Classroom* as a whole, in this chapter we describe the elements of Morning Meeting, both because it is a fundamental part of the *Responsive Classroom* and because of its potential to generate conditions to establish a community of learners and provide the foundation for teachers to promote the prevention of behavior problems. Numerous examples for other elements of the *Responsive Classroom* can be found throughout this book, and when put together, they can provide any elementary classroom with the basic preventive elements for managing behavior successfully.

Morning Meeting is one way to establish time in an elementary classroom for students and teachers to greet one another, share information, think together, and have fun. According to Kriete and Bechtel (2002), Morning Meeting can:

- Build classroom community.
- Provide a vehicle to establish trust among teacher and students.
- Improve student speaking skills and confidence.
- Encourage cooperation.
- Establish respectful patterns of communication.

Although Morning Meeting can be a brief classroom activity, it does require some planning. Both planning for and spending time on Morning Meeting is an investment in relationship building and can help to eliminate, or prevent the emergence of, student problem behavior. It can become a scheduled time when students and the teacher can interact in a democratic community and when the teacher can model appropriate social skills and provide students with feedback and guidance. Morning Meeting establishes trust within the classroom community and sets the tone for the rest of the day. According to Kriete and Bechtel (2002), when students walk into the classroom in the morning, they are greeted by their peers and given an opportunity to observe, reflect, speak, and listen as Morning Meeting brings together opportunities for social, emotional, and intellectual learning for everyone's benefit. Many of the principles of the *Responsive Classroom* are manifested in the workings of a Morning Meeting, which typically is made up of four components: (a) Greeting, (b) Sharing, (c) Group Activity, and (d) News and Announcements.

Greeting

Greeting is a way to acknowledge and welcome each other to the beginning of a new day of learning. Greeting one another sets a positive tone for the day, establishes friendships, and is a way to learn and use everyone's name. Greetings can be as simple as shaking hands, making eye contact, and saying, for example, *Good morning, Kirk*, with a *Good morning, Nick* reply. Greetings can be high fives or down lows, and teachers can introduce a variety of languages into the greetings, such as *Bonjour, Shalom, Buenos dias, Guten morgen*, or sign language. The ultimate goal of greeting each other in the classroom is that everyone greets and is greeted equally.

At the beginning of the school year, Greeting is a great way for students to get to know each other. As students learn each other's names, they will be able to call upon each other to ask a question, recognize one another in a group discussion, request help, and offer congratulations or an apology. As students become familiar with each other, they will be open to listening and speaking within a supportive group setting. Hearing our name lets us know that someone values speaking to us and makes us feel part of the larger community. The basic idea behind a formalized Greeting in the morning is to have our name out there and to make sure that all the students in the classroom are individually identified and understood.

By welcoming each other on a daily basis with a clear voice and a friendly smile, students are practicing the art of hospitality. Students learn how to be caretakers of each other in the community. Teachers should keep greetings simple at first, model the greeting, help students remember names with name tags, and have students greet different people each day. As shown in Table 5.1, Kriete and Bechtel (2002) suggest a number of different types of greetings, all designed for everyone to acknowledge one another and to be acknowledged as members of a community of learners.

Sharing

Sharing allows students to know others and be known by learning about each other's interests. Sharing also provides an opportunity to value others' opinions and articulate thoughts, feelings, and ideas in a relaxed environment. Sharing during Morning Meeting can help students develop an ability to speak in a group, learn more about each other, and develop self-esteem and respect for others. For example, on her day to share, Clarise brought in a number of shells she had collected at the beach during her summer vacation. She explained where she went and how she collected her shells and then invited questions and comments from her classmates. Clarise needed instruction and preparation to share her information, and her classmates needed to know how to make appropriate comments and ask good questions. During Sharing, students should be reminded to listen to the speaker and ask questions relevant to the topic. Students

TABLE 5.1	Greetings for Morning Meeting
Type of Greeting	**Description**
Formal	Students greet each other using last names (e.g., *Good Morning, Mr. Russell; Good Morning, Ms. Rivas*).
Name card	The teacher places name cards in the center of a circle. Students, in turn, choose the top card from the pile and greet the person.
Introductions	Each student interviews a partner to prepare for a greeting.
Cross-circle	Students greet someone across the circle from them.
Silent	Greetings are done silently, using only the face or body.
Alphabetical	Students greet each other in alphabetical order.
Ball toss	Students pass a ball around to greet each other.

should state their thoughts with clarity, listen actively for questions, and consider others' perspectives. Sharing thus requires instruction and modeling from the teacher, but with practice, students learn to be comfortable and develop a sense of significance within the classroom.

All students should have a turn sharing, because it provides practice in speaking to a group in a strong and individual voice and strengthens vocabulary development and reading success as students work at expressing themselves and understanding others through conversation. Students will practice forming good questions and comments as well as extending connections they have with their peers. Appropriate questions for Clarise could include how many shells she had collected and what was her favorite shell and why. As students learn about each other's interests and lives outside of school, they will be more willing to share their experiences with their classmates. Teachers can guide students' sharing by selecting varied topics, such as "Bring Your Favorite Family Vacation Pictures" or "Talk about Your Favorite Relative."

As one example of how to conduct a Sharing session, the classroom teacher might have students sign up to share during the week or simply rotate sharing according to alphabetical order. With Morning Meeting, everyone should have several opportunities during the school year to share. The example in Table 5.2 shows how the teacher can facilitate sharing and remind students to engage in good, active listening. Over time,

---

TABLE 5.2 **Sample Sharing Script for Elementary Morning Meeting**

Teacher: Boys and girls, it is sharing time, and it looks like it is Jacquez's turn today, so let's do our best to listen and ask good questions.

Jacquez: Last night I went to my big brother's high-school football game. We ate hot dogs and I saw the band during half-time. I also got a snow cone. I got a program and my brother's name is in it [*Jacquez holds up the program.*] I had a lot of fun with my family.

Teacher: Thank you for sharing, Jacquez. You can take three questions. Remember, hold up three fingers so you can keep track. Alright, who has a question for Jacquez? [*Students' hands go up.*] Okay, Jacquez, call on the first person.

Jacquez: Marty.

Marty: Who did your brother's team play against?

Jacquez: They played the Blue Devils.

Teacher: Okay, that's one. Put one finger down, and call on somebody else.

Jacquez: [*Puts one finger down and looks around the circle.*] Raymond.

Raymond: Did your brother score a touchdown?

Jacquez: No, he plays defense, but he did tackle the other team's quarterback twice.

Teacher: Great question! Jacquez, put another finger down, and call on someone for your last question.

Jacquez: Ashley.

Ashley: Who won the football game?

Jacquez: My brother's team won. They are the Rams. The score was 13-6. He was really happy.

Teacher: Great questions, boys and girls. I can tell you were really listening to Jacquez by the questions you asked. Let's tell Jacquez thank you for sharing.

Class: Thank you for sharing, Jacquez!

the teacher can slowly lessen such guidance as the students learn the routine. The goal is for the students to completely take over the sharing on their own.

One thing for teachers to consider is that some news might not be suitable for group sharing. Teachers should make sure that students understand some topics can be shared with everyone but that others, like family topics or events, may not be appropriate and should be shared with the teacher privately. Also, because there are always time concerns for conducting a full Morning Meeting, teachers may find holding a separate meeting for Sharing later in the day to be more effective, because students may be able to give each other more attention then.

Group Activity

Group Activity allows students to have fun, fosters active participation, builds class cohesion and spirit, encourages cooperation rather than competition, and lets all students participate at their own level. According to Kriete and Bechtel (2002), teachers should model appropriate behaviors and discuss with students relevant topics such as appropriate voice or noise level during the activity, physical controls that might be needed, issues around taking turns and what happens if someone makes a mistake, and finally, what cooperative play is all about. Teachers should choose activities that have a reasonable assurance the group will experience success without an excessive amount of preparation. These activities can be physical, with lots of high-energy fun, or they can be intellectual games or puzzles for students to solve. Group Activity can also be something creative, artistic, or in some cases, just plain silly. For Group Activity to contribute to the overall goal of establishing a positive classroom community, the activities, over time, should ensure that all students have a role as a leader and participant.

Group activities are for everyone in the class and should be brief and fast-paced. One such activity, *Zoom*, is a fast-paced game designed to generate laughter. Students sit in a circle and see how fast they can get the word *Zoom*, the sound of a race car, around the group. One person starts by turning his or her head to the side and saying *Zoom* to the person sitting on that side; this continues until everyone has passed *Zoom* around the circle. A student or teacher could use a stopwatch to see how fast the students can pass *Zoom* around the circle and, perhaps, establish classroom records. *Eek*, the sound of screeching tires, can be used in some *Zoom* activities to reverse the direction around the circle. Students have to pay close attention, and everyone can have great fun when a student in the circle says *Eek* as *Zoom* goes around. As a substitute for *Zoom*, handshakes can be used, or students can play Speed Pass, in which a small object is passed as fast as possible around the circle.

Pantomimes, in which students act out what they like to do (e.g., swing, listen to music, ride a bike), places they often go (e.g., grocery store, drive-thru window, restaurant), or using a certain object (e.g., vacuum, paint brush, computer) and the other students guess the activity, are also enjoyable. Additional possibilities include Hot and Cold and other detective games in which students must discover hidden clues or ask questions about a mystery. Besides the obvious opportunity for fun in the classroom, Group Activity also offers opportunities for students to practice skills like listening, following directions, and exercising self-control. As shown in Table 5.3, there are numerous group activities for lower and upper elementary grades, such as Human Protractor, Cooperative Spider Web, Birthday Line Up, and Dead Fish.

TABLE 5.3	Examples of Group Activities	
Lower Elementary Grades		**Upper Elementary Grades**
Clapping Names: Clap on beat for each syllable in a person's name.		**Cooperative Spider Web:** Have students create a spider web by rolling a ball of string to each other.
Hot and Cold: Guide a seeker to a hidden object by saying *hot* or *cold*.		**Dead Fish:** Have students lie on the floor as lifeless as dead fish. The teacher tags out those who move or giggle. Allow those who are out to get others to laugh or move.
Pantomime This Object: Have students take turns pantomiming with an object.		**Memory Name Game:** Have students repeat what each person before them has replied so that that last person remembers what everyone has said.
The Telephone Game: Have students sit in a circle. Begin with a simple sentence, and pass the message around in a whisper. The goal is to have the last child receive the message accurately.		**Birthday Line Up:** Form students in a line. Instruct them to rearrange the line in order by birthdays, height, name, age, and so on.
Human Protractor: Have students sit in a circle with hands touching toes. Have students raise their hands gradually while you count from 1 to 20, and then have the group assume the position of each number while you randomly call them out.		**Occupation Pantomime:** Have students take turns acting out an occupation while others guess what it is.

News and Announcements

News and Announcements is a part of Morning Meeting that can help orient and transition students to the school day. News and Announcements ensures that students are aware of special events or changes in classroom routine; reinforces language, math, and thinking skills; and makes the connection between written and spoken language. As shown in Table 5.4, the teacher can write on a chart each morning with a variety of formats and content. When students walk into the classroom each day, they can follow the instructions on the chart, such as completing a simple reading or engaging in a spelling, math, or writing task.

At the end of Morning Meeting, students may review the chart to read about special events of the day and any academic work, such as completing the day's date, discovering the day's secret word, or as shown in Table 5.5, finding mistakes in a short passage. Each of these components can facilitate practicing the skills of greeting fellow students, listening and engaging in conversation, group problem solving, and noticing and anticipating.

According to Kriete and Bechtel (2002), students who start their day with a feeling of success and accomplishment begin to develop a sense of competence and mastery. For this to occur, teachers can choose questions and activities during News and Announcements that include a range of skills and challenges but that also allow success.

TABLE 5.4	Examples of News and Announcements Charts for Morning Meeting	
Lower Elementary Classrooms		**Upper Elementary Classrooms**

Lower Elementary Classrooms	Upper Elementary Classrooms

Good morning, class!
Today is Friday, October 30th. Tomorrow is _____.
We have a fall party at 1:00 P.M. No music today. Mr. Ramirez is sick.
  1. Put your homework in the basket. Put your name on it.
  2. Copy your spelling words into your planner.
  3. Write your homework under today's date.
  4. Read a book quietly at your seat.
Gracias,
Ms. Hannum
	Bonjour!
	Welcome to math. Today is Monday, December 7th. Our schedule for today is:
	  1. Review homework from last night.
	  2. Complete Lesson 3.2.
	  3. Have group activity.
	You have two minutes after the bell rings to complete the problem of the day:
	What number is 4 less than 12, times 3, plus 400? _____.
	Write your answer on a sticky note, and place it on the board.

Hola! Today is Monday, January 4th. I'm at a workshop today. Be your best for Mr. Harmon, your substitute. You'll have PE with Coach Frazier today. Have fun and be good. Have a great day. I'll see you tomorrow! Adios! Mr. Gates P.S. There are three contractions today. Please rewrite them as two words.	Good Morning! ☺ Today is Wednesday, November 25th. It is the last day before Thanksgiving Break, so we will have our spelling test today instead of Friday. Please sign your initials under the book you liked best that we have read this year. *Shiloh Maniac Island of the Frindle* * Magee Blue Dolphins* We will talk about each book today, so be ready! Sincerely, Ms. Hankinson

TABLE 5.5	Finding Mistakes in a News and Announcements Chart

good morning class!

today is friday, september 18, 2012. we have art with ms. Lindquist at 9:30

1. Copy down your homework.

2. Find all of the mistakes in the morning message.

3. Read a book quietly at your seat.

Reminder: There is a spelling test today!

Have a Great Day!

This may include sentence patterns that list the student leaders for the day, filling in the correct numbers on the calendar, a simple but interesting math problem to solve, or using fill-in-the-blanks to remind students about an upcoming writing assignment.

News and Announcements allows students to stay informed and practice responsibility in their classrooms. It is important that teachers use this time for simple skill practice and peer learning rather than for instruction. At the end of Morning Meeting, after students have greeted one another, taken part in a fun activity, participated in News and Announcements, and maybe, a student has shared with other students, everyone should be ready to transition into a productive school day.

Some Morning Meeting Ideas

Teachers should introduce Morning Meeting to their students as a way to get to know each person in the class and have fun together. According to Kriete and Bechtel (2002) as well as Charney (2002), Morning Meeting will meet all students' needs by giving them a sense of belonging in the classroom and a chance to have fun. Students who feel valued and appreciated by their peers will be motivated to learn and refrain from destructive behaviors in the classroom, thus setting the stage for preventing behavior problems in the classroom. As students begin to grasp the format and goals of Morning Meeting, they will become accustomed to assembling every day to share their hopes and ideas and practice teamwork as well as social and academic skills.

In the elementary classroom, Morning Meeting should occur just about every morning for 15 to 30 minutes. Teachers should be careful to limit Morning Meeting, because students may lose focus and attentiveness. In some classrooms, children may take turns leading some or all of Morning Meeting, and teachers are responsible for discerning and guiding the dynamics of Morning Meeting. Kriete and Bechtel (2002) suggest that for lower grades, teachers may have students sit in a circle and sing a song on the first day. Teachers may teach students a greeting on the second day and slowly move into a full Morning Meeting within several weeks. Teachers can begin Morning Meeting with a signal that shows students it is time to assemble. For example, the teacher may clap a number of times and have students repeat, or the teacher may begin a song or chant, such as *Time now, time now, time now for Morning Meeting*, or there could even be a rhyme, such as *1, 2, 3, 4 . . . Find your spot near the door*, or *Morning Meeting is ready to meet. Get on the floor and find your seat.*

Q: *My school, because of state and district mandates, sets our daily academic schedule. I do not have 15 minutes, much less 30 minutes, to conduct Morning Meeting.*

A: Although Morning Meeting is suggested to take about 15 to 30 minutes, many teachers choose to do parts of Morning Meeting throughout the school day. When doing so, all the steps can still be incorporated throughout the week, but they may not be followed every day. Greeting and News and Announcements should be a consistent morning ritual, because these components set the tone for the day. Sharing can take place at any time during the day, but it may be a good idea to make the time consistent so that students can anticipate when Sharing is to occur. Group Activity can be accomplished on the playground, during teacher-led physical education, during a transition, or as a brain break in between lessons.

Morning Meeting might start with Greeting, then Group Activity, and end in calendar and weather reading along with a brief academic task during News and Announcements. Sharing might take place later during the day. For younger students, the teacher may need to define skills and practice components of Greeting, Sharing, and even Group Activity. Teachers should always provide feedback to students during Morning Meeting to convey expectations for the meeting and student behavior. This can be accomplished by reminding students about the need for positive behavior, redirecting students who are off task, and reinforcing those who behave according to expectations.

Student seating may need to be rearranged before Morning Meeting begins so that all students will be able to listen, follow along, and connect with all their fellow students. For example, you might have mornings with special directions for girls to sit next to boys or find a new friend, or teachers can simply rotate student seating so that students are not always sitting next to their close friends. During Sharing, some students may need to rehearse a few minutes beforehand or practice appropriate sharing behaviors with a teacher before joining the group. It may be a good idea to have a scheduled Sharing time so that students can anticipate their opportunity to communicate with their classmates. For those students who attend special classes during the day or leave for other reasons, teachers should plan accordingly so that all students are in attendance during the parts of Morning Meeting.

MORNING MEETING AND MS. SHAPIRO

If Ms. Shapiro would initiate Morning Meeting, her morning routine might be quite different than what is illustrated in the scenario that opened this chapter. The interpersonal dynamic could be different in her room each morning, because Morning Meeting is designed to build a community, have students know each other and be known in positive ways, share beliefs, take risks in a supportive and safe environment, cooperate, learn independence, and develop cohesiveness. Do not forget that Morning Meeting also has an activity component, which allows students to enjoy an activity with the class for the sole purpose of having fun while, at the same time, still learning important social skills. Although Group Activity can be fun and exciting for students, it is not without its learning opportunities. Morning Meeting demands positive and nurturing adult–student collaboration, and it also demands positive peer-to-peer interactions that are conscious efforts of all involved in a classroom. As such, JaKerri, Jason, Coco, Paul, and DeShawn might treat each other differently as an effect of the demands of Morning Meeting over time, and the classroom could become a true community where everyone

---

Q: *I have behavior problems in my classroom, and I think Morning Meeting is a great foundation to have to set a positive tone for each school day. However, I do not see how this meeting time can have any real effect on my students' social skills.*

A: The good news is that schools are becoming more sensitive to and interested in students' social and emotional needs as part of their education. There is little doubt that the main focus will also be on academic achievement, yet the social and emotional curriculum can still be a priority in your classroom. Holding Morning Meeting, and using that time to be explicit in your teaching of the social skills that will help your children learn to get along with each other, will ultimately improve your academic instruction. Running a smooth and successful classroom where children feel safe, valued, and comfortable is a prerequisite to effective learning and teaching. Morning Meeting, then, is an investment and can create a healthy and positive learning environment where students are more able to channel their energy into academic learning.

has positive connections with each other. Ms. Shapiro, then, could start each school day off more positively through structure, high expectations, and fun opportunities for her students. In this way, Ms. Shapiro might prevent the situation described in the scenario and eliminate many behavior problems before they become chronic distractions that interfere with effective teaching.

Summary

Morning Meeting allows students to engage in a democratic process that invites participation, new learning, and open discussions while, at the same time, engages students in learning about respect, responsibility, and mutual caring for others. Morning Meeting allows the opportunity during the school day to know and be known and to have simple fun while doing an activity.

Although there are limited instructional hours in the school day, young children can benefit from Morning Meeting in a variety of ways, such as through Greeting, Sharing, Group Activity, and News and Announcements, and they are still engaged in learning essential social and emotional skills. Morning Meeting is a way for teachers to lay the groundwork so that problematic behaviors are less likely to occur. For Ms. Shapiro, the use of class time for Morning Meeting may help prevent some of the problems she has encountered and provide her students with a valuable learning experience not often found in classrooms today.

Additional Resources

On the Web		
Page Title	**Annotations**	**Web Address**
Morning Meeting	Forum where teachers discuss ideas for Morning Meeting	http://www.proteacher.org/c/579_Morning_Meeting.html
Morning Meeting Greetings	Slideshow of numerous silly Morning Meeting greetings	http://www.slideshare.net/MandieFunk/morning-meeting-greetings
Morning Meeting: Group Activities	Slideshow of songs and games to play during Morning Meeting	http://www.slideshare.net/MandieFunk/morning-meeting-activities-karie
Morning Message	Forum where teachers discuss ideas for incorporating academic content into the morning message	http://www.proteacher.net/discussions/showthread.php?t=252485&highlight=morning+meeting

In the Literature

Kriete, R. (2003). Start the day with community. *Educational Leadership, 61*(1), 68–70.
This article focuses on developing a sense of community in classrooms through the use of Morning Meeting. The author includes the components, requirements, and benefits of Morning Meeting in the classroom.

McTigue, E. M., & Rimm-Kaufman, S. E. (2011). The *Responsive Classroom* approach and its implications for improving reading and writing. *Reading & Writing Quarterly, 27*(1/2), 5–24.
This article describes how the use of Morning Meeting in the classroom can be tailored toward promoting literacy skills. The authors emphasize how teachers can intertwine literacy learning as well as social and emotional development in students through the use of Morning Meeting.

References

Brock, L. L., Nishida, T. K., Chiong, C., Grimm, K. J., & Rimm-Kaufman, S. E. (2008). Children's perceptions of the classroom environment and social and academic performance: A longitudinal analysis of the contribution of the Responsive Classroom approach. *Journal of School Psychology, 46*, 129–149.

Charney, R. S. (2002). *Teaching children to care: Classroom management for ethical and academic growth, K-8.* Turner Falls, MA: Northeast Foundation for Children.

Kriete, R., & Bechtel, L. (2002). *The Morning Meeting book*. Turner Falls, MA: Northeast Foundation for Children.

Northeast Foundation for Children. (2012, February 17). *Responsive Classroom* Fact Sheet. Retrieved from http://www.responsiveclassroom.org/sites/default/files/pdffiles/rcfactsheet.pdf

Pianta, R. C. (2006). Classroom management and relationships between children and teachers: Implications of research and practice. In C. M. Evertson & C. S. Weinstein (Eds.), *Handbook of classroom management: Research, practice, and contemporary issues* (pp. 685–709). Mahwah, NJ: Lawrence Erlbaum.

Rimm-Kaufman, S. E., & Chiu, Y. I. (2007). Promoting social and academic competence in the classroom: An intervention study examining the contribution of the *Responsive Classroom* approach. *Psychology in the Schools, 44*, 397–413.

Rimm-Kaufman, S. E., Fan, X., Chiu, Y. I., & You, W. (2007). The contribution of the *Responsive Classroom* approach on children's academic achievement: Results from a three year longitudinal study. *Journal of School Psychology, 45*, 401–421.

Rimm-Kaufman, S. E., & Sawyer, B. E. (2004). Primary-grade teachers' self-efficacy beliefs, attitudes toward teaching, and discipline and teaching practice priorities in relation to the *Responsive Classroom* approach. *Elementary School Journal, 104*, 321–341.

Smith, S. W. (2001). An interview with . . . Stephen W. Smith: Strategies for building a positive classroom environment by preventing behavior problems. *Intervention in School and Clinic, 37*, 31–35.

Watson, M., & Battistich, V. (2006). Building and sustaining caring communities. In C. M. Evertson & C. S. Weinstein (Eds.), *Handbook of classroom management: Research, practice, and contemporary issues* (pp. 253–279). Mahwah, NJ: Lawrence Erlbaum.

CHAPTER

6

Preventing Problem Behavior Through Effective Teaching

with R. Allan Allday

GOALS

- Explain how teachers can prevent student behavior problems by being effective teachers.

- Describe the management of classroom time.

- Explain how managing the instructional environment can prevent student behavior problems.

- Describe six teaching functions to improve academic achievement.

SCENARIO

It is Monday morning, and Mr. Wright is trying frantically to get his lessons organized for the day. Not prepared when the students enter the room, Mr. Wright tries to get everyone organized and start on his math lesson. While going through some slides and having students work on some problems, he suddenly remembers to announce the schoolwide assembly that will take place later that morning. After making the announcement, Mr. Wright talks a bit about his fishing trip over the weekend and then gets back to the lesson. During this, Hendrick says that he likes to fish, and Taylor starts talking about his uncle's fishing boat. At this point, some students are getting out of their seats, and most of the others are off task. Mr. Wright looks at the clock and realizes that he needs to finish math to start reading and get his class to the assembly on time. *We still have reading to do,* he says, *so let's pay attention so we can get through this material.* After a few minutes, however, students are moving around the room and talking loudly to each other. *Hey,* Mr. Wright tells them, *I do not know why everyone is talking! You have a worksheet to finish, and everyone needs to hurry up.*

A few moments later, some students are making progress, but others are struggling and starting to create some problems. Because Mr. Wright is behind on his lesson planning, he is working at his desk rather than walking around the room and helping students with their worksheet. Sammy and Rosiland want to ask questions, but Mr. Wright says he does not have enough time and instructs them to just finish their work. More and more students are talking to each other now and ignoring the work to be finished before reading starts. Mr. Wright is becoming agitated and threatens to send Sammy and Rosiland out of the room for not following directions. In the back of the room, Roberta tells Jamal to stop kicking her desk, and Jamal tells her to be quiet and crumples up his worksheet.

Our focus throughout this book has been on the importance of preventing mis-behavior by establishing and maintaining an effective classroom environ-ment. We have stressed that teachers who run their classrooms in a systematic manner are successful classroom managers. The basic question we ask is why wait for problem behaviors to occur and then react with disciplinary procedures that could, in turn, escalate the problems into more serious situations? Teachers whose classrooms are characterized by order, care and respect, and few interruptions due to behavior problems have more time to devote to teaching academic content, and students in these classrooms have more opportunities to learn the curriculum at hand. Thus, teachers like Mr. Wright need to understand the link between effective instruction and successful classroom management, both of which are vital for successful teaching.

As Savage and Savage (2010) observed, teachers cannot deliver effective instruc-tion unless there is classroom order, and good teaching facilitates good order. This is because well-planned and well-executed instruction motivates students, increases aca-demic achievement, and promotes on-task behavior. In the scenario that opened this chapter, Mr. Wright began his lesson, suddenly remembered to tell his students about the assembly, and then talked briefly about his weekend fishing trip. From that point on, it seems that Mr. Wright was losing control and student behavior problems were starting to emerge. Simply put, the emerging behavior problems were caused by prob-lems in the teacher's lessons. In this chapter, we present research-based strategies that teachers can use to avoid classroom disruptions and behavior problems, improve their instruction, and encourage appropriate student behavior.

According to Witt, VanDerHeyden, and Gilbertson (2004), research on teaching and classroom behavior has demonstrated a number of ways that teachers can manage instructional variables to facilitate learning while promoting positive classroom beha-vior. When teachers focus on improving instruction to decrease classroom management problems, they influence not only student behavior but academic achievement as well. Our discussion about the link between improving academic achievement and student behavior focuses on four areas: (a) managing teacher behavior; (b) managing instruc-tional time; (c) managing lessons, teaching, and academic content; and (d) using teach-ing functions.

MANAGING TEACHER BEHAVIOR

In Chapter 1, we examined the research of Jacob Kounin (1970). His findings were piv-otal to our understanding of how teacher behavior affects student behavior. Kounin suggested that teachers should be aware of their environment and how their move-ment and interactions within the environment impact instructional effectiveness. If Mr. Wright had had Jacob Kounin's findings in mind, his classroom problems likely would not have occurred. In this section, we review teacher behaviors that are important to improving students' instructional outcomes and maintaining an orderly and disruption-free classroom. These behaviors include (a) demonstrating withitness, (b) using proximity control, and (c) praising effectively.

Demonstrating Withitness

As we explained in Chapter 1, Kounin's keystone finding was that the most effective classroom managers exhibited "withitness." That is, they had a high degree of awareness and were able to observe, direct, and manage student behavior in an effective and efficient manner while simultaneously delivering an effective lesson. Essentially, this means that teachers need to constantly engage in active supervision of their students, which requires awareness of students' academic and social behaviors. Active supervision entails a variety of teacher behaviors, including proximity control, which refers to moving around the classroom and standing in close proximity to students, and providing quick and effective redirection of problem behavior (see Chapters 7 and 8). If Mr. Wright had exhibited withitness, he would have noticed the first students become off task and addressed the problem before it spread to others.

Effective classroom managers also exhibited another supervisory characteristic that Kounin referred to as "overlapping." Kounin found that teachers who displayed an ability to overlap were able to attend to more than one task at a time. For example, if a teacher is going through a lesson in social studies class and notices two students whispering to each other, the teacher would move close to the students while continuing to give the lecture. In short, overlapping, which is dependent on a teacher being withit, is the ability to multitask.

Withitness and overlapping require that teachers judge which behaviors need to be addressed immediately and that teachers accurately target where problem behaviors may be developing. Effective teachers make accurate and rapid judgments about such issues.

To increase active supervision, or withitness, in the classroom, teachers should:

- Be able to see all students, and ensure that all students can see the teacher.
- Move among the students during instructional and practice activities.
- Place desks and activity areas so that everyone can move easily and freely.
- Develop ways to maintain or increase movement in the class (e.g., place a sign in a conspicuous place that says "SCAN AND MOVE").

Using Proximity Control

Proximity control is a simple strategy that can decrease problem behaviors by increasing the effectiveness of corrective statements due to the close teacher–student proximity. In Chapter 3, we reviewed the physical setup of a classroom that encourages active supervision and teacher mobility. Using proximity control requires that teachers move throughout the classroom efficiently as they observe the academic and behavioral performance of students while providing corrective feedback to students based on their performance.

When teachers detect potential behavior problems, they move close to the offending student or students until the likelihood of problem behaviors has diminished. As the teacher moves toward a student, it is important to maintain the pace of the lesson by continuing instruction. When the potential problem has decreased, the teacher should continue moving and provide nonverbal praise (e.g., thumbs up, smile) to students exhibiting appropriate behavior.

Another important effect of teacher movement and proximity control is that it allows teachers to go from student to student to (a) supervise students' work, (b) provide corrective feedback, and (c) provide process feedback (i.e., the teacher restates the steps of the problem as the student proceeds). In addition to supervising students, the teacher should question students to check for understanding. Of course, checking for understanding is critically important, because it allows teachers to assess their students' understanding of the content and skills being taught and then provide specific feedback, adjust instruction, and if necessary, reteach the lesson. Good and Brophy (2008) noted it is crucial that teachers check for students' understanding and, if students are making errors, correct the errors as soon as possible. Not only does this allow the teacher to correct student errors quickly, it lessens the likelihood of student frustration, which may lead to problem behavior.

To increase teacher movement and proximity control, teachers can:

- Move around the classroom during instructional and practice activities.
- Actively and consciously scan the classroom.
- Move to a student's area when problems become noticeable while keeping the lesson going.
- Make brief but frequent contacts with students during practice activities.

Praising Effectively

With most students, providing teacher praise for exhibiting appropriate behavior will increase the likelihood that students will perform the behavior again in the future. According to Good and Brophy (2008), students generally prefer private praise delivered quietly rather than public praise delivered loudly and effusively. Additionally, students prefer specific praise for meaningful accomplishments rather than general praise. Although general praise statements, such as *Way to go*, *Good job*, *That's the way*, or *Excellent*, do communicate that students are engaged in a teacher-approved behavior, they do not specify what was "excellent" or what, exactly, was a "good job." Making specific praise statements that describe the exact preferred behavior and let students know precisely why they are being praised is an effective strategy for increasing compliance and on-task behavior and decreasing misbehavior. Researchers have demonstrated that training teachers to include the specific behavior when providing praise can increase students' rates of appropriate behavior (Sutherland, Alder, & Gunter, 2003).

Most teachers assume that praise always produces a positive effect on the student's behavior, yet this may not always be true. For instance, when withdrawn or shy students are overtly praised (e.g., *Way to go Samuel, you followed directions and got the assignment done on time!*), they may become embarrassed and not want to perform the behavior again for fear of being singled out and, perhaps, embarrassed. Teachers must be aware of students who find praise aversive and adjust the type of praise they use to maximize its effectiveness. Public praise can also be embarrassing if it calls attention to conformity rather than actual accomplishments (e.g., *Randall, I like how you are staying in your seat this afternoon*).

According to Brophy (1981), the strategies that teachers use to elicit desired behavior are more important than praise for such behaviors after they occur. Nonetheless, when praise is delivered, the key to its effectiveness lies in its quality rather than its frequency. Moreover, effective praise (a) calls attention to development in the student's learning progress or skill mastery, (b) expresses appreciation for efforts or accomplishments in ways that call attention to those efforts or accomplishments rather than the student's role in pleasing the teacher, and (c) is delivered with spontaneity, genuineness, and warmth.

Teachers should be mindful about their use of praise statements with students. Sugai and Horner (2002) asserted that in interactions with students, teachers should strive for a ratio of four to five positive interactions for every negative one. By attending to the positive aspects of behavior and to those students who are meeting behavioral expectations, the teacher shifts the focus of students' attention to the behaviors that are valued and reinforced in the classroom and school.

Teachers should also ask themselves if the praise they deliver is achieving the goal of having students be academically engaged and well behaved. This question forces teachers to examine the use of praise with each student; there are times when teachers get stuck telling each student *Good job* or *Way to go*. Teachers should also determine if the praise they deliver actually increases the problem behaviors of certain students. When delivering praise, teachers should (a) monitor which behaviors they are more likely to praise; (b) determine the length of time between the behavior and the statement, because too much time may reduce the effectiveness of the praise; (c) assess the student's reaction to the praise, and (d) note the specificity of the praise statements they use.

To deliver effective praise, teachers should:

- Praise students simply and directly.
- Praise students in a quiet and natural voice.
- Specify the accomplishment or effort when praising.
- Call attention to the development of a skill or evidence of progress.
- Provide nonverbal communication of approval.
- Praise privately in most situations.

MANAGING INSTRUCTIONAL TIME

Most school days require students to be on campus for seven to eight hours, but during much of this time, unfortunately, students are not engaged in academic activities. In fact, according to one study, students are not engaged in academic activities for one-fourth to one-half of the school day (Jones, Valdez, Nowakowski, & Rasmussen, 1994). Making the best possible use of time is essential to increasing academic achievement and preventing problem behavior. Obviously, the more time that students devote to a particular subject or skill, the more likely they are to master that subject or skill. In classrooms of the most effective teachers and classroom managers, students spend most of their available time engaged in instructional activities rather than nonproductive or down time (Good & Brophy, 2008).

Two types of time that teachers need to be aware of are allocated time and academic engaged time. When teachers understand these types of classroom time, they can better assess where instructional time is lost and how best to fill the time that they have with meaningful activities.

Allocated Time

Allocated time is the amount of classroom time that is allocated for teaching. For example, a teacher may decide that 40 minutes each day will be allocated for a social studies lesson. Teachers sometimes have little control over allocated time, because they may be limited in the amount of time each day that they can focus on specific subject areas. In elementary settings, instructional time may be divided into periods of 50 to 60 minutes or blocks of 90 minutes. Teachers do, however, need time to conduct procedural activities, such as taking attendance, receiving and returning assignments, and allowing restroom breaks, each of which is a cost to instructional time (see Chapter 3 for establishing effective transitions). Teachers like Mr. Wright should take into account the myriad of interfering events throughout the day that cut into the allocated time, and they should keep in mind the goal of increasing the time that students spend actually learning. When teachers are effective planners, they are able to *determine* where time will go rather than *asking* where it went!

Academic Engaged Time

Academic engaged time is the amount of time in which students are actively and successfully involved in learning activities. Academic engaged time includes attending to the teacher and instructional materials, answering teacher's questions, reading aloud, asking questions, taking notes, and completing independent work. The greater the amount of time that a student is actively engaged in instructional activities, the greater the amount of learning.

Maximization of academic engaged time is the key to improving classroom behavior and increasing academic performance. Mastropieri and Scruggs (2007) asserted that teachers could actually double the amount of classroom learning simply by increasing student engagement in learning activities throughout the allocated time period. In other words, within the allocated time for instruction, teachers should work to reduce or make as efficient as possible nonacademic activities, such as transitions, distributing materials, and digressions, and increase, to the maximum possible the amount of time in which students are actively engaged in a learning activity. According to Paine, Radicchi, Rosellini, Deutchman, and Darch (1983), classroom time is like money—you have to be careful in your management of it, or it can slip through your fingers!

What is equally important about academic engaged time in the classroom is that when there is more of it, there is a likelihood that students will engage in less problematic behaviors. Kounin (1970) suggested that teachers who kept their students engaged were more effective classroom managers than teachers who allowed more down time. This logic is easy to follow, because task engagement and task disengagement are incompatible behaviors. Students cannot be on task and off task simultaneously. Thus, if Mr. Wright could have kept his students better engaged in the math lesson, then his students' off-task behaviors would have been minimized.

To increase academic engaged time, teachers can:

- Minimize time spent in organizational activities by developing and streamlining procedures (see Chapter 3).

- Teach, practice, and encourage students to transition between activities efficiently (see Chapter 3).
- Discourage classroom interruptions.
- Select learning activities that maximize engaged time and minimize free or down time.
- Start and stop all instructional activities on time.
- Build in frequent opportunities for students to respond during instructional activities.

Q: *I have noticed that during the hour-long math block in my class, I can never seem to complete a lesson and usually need an extra 15 minutes. Sometimes, this creates some student behavior problems. How can we can finish our math lesson on time and move into social studies?*

A: Increasing academic engaged time during the math lesson will help to end the lesson on time and move into social studies without the added stressors of limited time and tired students. To increase academic engaged time, use the concepts that we have discussed in this book. Teach and reteach procedures for starting the lesson, passing out materials, and turning in homework. Having procedures for the "housekeeping" parts of the lesson will increase the time available for instruction. Also, use questioning during the lesson to ensure that students are attending. Asking numerous, fast-paced questions during the lesson will keep students engaged and interested. Following the lesson, guided practice is essential to ensure the skill being taught is practiced. It also helps to transition students into the next activity.

MANAGING LESSONS, TEACHING, AND ACADEMIC CONTENT

So far, we have examined how teachers may improve academic achievement and student behavior through the judicious use of teacher behaviors, such as withitness, proximity control, and praise, and by increasing the time in which students are actively engaged in learning. In this section, we address how teachers can manage instruction to increase achievement and lessen student misbehavior by (a) planning instruction carefully and thoughtfully; (b) planning lessons at an appropriate level of difficulty; (c) increasing opportunities for students to respond correctly; (d) teaching at a brisk pace, and keeping lessons moving forward smoothly; (e) providing interesting lessons and activities; and (f) holding students accountable for learning.

Planning Instruction Carefully and Thoroughly

To increase the likelihood that students will learn academic content, teachers must carefully plan every aspect of the academic lesson. Planning begins before the lesson and is carried throughout the instruction. A well-planned lesson can lead to increased academic engagement, because the teacher is more comfortable with the content and does not feel "bound" to the lectern. Additionally, five specific benefits of well-planned instruction can engender academic achievement and, thus, prevent student behavior problems in the classroom.

First, teachers will be more comfortable and efficacious when their lessons are planned thoroughly. Planning lessons thoroughly leads to greater academic engaged time, because the teacher will have an unobstructed idea of what needs to be accomplished.

Second, careful planning means that all materials are ready before the start of the lesson. When teachers know where teaching materials and supplies are located, they avoid tracking and collecting these materials.

Third, the likelihood of keeping the pace of instruction moving is increased when teachers plan carefully and thoroughly. Briskly paced lessons can maximize instruction time and minimize problem behavior. When teachers become more comfortable with the content, they can address behavior problems quickly and efficiently while continuing the lesson (i.e., overlapping).

Fourth, when teachers prepare thoroughly for their lessons, this increases the likelihood of their asking content-specific questions that can reengage students who are beginning off-task behavior during the lesson. Effective questioning increases a student's opportunities to respond, which can result in greater student learning.

Fifth, a well-planned lesson minimizes the likelihood of student down time. As we have noted, student down time often leads to off-task and disruptive behaviors, because students have no planned or structured activity to complete. Anything teachers can do to minimize student down time will lead to better classroom management. As shown in Table 6.1, planning instruction carefully and thoroughly can provide many instructional benefits that, in turn, can lead to better preventive measures in the classroom.

Planning Lessons at an Appropriate Level of Difficulty

One frequent reason that students have behavior problems in class is that their academic tasks are too difficult to complete successfully within the time allocated and, thus, they become frustrated. In fact, a majority of researchers who have investigated the relationship between instructional variables and problem behavior have concentrated on task difficulty, because problem behavior can provide students a means to escape, avoid, or postpone the difficult academic task (Witt et al., 2004). Generally, researchers have found academic tasks that frustrate students are associated with increased incidences of problem behavior in the classroom (Witt et al., 2004). Thus, requiring students to do academic tasks that are too difficult for them hinders skill acquisition and increases disruptive problem behavior.

TABLE 6.1	The Multiple Components of Well-Planned Lessons
A well-planned lesson can . . .	
• Help teachers feel more comfortable with the material.	• Prevent having to locate materials during the lesson.
• Increase academic engaged time.	• Help maintain a quick pace of instruction.
• Minimize behavior problems.	• Maximize instructional opportunities.
• Increase teacher knowledge and understanding of the content.	• Allow teachers to overlap content and behavior instruction.
• Improve the quantity and quality of content-specific questions.	• Increase student opportunities to respond to questioning.
• Minimize instructional down time.	• Amplify student learning.

Clearly, it is important that teachers match the academic tasks they assign with the students' abilities. Doing so decreases the likelihood of students engaging in problem behavior and increases academic achievement. To ensure that the academic tasks are at an appropriate level of difficulty, Gunter, Denny, Kenton, and Venn (2000) suggested that teachers systematically plan activities that are appropriate to students' abilities and then monitor correct responses and error rates to ensure the instructional tasks are appropriate. Teachers can also assess students' performance on academic tasks using teacher-made tests and curriculum-based assessment. If students are responding at below an 80 percent level of success, the task may be too difficult for them, and they are close to reaching their frustration level (Good & Brophy, 2008).

A number of potential solutions are available when teachers believe that academic tasks are too difficult for their students. First, teachers should reteach the content until students are comfortable with the academic tasks. Researchers have found that when students' work is completed correctly and quickly (i.e., accuracy, fluency), students display greater amounts of on-task behavior and decreased amounts of problem behavior (Gunter et al., 2000). Second, teachers can modify academic tasks in ways that have been shown to decrease the amount of effort needed, such as shortening the task or providing breaks. Third, the task can be modified to make it less frustrating. For example, easier problems that students enjoy can be interspersed with more difficult problems or tasks. As Witt and colleagues (2004) observed, it is futile to manage student behavior when students are working at a frustration level that hinders academic acquisition. Ensuring that the difficulty level of academic tasks matches students' abilities is crucial to being a successful classroom manager.

In summary, a number of strategies can reduce student frustration with academic tasks. These include:

- Back up and reteach if students do not seem to understand a skill or activity.
- Make sure students are successful at or above the 80 percent level when they practice academic activities.
- Modify the academic tasks to decrease student effort when they seem to be getting frustrated.

Increasing Opportunities for Students to Respond Correctly

As established earlier in this chapter, the time allocated for academic instruction is precious, and teachers must work to ensure that students have adequate opportunities to engage in the material being taught. One method to do this is by increasing students' opportunities to respond. By increasing the number of active responses, teachers can increase students' academic achievement. Sutherland and colleagues (2003) investigated opportunities to respond in an elementary classroom for students with behavior problems. They found that when the teacher increased the opportunities for students to actively respond to academic requests, students had fewer disruptions, increased on-task rates, and more correct responses.

Teachers should ask many material-related questions during a lesson—something Mr. Wright failed to do, because he was ill-prepared and hurried. Teachers can require students to answer in groups or write individual responses, and they can request students to use different response formats. For example, teachers could ask for group choral responding, group written responding, or answers on response cards. These formats require that all students in a classroom respond simultaneously. Students should be provided with four to six opportunities to respond per minute. Increasing opportunities to respond is important, but it is crucial that students are responding correctly and accurately to these increased opportunities. When teachers increase opportunities to respond, students must also experience a high rate of success in their academic task. If students know the material they should be correct more than 90 percent of the time. If the material has recently been introduced, students should be correct 80 percent of the time. If percentages are lower than 80 percent, the material should be taught again.

There is a clear and positive relationship between high levels of correct responding and increased academic achievement. Similarly, there is a clear and positive relationship between high levels of correct responding and appropriate student behavior. Thus, teachers should strive to maintain high levels of student responding and ensure, as much as possible, that the vast majority of student responses are correct.

To facilitate greater opportunities to respond in the classroom, teachers can:

- Keep a brisk pace during instruction, and strive to ask numerous questions.
- Provide group opportunities to respond by using choral responding, written responding, or response cards.
- Monitor students' answers to ensure high rates of correct responses.
- Acknowledge correct responding.

Teaching at a Brisk Pace, and Keeping Lessons Moving Forward Smoothly

Lesson pacing is important to keep students on task during instruction. Teachers should take care not to set too rapid a pace, because it can lead to student frustration with the task and create behavior problems. Yet too slow a pace may lead to boredom and problems as well. Thus, teachers should try to obtain a brisk pace that is appropriate to the students' abilities. Not only is a brisk pace associated with greater student achievement, a teacher is able to cover more material, and it facilitates student engagement and opportunities to respond (Good & Brophy, 2008). Brisk pacing also facilitates the efficient use of instructional time, maintains student attention and interest, and decreases off-task behavior.

As far back as 1970, Jacob Kounin found that the most effective classroom managers taught their lessons at a brisk pace and maintained good lesson momentum. That is, the lessons moved ahead at an invigorating and efficient pace, with no breaks in the flow of the lesson. On the other hand, Kounin reported that the lessons of poor classroom managers were characterized by fragmentation and overdwelling. Fragmentation refers to breaking a lesson into several unnecessary, small steps, thus slowing the momentum of the lesson. Having a student complete a problem or task in front of the class is a way of creating fragmentation, because one student is engaged while the others simply watch and wait. Overdwelling refers to spending too much time on one aspect of a lesson or repeating part of a lesson that has already been taught. If a teacher dwells on an aspect of the lesson for too long a time, student boredom will certainly occur.

Savage and Savage (2010) observed that because today's classrooms contain a diversity of student ability, many teachers are unsure of what constitutes brisk, but appropriate, pacing. Clearly, instruction that is presented too rapidly may lose students and, thus, lead to students not learning the content. If instruction is presented too slowly, however, students who have mastered the content may become bored. A method that Savage and Savage suggested to find the correct pacing of instruction is for a teacher to choose a reference group. The reference group, composed primarily of students in the 25th percentile of the class, can be used to assess teaching pace. If the group is confused and lost with the material or task, the pace is probably too fast. Conversely, if the reference group is experiencing boredom, the pace may be too slow. If the group is attending, involved, and interested, however, then the pace is probably appropriate for 75 percent of the class. Savage and Savage also noted that by assessing teaching pace using the 25th percentile of the class as a reference group, a teacher's instructional pace may be slightly slow for high-achieving students, but it will result in a lesson that moves at an appropriate pace and provides for the success of most students.

Kounin (1970) found that in addition to moving forward at a brisk pace, the lessons taught by the most effective classroom managers flowed smoothly. Thus, lessons should be thematically connected so that one part of the lesson builds on a previous part and, thus, has a logical flow (Savage & Savage, 2010). Careful and thoughtful lesson planning can improve lesson smoothness, and as would be expected, thoughtless planning often results in less smooth instruction.

Specifically, Kounin (1970) reported that the lessons of less effective classroom managers were characterized by thrusts, dangles, and truncations. A thrust is a statement made by the teacher during a lesson that is not relevant to the lesson. In essence, the teacher gets off task and becomes distracted. For example, during a history lesson, the teacher suddenly says, *It is really getting dark outside. I guess we are in for a storm.* Or perhaps the teacher remembers an earlier school announcement and says, *Oh by the way, I forgot to tell you that tomorrow's assembly is postponed until next week.* Mr. Wright engaged in a thrust by telling his students about his fishing trip in the middle of his math lesson. A sudden announcement that comes over the school's public address system while the teacher is lecturing is also a thrust, because the lesson is interrupted while everyone listens to the announcement. When thrusts occur, refocusing may need to take place, which takes time away from the lesson, and students may get off task, which may lead to student misbehavior. Thus, it is important that teachers eliminate, as much as possible, thrusts from their teaching.

Dangles and truncations refer to breaks in the flow of the lesson when (a) the teacher abruptly switches the focus of a lesson, leaving the previous point dangling, and (b) the teacher never returns to the previous point, thereby truncating the lesson. An example of a dangle is when a teacher stops a science lesson to tell a story. An example of a truncation is that same teacher continuing with the story until the end of the class period and never returning to the science lesson.

When teaching a lesson, teachers must strive to teach briskly and move the lesson smoothly forward until it is concluded. Of course, any behaviors that break the smooth and brisk flow of the lesson must be avoided. When teachers interrupt the flow of the lesson, whether by overdwelling or slowing down or by engaging in thrusts, dangles, or truncations, students' learning may be affected, and problem behavior may occur.

Providing Interesting Lessons and Activities

Well-planned, interesting, and well-executed lessons not only keep students motivated and increase academic achievement but also prevent misbehavior (Evertson & Emmer, 2009; Good & Brophy, 2008; Kounin, 1970). In his seminal research, Kounin (1970) found that successful classroom managers developed more interesting and varied lessons than did less successful managers. That is, when lessons are well-planned, interesting, and include a variety of activities, these lessons attract and maintain students' attention, resulting in more on-task behavior and less problem behavior. Kounin referred to this as "valence." On the other hand, teachers who taught uninteresting lessons and had students do the same thing over and over again tended to lose their students' attention because of the tedious nature of the activities. Kounin called this "satiation," and he observed that it led to decreased work quality and increased off-task and problematic behavior.

It is important, therefore, that teachers include a variety of interesting and challenging activities in each lesson. According to Savage and Savage (2010), a good rule of thumb is not to require that elementary students do any single activity for more than 15 minutes. This means that if a teacher has a 45-minute reading lesson, the lesson should involve students in at least three different activities (e.g., oral reading, skills practice, question answering, discussion, writing). If teachers have students do the same task repeatedly, boredom may become a problem, which may lead in turn to decreased work quality, increased errors, and off-task and problem behavior.

To provide interesting lessons and activities, teachers can:

- Use short but motivating introductions before a lesson (e.g., *Now, you are going to find this interesting*).
- Vary activities within a lesson (e.g., do not stay with any particular activity for more 10 to 15 minutes).
- Provide group opportunities to respond by using choral responding, response cards, or similar methods that encourage involvement.
- Be enthusiastic.
- Move around the classroom, and make brief, positive contacts with students.
- Use motivating phrases during a lesson (e.g., *Now, I bet none of you have ever heard of what we are going to talk about next*).

Holding Students Accountable for Learning

Kounin (1970) also found that students were more likely to remain engaged in learning activities when they knew they might be held accountable for attending to the lesson. He found that teachers who had maintained high levels of student attention and involvement throughout the lesson were more successful classroom managers, because their classes were characterized by high rates of student involvement and low rates of problem behavior. Effective managers accomplished this by involving all students in a learning task.

One procedure that Kounin (1970) described to maintain student attention is group alerting. When using this procedure, teachers alert students that someone will be called on to answer a question or perform a skill—and that it could be anyone in the class. Thus, according to Kounin, group alerting keeps the students "on their toes" (p. 117) by asking questions and calling on students in a random rather than an obvious manner (e.g., going down rows of the class). If students never know when their teacher may require them to respond to questions or perform a task related to the learning activity, they are much more likely to attend and remain engaged. On the other hand, if students know that during a lesson there is little likelihood that they will be held accountable for what is being taught, their attention may wander and rates of academic engagement will decrease.

Savage and Savage (2010) suggested that teachers always stay alert for opportunities to involve students and never expect students to sit passively during an activity. It is the teacher's responsibility, therefore, to work to maintain high rates of student engagement. By using time wisely and keeping students involved in classroom activities, teachers will keep rates of student engagement high and instances of student misbehavior low. To accomplish this, teachers need to plan their lessons well and do all they can to ensure high rates of academic engagement.

Teachers can maintain students' focus on a task by:

- Asking questions.
- Requesting that students paraphrase given information.
- Having students signify agreement or disagreement with a statement.
- Asking students to perform a skill (e.g., work a problem on the board).

Mr. Wright in particular could have included a number of specific strategies to accomplish accountability in his classroom, such as:

- Asking frequent questions that require students to respond during lessons.
- Pausing before asking questions as a cue to let students know a question is coming.
- Alternating between asking individual students questions and asking the entire group to respond.
- Requiring group responses, such as choral responding, response cards, and thumbs up for yes or thumbs down for no.
- Avoiding asking questions in a predictable manner.
- Avoiding calling only on students who raise their hand.
- Asking students to respond to the answers provided by other students.

Q: *The behavior of my class seems to decline after lunch. We have to finish our science lesson before the end of the day and are often rushed for time. To make up for the limited time, I try to maintain fast-paced instruction so that we can cover all the necessary material. During science, the majority of the class is distracted, off task, and talking with other students. How can I prevent the problem behaviors that happen during our science lesson?*

A: Inappropriate instructional pacing in the classroom can account for the off-task behavior that is occurring during your science lesson. When the lesson is rushed, the pace may be too difficult for most students. You could adjust the difficulty of the lesson by breaking it into smaller, more manageable parts. By monitoring the progress of the 25th percentile of your class, you might find it would be advantageous to slow the pace of the lesson. Monitor the understanding and achievement of this group to ensure that the lesson is paced appropriately for the majority of the class. Remember, the point of the lesson is for students to learn the content. Students are not learning the content to a mastery level if the lesson is moving too quickly for them to understand.

USING TEACHING FUNCTIONS

A great amount of research has been conducted over the past 40 years about teacher effectiveness. In 1986, Rosenshine and Steven reviewed and synthesized the teacher effectiveness literature and concluded that when teachers teach systematically, student achievement and classroom management improves. These authors also summarized the available research and categorized the findings about effective instruction into what they called "teaching functions."

Teaching functions include (a) daily review, (b) presentation, (c) guided practice, (d) feedback and corrections, (e) independent practice, and (f) weekly and monthly review. Good and Brophy (2008) noted that the students of teachers who implemented teaching functions showed greater achievement gains than the students of teachers who used methods they had developed on their own.

Teaching Function 1: Daily Review

According to Rosenshine and Stevens (1986), teachers should begin lessons with a daily review of previous material. The purpose of a daily review is to make certain that the students are firm in their knowledge of previously taught skills. Additionally, a daily review session provides additional practice on the previous material and it allows the teacher to determine if the students need still more practice activities and reteaching.

When conducting daily review activities, teachers should begin each lesson with a five- to eight-minute review of content or skills covered during the previous lesson. Depending on the content of the previous lesson, this review may include (a) correcting homework, (b) questioning students, (c) providing additional practice, (d) reexamining recently acquired vocabulary or skills, or (e) giving a short quiz.

Teaching Function 2: Presentation

The goal of presentation is to teach novel skills or new knowledge. Presenting new material is an effective way to expose students to content or a skill while allowing the teacher to control the material being taught (Good & Brophy, 2008). To conduct a presentation in an efficient manner, teachers must focus on the learner and teach one point at a time. Further, teachers should present materials in short steps interspersed with questions or activities. Good and Brophy (2008) reported that low-ability or low-achieving students learn more by having less material taught to them in smaller steps that they can master without becoming frustrated. These researchers also concluded that teachers of low-achieving students should err on the side of overteaching rather than moving too quickly.

An effective presentation involves several elements. These include (a) focusing, (b) pacing, (c) attention, (d) clarity, and (e) demonstration.

FOCUSING   Begin the presentation by getting all the students' attention. Teachers should first establish the "why" of the presentation by discussing the importance of the content being covered and the lesson objectives, including a specific rationale and the context for the lesson.

PACING After gaining the students' attention, the teacher should move briskly through the presentation. When we talked about teaching at a brisk pace and keeping lessons moving forward smoothly, we mentioned that it is important to maintain student focus and lesson momentum. The teacher should present the material in a lively and enthusiastic manner, without dwelling, slowing down, or engaging in thrusts, dangles, or truncations.

ATTENTION Teachers must monitor their students' attention during the lesson. If teachers display withitness, their students are more likely to pay attention. When the teacher occasionally changes something in the presentation, such as questioning or modulating voice tone and volume, it can increase students' attention. Teachers need to avoid becoming predictable and repetitive, because students' minds will wander.

CLARITY The teacher's presentation must be clear so that the students will understand the concepts and skills being taught. Presentations that are confusing, unclear, or ambiguous will result in student misunderstanding. To ensure that lessons are clear, effective teachers often (a) present new material in small steps, (b) give clear and detailed instructions and explanations, and (c) provide practice activities for students after each step. Additionally, effective teachers eliminate, as much as possible, digressions (e.g., dangles, truncations) during presentations that can increase student confusion.

DEMONSTRATION According to Rosenshine and Stevens (1986), when effective teachers provide demonstrations, they include numerous explanations, redundant explanations, and sufficient instruction, resulting in greater student learning. These researchers also observed that the most effective teachers clearly stated the primary goals and main points to be learned during the presentation. Effective teachers presented material for practice in small steps, and they modeled the skill or process while, at the same time, giving many detailed and concrete explanations. Teachers should also check frequently for student understanding of the skill during the demonstration; in this way, teachers can provide feedback and corrections.

Teaching Function 3: Guided Practice

Teachers should use guided practice activities after they are convinced that their students have mastered the material that was taught (e.g., after students have a high rate of correct academic responding to teacher questions). The purpose of guided practice is to provide the active practice, enhancement, and elaboration that students need to become fluent. During guided practice activities, the teacher can move among the students correcting errors, reteaching if needed, and providing sufficient practice activities so that students can move on to the next function, which is independent practice.

A math teacher, for example, could use guided practice after teaching a skills lesson in mathematics. The guided practice activity could consist of math problems on a worksheet or projected on a screen. The teacher would tell the students to complete the problems and then go from student to student to supervise the work and provide appropriate feedback. In this way, the teacher can determine if the students are ready to move on to independent practice or if they need additional practice or reteaching.

Rosenshine and Stevens (1986) asserted that more effective teachers devote more time to guided practice. Specifically, more effective teachers spend more time asking questions, correcting errors, repeating the new material, and helping students work out problems than less effective teachers. Rosenshine and Stevens also noted that although

all teachers ask questions, the most effective teachers ask many more questions than the less effective ones Clearly, teachers should ask many questions during guided practice activities and provide feedback when students respond.

During guided practice, contact with individual students should be brief so that teachers can get to all their students within a few minutes. According to Jones (2007), teachers spend an average of 4 minutes and 23 seconds with every student who raises his or her hand for assistance. In a 25-minute practice activity, that means the teacher can only get to five students! To reduce the amount of time that teachers spend with students, Jones developed a procedure for providing assistance that he called "praise–prompt–leave." This strategy consisted of arranging student seating so that the teacher could easily see all the students and get to them quickly. The teacher used a signal system for students to indicate when they needed assistance. After a student signals the need for assistance, the teacher goes to the student's desk as soon as possible. First, the teacher praises the student for something that has been done correctly. Second, the teacher prompts the student about the next step or gives a quick correction. Third, the teacher leaves the student and moves on to assist another student. The teacher later checks back with the student who needed help to determine that student's progress and reteach if necessary. Jones advised that teachers should attempt to keep student contacts to between 60 and 90 seconds.

Teaching Function 4: Feedback and Corrections

The fourth teaching function involves providing feedback to student answers and corrections to student errors. The goal of providing feedback and corrections is to ensure that students are practicing the new skill correctly. To accomplish this, teachers must carefully assess their students' understanding of the skills or content being taught, provide specific feedback, and then adjust instruction and reteach lessons if necessary. Mr. Wright did little of this; thus, there was an increase in behavior problems in his classroom.

A teacher should differentiate between positive feedback, which is contingent on student performance, and corrective feedback, which should be coupled with constructive comments. For example, if an answer is correct, the teacher can move on or give a short statement of praise. If the answer is incorrect, the teacher should provide hints, ask the question in a different way, or explain again the steps to be followed. A less effective teacher would simply call on another student and move on without providing specific corrective feedback.

In their review of the literature, Rosenshine and Stevens (1986) found four types of student responses to teacher questions (see Table 6.2). First, students may respond with a quick and firm answer that is correct. In most cases, a teacher should provide a praise statement (*Good, that is a correct answer!*) and move on. Second, the student may make a hesitant but correct response; the hesitancy may indicate that the student is unsure. In this case, a teacher should provide a praise statement followed by process feedback, in which the steps used to arrive at the correct answer are reviewed. This teacher response will help the student overlearn the correct steps in the process. Third, the student may make an incorrect response due to carelessness. In this case, the teacher should correct the student and move on. Fourth, the student may make an incorrect response because of lack of skill or concept knowledge. In this case, the teacher should first try to prompt the correct answer by giving process feedback, encouraging the student to keep trying, and explaining that the student is on the right track. The teacher should then leave, make brief contacts with the other students, but later return to the student who does not have the skill and reteach the material.

TABLE 6.2	Student Responses to Teacher Questions and Appropriate Teacher Actions

Student Response to Questions	Teacher Action
Quick and firm answer that is correct	Praise student, and continue questioning other students.
Hesitant but correct answer	Praise student, and then review the steps used to find the correct answer.
Incorrect answer due to carelessness	Correct the student and move on.
Incorrect answer due to lack of skill or concept knowledge	Prompt the student toward the correct answer and praise throughout. Then, assist other students, and return to the struggling student later for reteaching.

In large classrooms, reteaching can be a problem. How does a teacher reteach one student with so many other students in the class? Three options are to:

- Reteach the skill or concept to the student when the other students are engaged in independent activities.
- Have peer tutors reteach the student.
- Provide reteaching to a group of students having difficulty, but at a later time.

Good and Brophy (2008) asserted that it is crucial teachers check for all students' understanding and, if a student or students are making errors, correct the errors as soon as possible. It is not effective to give only the student making the error the correct answer and then move on. Teachers should take the opportunity to explain the error to all students and reteach the content. Good and Brophy also noted that if student errors go uncorrected, they can become difficult to correct later, and they may lead to interference with subsequent learning. The point is that students learn more effectively when teachers check for understanding and give immediate corrective feedback.

> Q: *I try to be sure to praise my students when they answer questions correctly in class. How can I be sure to differentiate between feedback for students who answer correctly with confidence and those students who are hesitant but correct in their answer?*
>
> A: When students answer questions correctly in the classroom, be sure to praise them for their efforts. When students answer with confidence, it is best to praise the student for the effort and response and then move on to the next student. A good example may be to give a quick *That is correct, Katie*, and move on to the next student. When a student answers with hesitation, however, praise the student for the effort and then give him or her feedback on how the answer was reached. Review the content knowledge necessary to answer the question with confidence before moving on to the next student or question. The point is to be sure to praise the student for the effort and ensure that student has mastered the content with confidence.

Teaching Function 5: Independent Practice

After students have shown proficiency in the content or skill areas in the guided practice sessions, the teacher should move to independent practice. The goals of independent practice are (a) to provide the additional practice that students need to become fluent at a skill (i.e., automaticity) and (b) to integrate the new information or skills with previous knowledge or skills.

In independent practice, teachers provide students with the same work covered during guided practice; however, the students work without the extensive teacher assistance. During independent practice, the teacher should circulate around the room, ensuring that there is consistent but short (e.g., 30 seconds) student–teacher contact and that students are achieving rates of success in the 85 to 90 percent range. The teacher should make brief contact with each student in the first few minutes of independent practice. Because one of the purposes of independent practice is to help students perform smoothly and confidently, independent practice should occur only after sufficient guided practice, and the teacher should carefully monitor recently acquired skills before assigning them as homework.

According to Good and Brophy (2008), independent assignments should be basic parts of the curriculum, not merely time fillers. Thus, teachers should (a) plan their independent assignments carefully so that they provide their students with meaningful opportunities to practice at the correct level of difficulty (i.e., not too difficult and not too easy), (b) make the importance of the independent practice activities clear to the students, and (c) monitor student progress on the assignments and provide feedback to students who experience problems.

It is important that teachers maintain high rates of student engagement during independent practice. Rosenshine and Stevens (1986) asserted that students' level of engagement is affected by how adequately prepared they are to do the seatwork activities and how effectively the teacher keeps students on task. Teachers should also establish a set routine that students are instructed to follow during seatwork activities. Routines, as we described in Chapter 3, prescribe how students should conduct themselves during seatwork, in what activities they should engage, how they can get assistance from the teacher if needed, and what they should do if they complete the work early.

Teaching Function 6: Weekly and Monthly Reviews

The purpose of weekly and monthly reviews is to make certain that a student is learning and practicing the skills that are being taught. To accomplish this, teachers could review the previous week's work every Monday and the previous month's work every fourth Monday. The teacher should ensure that such reviews provide the additional, successful practice that students need to become smooth performers who are capable of applying their skills to new areas. If reviews indicate that a student's skills are breaking down, then the teacher should reteach. Frequent reviews are especially important for low-achieving students to determine if they mastered a skill or a lesson (Rosenshine & Stevens, 1986).

Summary

In this book, we have stressed that the key to effective classroom management is prevention. The attitudes and behaviors that teachers exhibit toward their students; the structure of their classroom, including procedures, rules, and consequences; and the classroom environment all contribute positively to classroom management. In such environments, academic engagement and achievement are increased, and disruptions are minimized.

Researchers examining the effects of instruction on classroom behavior have demonstrated clearly how teachers can manage instructional variables in ways that facilitate student learning while promoting positive classroom behavior. When teachers focus on improving instruction to decrease classroom management problems, it influences not only student behavior but academic achievement as well. Teachers cannot deliver effective instruction without order in the classroom, and good teaching facilitates good order. In this chapter, we have explained how well-planned and well-executed lessons motivate students, increase academic achievement, and promote on-task behavior.

Additional Resources

	On the Web	
Page Title	**Annotations**	**Web Address**
How to Give Effective Praise in the Classroom	Step-by-step analysis of giving effective praise in the classroom	http://www.ehow.com/how_8005024_give-effective-praise-classroom.html
Lesson Plan Templates	Database of online lesson planning programs, templates, and downloads	http://www.internet4classrooms.com/links_grades_kindergarten_12/lesson_plan_templates_teacher_tools.htm
Possible Activities for Independent or Guided Practice	Quick, simple, and interactive activities teachers can use for guided or independent practice	http://rwd1.needham.k12.ma.us/program_dev/documents/curriculumbinder/spelling/activities.pdf
Teacher Toolkit Document	Activities and games teachers can use to increase academic engaged time in the classroom	http://www.creducation.org/resources/cre_infusion/teachers_engagement_toolkit.pdf
Ways to Assess Student Learning During Class	Interesting and fun ways to assess students' understanding and learning	http://tep.uoregon.edu/pdf/assessment/Ways_to_Assess_Student_Learning_During_Class.pdf
Withitness	Discussion of Jacob Kounin's idea of withitness and its effectiveness in the classroom	http://wik.ed.uiuc.edu/index.php/Withitness

In the Literature

Partin, T. C. M., Robertson, R. E., Maggin, D. M., Oliver, R., & Wehby, J. H. (2010). Using teacher praise and opportunities to respond to promote appropriate student behavior. *Preventing School Failure, 54*(3), 172–178.

This article details how increasing rates of teacher praise and opportunities to respond to academic requests can prevent problem behavior. The focus is on how changes to these two teacher behaviors can assist in improving instructional management.

Sutherland, K. S., Lewis-Palmer, T., Stichter, J., & Morgan, P. L. (2008). Examining the influence of teacher behavior and classroom context on the behavioral and academic outcomes for students with emotional or behavioral disorders. *Journal of Special Education, 41*(4), 223–233.

This article addresses teacher and classroom variables that can impact student academic and social behaviors. A second focus of this article is on assessment of classroom contexts.

References

Brophy, J. E. (1981). Teacher praise: A functional analysis. *Review of Educational Research, 51*, 5–32.

Evertson, C. M., & Emmer, E. T. (2009). *Classroom management for elementary teachers*. Upper Saddle River, NJ: Pearson/Merrill Education.

Good, T. L., & Brophy, J. E. (2008). *Looking in classrooms* (10th ed.). Upper Saddle River, NJ: Pearson/Merrill Education.

Gunter, P. L., Denny, R. K., Kenton, R., & Venn, M. L. (2000). Modifications of instructional materials and procedures for curricular success of students with emotional and behavioral disorders. *Preventing School Failure, 44*(3), 116–121.

Jones, F. H. (2007). *Tools for teaching* (2nd ed.). Santa Cruz, CA: Frederick H. Jones & Associates.

Jones, B., Valdez, G., Nowakowski, J., & Rasmussen, C. (1994). *Designing learning and technology for educational reform*. Oak Brook, IL: North Central Regional Educational Laboratory.

Kounin, J. (1970). *Discipline and group management in classrooms*. New York: Holt, Rinehart, & Winston.

Mastropieri, M. A., & Scruggs, T. E. (2007). *Effective instruction for special education* (3rd ed.). Austin, TX: Pro-Ed.

Paine, S. C., Radicchi, J., Rosellini, L. C., Deutchman, L., & Darch, C. B. (1983). *Structuring your classroom for academic success*. Champaign, IL: Research Press.

Rosenshine, B., & Stevens, R. (1986). Teaching functions. In M. C. Wittrock (Ed.), *The handbook of research in teaching* (pp. 376–391). New York: Macmillan.

Savage, T. V., & Savage, M. K. (2010). *Successful classroom management and discipline: Teaching self-control and responsibility* (3rd ed.). Los Angeles: Sage.

Sugai, G., & Horner, R. H. (2002). The evolution of discipline practices: Schoolwide positive behavior supports. *Child and Family Behavior Therapy, 24*, 23–50.

Sutherland, K., Alder, N., & Gunter, P. (2003). The effect of varying rates of opportunities to respond to academic requests on the classroom behavior of students with EBD. *Journal of Emotional and Behavioral Disorders, 11*, 239–248.

Witt, J. C., VanDerHeyden, A. M., & Gilbertson, D. (2004). Instruction and classroom management. In R. B. Rutherford, Jr., M. M. Quinn, & S. R. Mathur (Eds.), *Handbook of research in emotional and behavioral disorders* (pp. 426–451). New York: Guilford Press.

Using Specific Prevention and Intervention Techniques

GOALS

- Provide a rationale for modeling teacher self-discipline and self-control.
- Describe strategies to redirect student behavior.
- Provide strategies to increase choice making.
- Describe the types of group-oriented interventions.
- Explain the steps for developing student behavioral contracts.

SCENARIO

Ms. Dickinson often talks to her students about keeping their cool when they get angry at their peers. She frequently discusses with her whole class about how acting in a hostile manner when feeling angry toward others is not a good way to get what they want. She will point out that students need to try to be rational and think clearly when angry so that they can make good decisions. On occasion, however, Ms. Dickinson also loses her cool in front of her class and tells students to leave the room or even sometimes shouts. She gets angry most often when students are talking, getting up out of their seats, or bothering other students. She sometimes reprimands students in front of the whole class by saying sarcastic things like *Demarcus, is there a reason you cannot stay in your seat?* or *Haley, will you be quiet? I have seen you not talk, so I know it is possible!* Sometimes, students say something back to Ms. Dickinson about how getting angry doesn't help matters and remind Ms. Dickinson of her own message to them about staying cool to get what you want. That only makes Ms. Dickinson angrier.

With instructional tasks, Ms. Dickinson rarely allows her students a choice in how they can engage in an assignment. It usually has to be done the way she wants it done, even though her students sometimes ask if they can do things differently. Her students are sometimes heard saying *Why are we doing it this way? This is stupid.*

A lthough Ms. Dickinson's manner in her class has not contributed to out-of-control student behavior, some changes could be implemented to prevent student disruption in the classroom or reduce the occurrence of problem behavior. In this chapter, we examine four strategies that teachers can use to prevent problem behaviors, and we address two classwide intervention strategies that, when successfully implemented, can increase appropriate student behavior and decrease inappropriate ones.

PREVENTION STRATEGIES

This section presents four prevention strategies that Ms. Dickinson could use to prevent behavior problems from occurring and to manage her classroom successfully. Ms. Dickinson could:

1. Model appropriate behavior for students to observe.
2. Use self-discipline and self-control.
3. Implement strategies to redirect student behavior instead of reprimanding them.
4. Increase choice making in the classroom.

Each of these four techniques can prevent small behavioral situations in the classroom from turning into larger ones, and each could be a foundation for managing Ms. Dickinson's classroom.

Modeling Appropriate Behavior

Besides parents and caregivers, teachers spend the most amount of time interacting with children. With this in mind, the opportunity for students to watch teachers behave in the classroom over the course of a school year is enormous. According to Cullinan (2007), learning through observation is critical to development, because many behavior patterns are so complex that learning without an opportunity to observe a model's demonstration would be difficult. What is needed in the classroom, then, are role models, adults who can show students a controlled way to handle situations that may be complex, difficult to handle, or anger provoking.

As is widely known, observational learning is a powerful teaching tool (see, e.g., Bandura, 1986), one that teachers should be constantly aware of, and they should not discount its importance. In everyday interactions, whether during the formal instructional parts of the day (e.g., whole-class instruction, small group work) or in more informal activities, it is important for teachers to model self-control in their everyday interactions in the classroom. Not just teachers like Ms. Dickinson but everyone, no matter their occupation or the conditions of their personal lives, can benefit from self-discipline and practicing the skill of self-control to manage emotions. When teachers in particular exhibit self-control, they become effective guidance models for their students.

According to Albert Bandura (1986), an internationally known psychologist, observing other people's behavior is better for acquiring cognitive skills and new behavior patterns than learning from the consequences of trial and error. Bandura's work began in the 1960s, as he explored people's imitation of behavior they had observed. According to Cullinan (2007), Bandura developed a general modeling theory that led to a more general theory of human functioning called social cognitive theory.

As part of social cognitive theory, Bandura explains that learning takes place when individuals change their thoughts, behaviors, and emotions as a result of observing a model. Bandura revealed that people imitate the observed behavior of others because:

- Individuals observe a behavior in the environment.
- Individuals remember what was observed.
- Individuals engage in a behavior that imitates the observed behavior.
- Individuals imitate, or do not imitate, the observed behavior because something in the environment reinforces, or punishes, the behavior.

One of the benefits of modeling self-control in the classroom is that students can learn the approximated behaviors—that is, the behaviors they see modeled—before they actually perform the behavior themselves. In this way, they do not have to go through the difficulties that may arise while learning the behavior on their own; thus, learning efficiency is increased. Suffice it to say that an in-depth examination of social cognitive theory and the psychological aspects of modeling are beyond the scope of this book, yet a few tips would be useful for a teacher like Ms. Dickinson to use in teaching students social skills and preventing problem behaviors in the classroom.

First, students are likely to model teacher behavior, because in most instances, teachers are viewed as important figures in students' lives and most students want to please adults. Bandura (1997) pointed out that children learn from adults who are perceived as nurturing figures and who tend to be rewarding. Teachers who are caring and responsive in the classroom can have a greater influence on students than teachers who are perceived neutrally or negatively.

Second, repeated exposure to the wanted behavior is necessary for children to learn through modeling. What students may need are many episodes of a teacher effectively managing complex and difficult situations in the classroom, especially situations where strong emotions may be present. Seeing these types of situations handled with skill by teachers allows students to become familiar with the behavioral patterns that the teacher displays, and they can then begin to recognize the finer points of the modeling behavior.

Lastly, students may need many and varied opportunities to:

- Practice the skills they have witnessed.
- Learn to master the skills through performance feedback from their teachers.
- Be rewarded when they engage in the appropriate behavior.

Because of the known power of observational learning, teachers should do as much as they can to show students, through their own behavior, how to handle strong emotions in the classroom. This can be accomplished through modeling of appropriate self-discipline and self-control.

Using Self-Discipline and Self-Control

The terms *self-discipline* and *self-control* are often used synonymously, but depending on what source is accessed, they can be conceptually different.

TEACHER SELF-DISCIPLINE Self-discipline can be thought of as the willpower needed to overcome other desires, and it can be described as doing something that you do not want to do but know is in your best interest. Basically, it is the act that overcomes the desire to not do something. One example that most everyone can relate to is going to the gym for a workout after an exhausting day at work when it would be much easier to go home and rest. Sticking to a daily smoking cessation plan or washing dishes when you would rather be sitting down watching TV are other examples of self-discipline. Sometimes, just getting out of bed in the morning immediately, when the alarm sounds, can be an example of practicing self-discipline.

For students to observe effective self-control in the classroom, self-discipline by the teacher comes first. Teachers who want to have better self-control of their emotions in the classroom to model restraint for students, especially in anger-provoking situations, require a great deal of self-discipline, because teachers may not want to engage in daily introspection about their own behavior when the teaching environment has so many other pressing demands. While self-discipline is thought of as doing something you do not necessarily want to do, self-control can be thought of as the skill component and is engaged when there is a need to gain immediate control over unwanted behaviors.

TEACHER SELF-CONTROL   Keeping emotions and actions under control in the classroom throughout the day can be challenging, especially when working with students whose behavior is sometimes difficult to manage. Being in control of our own behavior can result in gaining control over the things external to us, yet control over our inner selves comes first. Being in control of an internal self can contribute to positive self-esteem and self-mastery, better teaching confidence, endurance and inner strength, and willpower.

Managing emotions in the classroom and creating effective self-control starts with awareness about self-control and a conviction to become a skilled practitioner of it (i.e., self-discipline). The next step is making an effort to be knowledgeable and gaining an understanding about how to develop control over strong emotions that can flare up anytime and negatively affect responsive actions. When teachers make self-control an everyday goal, which would be self-discipline, it can:

- Provide them with a sense of mastery over their interactions with students in the classroom.
- Empower them to do more.
- Reduce any sense of helplessness.
- Prevent student behavior problems.

Simply put, problem behavior by students can occur in reaction to negative teacher behavior, and it may not occur when the teacher exhibits self-control.

For Ms. Dickinson, becoming knowledgeable about the ability to increase self-control, and about how that skill development could contribute to a stable and nurturing classroom, could transform her into a model of responsibility and trustworthiness. She could pair her verbal instructions to students about keeping their emotions in check and the need to be a rational, rather than an irrational, thinker with her own behavior modeling, self-control, and restraint.

Self-control can sometimes lead to better monitoring of mood and the elimination of negative thoughts about the ability to control emotions and behaviors. Unfortunately, for those who relapse time and time again, losing control when provoked ends up reinforcing that behavior through negative thoughts, such as *There I go again. I cannot do this.*

It is not getting any better. Fortunately, self-control is a skill that can be practiced, and over time, teachers can refine and readjust their skill while approaching any classroom situation. Negative thoughts, however, can get in the way, so the trick is turning those thoughts into more positive ones.

A large amount of research supports the use of inner speech, or self-talk, to modify thoughts that affect overt behavior (see Smith & Daunic, 2006). Theories generated by cognitive psychologists assert that the way people talk to themselves is fundamental to developing self-control and that defeating self-statements (what we tell ourselves) can contribute to poor self-esteem, impulsivity, and aggressive behavior. Bandura (1986) believes that people are capable of self-reflection about their own thinking and ability to achieve their goals and outcomes.

By becoming aware and making a conscious effort to modify negative thoughts, teachers can decrease their impulsive decisions and their impulsive actions. When teachers are able to use positive and helpful inner speech while making a decision in the classroom, they are less likely to lose control and react in a hasty and irrational way.

Inner speech can be useful for a teacher to develop self-control and, thus, be a role model for students of restraint and positive control. Evaluation about behavior, especially in anger-provoking situations, should be constant and ongoing, and the purposeful use of inner speech can assist teachers in gaining more and more self-control. Self-statements such as *I am improving and I am getting better at controlling myself during the school day. I am certainly not perfect, but that's okay. I just need to stay with it and get better every day* are much better than *I will never be able to get control like I want. I get so angry sometimes. This is not going to work.*

If teachers can recognize problems with their own negative behaviors, regardless of how big or how small, during the school day and can learn to listen to their own inner voice or self-talk, then change can happen. With a willingness to improve through self-discipline and constant practice of self-control, teachers can model appropriate behavior for their students and, thus, prevent disruptive and unwanted behavior in the classroom.

We discuss strategies for teaching self-control to students in Chapter 9. The key point here is that teachers need to focus on maintaining their personal self-control and self-discipline to be an effective model for students.

Q: *The classroom can be an emotional place sometimes, and some days it does get the best of me. I am not usually a reactionary person, but I do let off a little steam in front of my students once in a while in response to what they say or do. Since I do not consider myself wildly out of control, do you think I need to worry about modeling self-control for my students?*

A: As you said, the classroom can be an emotional environment, and even the most experienced teachers can always become better at modeling their self-control. You have taken the first step by questioning your abilities. Now, look further, judge for yourself what you could do better, and try to develop some self-discipline to get better at managing your emotions and showing students how to behave during an emotionally charged situation. For teachers who work with difficult-to-manage students on a daily basis, modeling how to control emotions so that students can observe and conduct themselves the same way is foundational to preventing further problems in the classroom.

Redirecting versus Reprimanding Student Behavior

According to Alberto and Troutman (2009), reprimanding students for behavioral infractions is one of the most commonly used punishment techniques found in classrooms today. Reprimands are typically delivered to stop behaviors, and they are intended to act as punishers. The definition of an intervention acting as a punisher—in this case, a reprimand—is that the student's behavior is significantly reduced or does not occur again in the future.

Reprimands to stop behavior can be quick, verbal instructions by teachers, such as *Mallory, stop it*, or *Quit bothering Shekeva*, or, *Alano, stop tapping your foot and get back to work*. Interestingly, however, a student's inappropriate behavior in the classroom may actually be reinforced by a teacher's reprimand, because the student is successful in gaining the teacher's attention. If the student is after attention in the classroom, a teacher's reprimand can, unintentionally, serve as a reward for the inappropriate behavior. For example, when a teacher reprimands Shelia for poking Tashawn and not focusing on her work, the teacher may actually be maintaining or reinforcing Shelia's behavior, because the student is gaining desired teacher attention. Shelia has learned that if she continues to poke and bother Tashawn, the teacher will continue to give her attention, which is something that Shelia desires. Teacher reprimands can stop behavior and reduce its future occurrence, but it is important for teachers to understand that if the behavior does continue, the reprimands may be inadvertently reinforcing the unwanted behavior.

Reprimands also have the ability to turn benign or annoying behaviors, such as tapping a pencil on the desk, making noises, or whispering to others, into serious behavioral issues. Because reprimands often take the form of public humiliation, the entire class is cued into a student's behavior. In the case of Alex, a fourth-grade student with a history of verbally aggressive behavior and noncompliance, a reprimand can quickly turn a simple infraction into a behavioral meltdown:

> TEACHER: Alex, I can't believe you're making those noises again. Do you really have to sound like a duck when you're working in your group? You're not a duck are you?
>
> ALEX: Maybe I am a duck! What's the big deal?
>
> TEACHER: Hey, I don't need to hear it anymore. If I do, you're going to the office.
>
> ALEX: (*BARELY AUDIBLE*) You're not the boss of me!

At the end of this scenario, the potential is there for Alex to "square off" against the teacher and require much more extensive teacher intervention to get back on track toward more desirable behavior. Also, Alex could end up being removed from the class for something that may not have been disruptive enough to necessarily merit removal.

In the case of Alex, a more effective approach, and one that could avoid a public power struggle, is to turn a reprimand into a redirect. A redirect is an attempt to divert a student back toward acceptable behavior without the intent to punish the student. For an infraction like Alex's, the teacher could have tried first to redirect the behavior with no intent to punish. In this way, Alex's violation of a classroom rule or expectation could have been diverted with Alex sitting back down in his seat and little or no public awareness. Redirecting small, common, everyday problems in the classroom can prevent more difficult and explosive student problems from occurring later. Redirecting student behavior is preferable to reprimanding students for small indiscretions in the classroom, such as talking, being out of their seat without permission, not paying attention, and generally bothering other students. By redirecting student behavior from less desirable to more desirable behavior, teachers like Ms. Dickinson can avoid encountering the issues associated with punishing students and perpetuating the culture of punishment that we discussed in Chapter 2.

Redirecting can be easily understood as a common parenting technique useful for the positive managing of toddler behavior in the home. Most toddlers want to explore the home environment using their newly discovered walking skills, yet safety is always a concern for the supervising adults. For example, if a small child was to approach a coffee table in the living room and reach for a water glass or, maybe, a hot cup of coffee, a parent or other adult may whisk the child away and say, *No, must not touch! Come over here and play with these blocks on the floor instead.* In this scenario, the intent is simply to redirect the toddler's behavior toward a more desirable behavior from a less desirable one. Reprimanding the toddler by being firm and yelling *Stop it! Sit down right now and stop reaching for things on the table!* is unnecessary, unproductive, and developmentally inappropriate. (Although a good example to understand the basics of redirecting behavior, this situation could have been prevented entirely if the water glass or hot coffee were not on the table in the first place with a small toddler around!)

To explore how to prevent behavior problems effectively using redirection, we use Kaplan's (1995) hints for managing benign behavior problems. These include (a) make privacy and simplicity paramount; (b) communicate first with eye contact; (c) be succinct; (d) use student-friendly language; (e) resist sarcasm; (f) use if-then statements; (g) speak calmly, and use a normal voice; (h) be mindful of your body language; (i) give the student time to comply; and (j) follow up with a thank you.

MAKE PRIVACY AND SIMPLICITY PARAMOUNT   When redirecting behavior, make privacy a priority, and keep it simple. Although it can be difficult to manage behavior privately in a classroom full of students, a focus should be on redirecting a student from problematic behavior with as little attention from other students as possible. Keeping the redirect personal and private means getting close to the student to talk, thus minimizing any public announcement in the classroom about that student's transgression. Accomplishing privacy helps to keep behaviors outside the public eye and to avoid students feeling the need to save face in front of their friends. Students are more likely to respond belligerently when they feel the need to show off for their peers. Taking a more private approach helps to eliminate the student's need to be defiant. When it is difficult to get close to the student to redirect a behavior, simple nonverbal cues or attention-seeking devices, such as snapping your fingers, calling the student's name, or if the student is looking, raising an eyebrow in a questioning fashion, can be effective.

COMMUNICATE FIRST WITH EYE CONTACT   Effective communication requires the speaker to establish eye contact with the listener. Communicative intent is less noticeable and more likely to be misdirected when eye contact is not established. Consider having a conversation with a friend or colleague while also typing on the computer. Head nodding and phrases such as *I agree* are used, but your friend or colleague may feel that you are not actually listening. When redirecting a student, make sure to have the student's attention. Gaining the student's attention could be as easy as calling the student's name or tapping the student on the arm so that he or she looks at you and, thus, establishes eye contact. Once eye contact is established, a redirection can occur. However, be sure to avoid using demanding phrases, such as *Look at me when I am speaking to you*. These phrases can turn a redirection into something more punitive or punishing.

BE SUCCINCT   Being brief with your redirect can be difficult, but it is necessary. Avoid using this as an opportunity for a lecture or to engage in questioning students about why they continue to make poor choices. When redirecting a student toward more desirable behaviors, be succinct and direct while still maintaining the intent of moving the student toward more appropriate behavior. In reference to Alex, the teacher could say, *Alex, I see you are out of your seat. Can I help you with your assignment?* The teacher has helped Alex get back on track with his assignment in a direct and concise way. Little time has been wasted and Alex is back on track.

USE STUDENT-FRIENDLY LANGUAGE   Sometimes, a teacher will use words to describe a student's work or behavior that are unfamiliar to the student. Remember to use student-friendly language, and take the student's comfort level with language into consideration. One way to make sure the student understands your message is to be precise in describing the behavior you desire the student to start or stop doing. For example, *Anna, you are tapping your foot and bothering other students*. Anna may be so involved in her assignment that she is unaware of what she is doing and that she is bothering other students. With a quick *Stop that Anna*, she might respond with *What? I'm not doing anything*. Anna's response would then require more direction and prompting to achieve the desired result of her stopping the tapping. With more difficult-to-manage students, this exchange could create more problems. To turn this situation into a redirection, the teacher could say *Anna, you need to start your math work. It is almost time to move into reading*.

RESIST SARCASM   Sarcasm directed toward a student might make them feel a need to respond with their own sarcastic remark. A teacher might say *Anna, stop tapping your foot. Can't you keep your feet still for even a second?* Anna might then feel the need to respond with *No, I can't. What about you?* This exchange can quickly turn into the teacher and student being caught in a potential lose–lose situation.

USE IF-THEN STATEMENTS   When redirecting students, use statements that are clear and focused on what might occur if the behavior continues or if it stops. A teacher might say *Paul, if you can't get your assignment done by the bell, you will have to take it home for homework* instead of *Paul, stop talking and get your work done*. Another example is *Emily, if you stop tapping your pencil, Erika can get her project finished, and you two can play at recess* instead of *Emily, quit tapping your pencil and annoying Erika*. Clearly identifying a connection between student behavior and an outcome may help to redirect behavior, and helping students understand the effects of their actions aids the teacher in turning a reprimand into a redirect.

SPEAK CALMLY, AND USE A NORMAL VOICE   Be sure to keep your goal in mind when redirecting students. Avoid losing sight of what you are trying to accomplish or reacting with a hostile or loud voice. Students have the ability to aggravate or annoy even veteran teachers through their actions, but the goal is to redirect students toward more appropriate behaviors. Approaching the student in a calm manner and using a normal voice works better than yelling or seeming angry.

BE MINDFUL OF YOUR BODY LANGUAGE   Professionals have the ability to intensify situations with students simply by using body language that conveys aggression or power, even while using a normal speaking voice. The message that is conveyed through body language is equally, or even more, important as what we verbally say to the student. When redirecting student behavior, our words can be saying one thing while our body language can be saying another. For example, a teacher may use a soft voice, saying *Carl, put away your book and get ready for PE,* while also invading the student's personal space or pointing at the student. This interaction opens the student to deriving a different message than what was intended. Using the same words while standing out of the student's personal space with arms at the side, however, allows the student to better gain the intended message. Students are more likely to respond favorably to the redirection when nonthreatening body language is used.

GIVE THE STUDENT TIME TO COMPLY   Teachers must be patient and wait for students to comply after an appropriate redirection is used. Students sometimes feel the need to attend to their own priorities first before they follow a teacher's request. If a teacher has not indicated a time frame in her request, then waiting for compliance is appropriate. For example, as can often occur, Kelly is complying with her teacher's redirection to go back to her desk, but Kelly is not moving fast enough for the teacher. This incident can quickly move from a simple redirection to a negative situation for the teacher and student unless the teacher waits patiently. Kelly may feel the need to maintain control of the situation by moving back to her desk as slowly as possible. In the classroom, patience is a strength of teachers, and waiting can be an effective strategy.

FOLLOW UP WITH A THANK YOU   It is essential that teachers follow up when students comply with a teacher request. A simple *Thank you* is a common courtesy that helps to strengthen the sense of community in the classroom, creates a pleasant social exchange, and acknowledges the effort the student put forth to comply with the teacher's request. Professionals must remember the power associated with a *Thank you* for a job well done. Students need the acknowledgment of a great job and may even shock the teacher with a *You're welcome!*

AN EXAMPLE OF A REDIRECT VERSUS A REPRIMAND   Table 7.1 shows an example of the different outcomes as a result of Ms. Beckman using a redirect versus a reprimand of student behavior. In the Table 7.1 example, Ms. Beckman is making an investment of time in redirecting the behavior of Maddie and Jatera. With a small amount of physical effort in a short period of time, Ms. Beckman is able to:

- Redirect the girls' behavior privately.
- Interact using nonthreatening body language.
- Explain what they were doing that was not appropriate.
- Offer assistance if needed.
- Use an if-then statement to explain how continuing their behavior will lead to a consequence they may not want.

TABLE 7.1	A Redirect versus a Reprimand

Situation

While conducting a reading group, Ms. Beckman notices that Maddie and Jatera, who are working together on a project in the back of the room, are pushing each other, knocking things off their worktable, and giggling loudly, which is bothering other students who want to get their work done before recess.

Redirect and Outcome	Reprimand and Outcome
Ms. Beckman quietly leaves the reading group, approaches the two students and then crouches down beside their worktable while making sure she has their attention and says, calmly, *Maddie and Jatera, you are bothering other people who are trying to get their work done. I can help you when I am done with the reading group if you want, but if you can't get your project finished before recess, you will have to take it home for homework.* The girls start to work immediately and remain focused until they finish their work. After Ms. Beckman finishes her reading group, she returns to the girls and says, *Thank you both for being so cooperative. Looks like you got your project done. That's fantastic!*	Ms. Beckman stands up at her reading table, points in Maddie and Jetera's direction, and says, loudly, *Can't you two stay quiet for five seconds? Every time I turn my back you seem to be fooling around and bothering people! Do you have a problem? Get back to work.* The two girls don't look at Ms. Beckman and continue to giggle. Maddie says, *We're not fooling around. We're talking about our project.* Ms. Beckman says, *If you don't settle down, I am coming over there, and I'm taking you to the office.* Ms. Beckman doesn't follow up, though, and a few minutes later, Maddie and Jatera are still bothering other students by giggling and pushing each other at their worktable.

Ms. Beckman's actions did interrupt her reading group, but it was in the hope of saving time and effort later on. And she stopped or redirected the students' behavior, thus preventing problems in the future. While dealing with problem behavior with redirection in mind offers no guaranteed results, it is a positive approach, and it is an attempt to prevent problem behaviors from escalating and getting out of control.

In summary, reprimanding students can sometimes lead to a rapid escalation of student misbehavior, ending in a power struggle with only adverse outcomes for both teacher and student. Redirecting students from unwanted behavior to more desirable ones is an attempt to be more positive when interacting with students in the classroom. Like moving the toddler away from reaching for a water glass or a hot cup of coffee on the table and toward age-appropriate toys on the floor, redirecting student behavior is recommended only for relatively inconsequential behaviors. In the case of Ms. Dickinson, for example, redirecting small behavioral indiscretions by her students rather than reprimanding them will develop a positive habit useful for preventing behavior problems in the classroom. Other, more problematic behaviors, such as student defiance, chronic violations of classroom rules, threats, or those involving issues of safety, may not be candidates for redirection.

> **Q:** *I never really noticed before, but I was reprimanding my students more often than I care to say when trying to handle those small, daily behavior problems. What was surprising is how often my students would act negatively to my attempts to stop their behavior and the situations would become increasingly problematic. Is there one particular aspect of redirecting behavior that I should focus on, and how do I know it is working?*
>
> **A:** Knowing more about reprimands allows you to analyze your behavior so that you can turn it around to a more redirecting approach. By doing this, you have already made gains in having the approach work for you to make your classroom a more positive environment. Because redirecting student behavior is an approach in which all the components are salient, being as private as you can with each student does seem to be foundational. It is not a comfortable situation for anyone to have behavioral transgressions made public. It may seem like no big deal, but think about it from an adult perspective. Would adults want it known by their peers that they made a mistake about something in the workplace? You know when it is working when your students respond in a positive way and comply with your redirection. One more thing: Do not forget to thank them when they do what you want them to do.

Increasing Choice Making

Allowing students to make choices about their learning during the school day is a powerful prevention technique and one that can contribute, in a meaningful way, to maintaining a positive classroom climate (Dunlap, dePerczel, Clarke, Wilson, White, & Gomez, 1994). Often thought of as a creative and enriching way to provide general academic instruction, choice making is overlooked as a way of managing student behavior and preventing classroom disruptions. According to Lane, Faulk, and Wehby (2006), open instruction allowing an array of possible learning avenues or choices can be found in classrooms where creativity is encouraged and students feel empowered and in charge of their own learning. When students feel like they have some power to make decisions in the classroom and have some control over events that affect them, behavior problems can be prevented (Hoy & Weinstein, 2006). Conversely, when students are constantly left with few options in the classroom, some students can feel increased resentment and even hostility about being told what to do, and they may act on those negative feelings, thus creating unwanted and undesirable behavior.

Allowing students to make meaningful choices or select from among a few alternatives is a way of teaching them that they can influence their environment without having to engage in inappropriate behaviors. Students can become more motivated when they experience some autonomy in their learning, and motivation can be compromised when students have little voice in the class structure or limited opportunities to make choices (Deci, 1992). Often, students engage in unwanted behavior because they want some control in the classroom or crave any opportunity to get attention (Dunlap et al., 1994). Providing students with opportunities to have a choice in what they want to do, or where they would like to do it and with whom, can give them the control they seek and provide the attention they deserve.

For many students, there are limited opportunities to make important choices during the school day. Most often, teachers tell students what tasks and activities need to be completed, with whom they can work, and what rewards there might be when the work is done. Most instructional activities are programmed in advance by teachers—and rightfully so. Teachers have an immense and varied job of providing academic instruction to, as well as social and emotional learning for, a large number of students, so it is understandable that providing choices to students may complicate further an already complex job. There is a need for predictability, routine, and order to avoid disorganization and confusion, yet providing students with choices does not necessarily contribute to a disorderly or unpredictable classroom routine. Giving students options from which they can choose can be as simple as allowing students to:

- Pick partners for completing an assignment.
- Sit where they want in the classroom during specific times of day.
- Take short breaks when engaged in independent work.
- Seek assistance from trusted peers.
- Select from an array of alternate assignments.
- Establish their own grading scale, due dates, and assignments (for more experienced students).

Providing instructional choices can be as simple as allowing students to choose from a menu of five or six stories the one that interests them the most. Other ideas may be to query students to find out what topic or topics, also from a menu, they may want to study in depth during science. A teacher may allow students to join small groups of students who have similar interests in a topic. One interesting idea is to assess learning by asking students if they are ready to move to the next idea or topic, need more time, or need additional explanation and to go over things one more time.

Another simple example is how a teacher could provide students with choices to practice their spelling words. The teacher could allow them to:

- Read the word, spell it to themselves, and then write it.
- Work with a peer who says the word while the first student writes it.
- Listen to the words found on a computer and write them on paper.

The teacher could also allow students to sit in an area of their choice in the classroom that is a designated area to work on their spelling assignment and to either hand their work in as completed or have a peer check it for accuracy against the master spelling word list.

Providing students with choices does not have to be all day, every day. Allowing too many choices too many times during the day or week can overload students, and they may perceive the learning environment as being without structure and find it unappealing. Teachers should think carefully about what situations are best suited for students to choose, and in what manner, and for whom. Obviously, some situations require specific outcomes, and teachers must dictate how the tasks need to be structured. Also, some students cannot, or will not, do well when offered choices to complete instructional tasks or activities. As most teachers know, there are students who, when given choices, make bad ones. Teachers must ask, for any individual student, which choices are appropriate to offer and how many choices should be available. Note that students should never be provided with a choice to *not* engage in an activity. Under most circumstances, it would be inappropriate to allow students an option of not doing something in the classroom that would affect a grade or an overall behavioral assessment. Teachers are required to present instruction and activities throughout the school day and have their students complete curricula, while students are expected to be active, not inactive, in their learning.

In several studies about how teachers increase student interest in the classroom, Flowerday and Schraw (2000) as well as Schraw, Flowerday and Lehman (2001) found that teachers believe allowing students to make choices in the classroom increases their intrinsic motivation and interest and, further, believe this is especially true for low-interest-in-learning and undermotivated students. Students who exhibit challenging behavior, and those who have low interest in learning and lack adequate motivation, will benefit from successfully making choices (Jolivette, Wehby, Canale, & Massey, 2001; Schraw et al., 2001). When behavior problems come from students who lack motivation and interest in learning, providing choices to pique their interest and promote ownership can be a significant behavioral prevention strategy.

Flowerday and Schraw (2000) reported that teachers in their study offered the following informal guidelines for providing students choice in the classroom:

- Simple choices should be offered first, and then teachers should work into more sophisticated ones.
- It is appropriate for teachers to offer choices to students of all ages, but it is especially important for those students who have low interest in the material or task.
- Teachers can present students with a variety of choices involving their academic work and completing homework and, if possible, involving student assessment and even the social area.
- Teachers should remember to provide instruction for students to learn how to make instructional choices, and there should be opportunities to learn from mistakes and get teacher feedback about their choices.
- For younger or inexperienced students, group or team members can help facilitate choice in the classroom.

Of course, allowing students to make choices would not be appropriate for curricular activities, such as explicit and direct reading, math, or science instruction. Sometimes, certain aspects of instruction need to get completed in a timely and efficient manner. A savvy teacher must anticipate how allowing choices in the classroom might affect high-stakes testing and other accountability standards for which most schools and districts are held responsible.

In some cases, especially during the early years of elementary school, students may have had little experience in making choices. Thus, it is up to the teacher to make sure that students understand how choice making works and then provide some assessment of their ability. At the outset, teachers may help students understand the advantages and disadvantages of each choice they may make. After the chosen project or activity is completed, teachers may ask students for an assessment of the choice they made. If students were not satisfied with their experience, the teacher might ask *What would you do different next time?* or say *Maybe next time you can try to do something different and see how that works for you.*

Making choices available for students in the classroom is most often thought of as a way to provide a rich and varied instructional environment, and facilitating the expression of choice or preference can be relatively simple for teachers to incorporate in their daily instructional routine. In fact, teachers should avoid complexity, because allowing too many choices can confuse students and contribute to behavior problems.

Making choices available for students in the classroom is less understood as a strategy to prevent behavior problems, but when students feel a sense of ownership over what they have to do during the school day, they are less apt to behave in inappropriate ways to gain attention and control. This is especially true for students who lack drive and enthusiasm for instruction and school-related tasks. A teacher's investment in permitting students to choose in the classroom really goes beyond just distinct acts of selection. Rather, it is a move toward the development of student self-direction, self-control, and autonomy.

In summary, teachers should be mindful about managing their emotions in the classroom and practicing self-control so that students can learn the behaviors they see modeled before they actually perform the behavior themselves. For some teachers, keeping emotions and actions under control throughout the school day can be difficult, especially when working with students who exhibit unwanted or inappropriate behavior. Being in control of our own behavior is a skill to be practiced that can lead to control over external events. Teachers should also be mindful to redirect rather than reprimand student behavior to prevent small problems in the classroom from becoming more difficult and, possibly, explosive. Finally, allowing students to make choices about how they complete classroom activities or projects is often overlooked as a way of preventing student behaviors. When students feel like they have some power in the classroom to make decisions, behavior problems can be prevented.

INTERVENTION STRATEGIES

In the first part of this chapter, we described four specific prevention strategies, yet two interventions are worth mentioning that, in actuality, can also be considered as prevention approaches. We think about group-oriented interventions and student behavioral contracting as ways to intervene when there are chronic behavior problems in the classroom, but they can also be viewed as strategies to encourage appropriate behaviors, which in turn prevents inappropriate student behavior.

Group-Oriented Interventions

Group-oriented interventions, or group contingencies, involve all students in the classroom; students are acknowledged, encouraged, and rewarded for the behavior of the entire group. Often, a class will be divided into two or three groups and one or more of the groups, contingent upon appropriate behavior, will be rewarded following an activity or period of time. In most cases, the teacher provides a reward such as free time, game time, or a class party.

One advantage of group-oriented interventions is that the students in the group exert positive influence over the behavior of group members and, thus, encourage cooperation and help develop group cohesiveness. Moreover, these interventions are well suited to situations where a teacher wants to reinforce similar behaviors by all students in the class, such as on-task and good learning behaviors. Researchers have found that group-oriented interventions can be used to improve a wide variety of student behavior, such as academic productivity and achievement, on-task behavior, cooperation, and social interactions, in a wide variety of settings, such as elementary- and middle-school classrooms, special education settings, school buses, the cafeteria, and at home (Alberto & Troutman, 2009; Cooper, Heron, & Heward, 2007; Fabiano, Pelham, Karmazin, Kreher, Panahon, & Carlson, 2008). In fact, as a result of a meta-analysis on the effects of interventions in school settings, Stage and Quiroz (1997) noted that group contingencies produced the largest effect sizes in student social behavior.

Group-oriented interventions are relatively easy to implement, and students tend to enjoy them (Thorne & Kamps, 2008). Teachers, however, need to be thoughtful about which students constitute the groups and then monitor closely student behavior within the groups. Monitoring is especially important, because the power of peer influence within groups—the ingredient that influences group outcome—can turn into undue peer pressure. When students are unable to perform the behavior expected of the group, pressure from students within the group can have negative effects. To avoid these problems, teachers must ensure that all students within a group are capable of performing the expected behavior.

TYPES OF GROUP-ORIENTED INTERVENTIONS The primary types of group-oriented interventions are (a) dependent, (b) independent, and (c) interdependent. In all three types of interventions, the teacher provides a reward or reinforcing event at the end of the group activity. The differences among dependent, independent, and interdependent group-oriented interventions are how students earn the reward.

Dependent Group-Oriented Interventions In a dependent group-oriented intervention, the performance of one student, or a small group of students, determines the reward that the entire group receives. For the group to receive the reward, the student or small group of students must reach a criteria level set by the teacher (e.g., the target student must earn 35 out of a possible 40 points in one week). If the target student or students meet or exceed this level, then the entire group receives the reward. If teachers do not believe a student should be singled out or want to work on the behavior of a number of students, they can randomly select students and not disclose their identity to the group. If the group earns the reward, the teacher could then identify the student or students whose behavior was monitored and conversely, keep the name or names confidential if the group does not earn the reward. In the following example, Ms. Dickinson uses a dependent group-oriented intervention to increase rate of homework completion:

Ms. Dickinson wants to increase her students' rate of homework completion using a dependent group-oriented intervention. She explains to her students that if assignments are completed and handed in on time, then students will earn a reward. The reward, however, depends on how a particular student in the group performs. Ms. Dickinson randomly picks a student's name, writes the name on a piece of paper, puts the piece of paper in an envelope, and then tapes the envelope to the bulletin board without revealing the identity of the student chosen. The following morning, Ms. Dickinson looks through all the returned homework assignments and then opens the envelope. The class will earn an extra five minutes of recess time if the selected student's homework is complete and on time. Ms. Dickinson might then reveal the name of the student who was responsible for the group reward to the class.

Independent Group-Oriented Interventions   In an independent group-oriented intervention, the reward is the same for all students, but students earn the reward on an individual basis, regardless of how the other students do on the behavior or task required. Thus, each individual student must earn the reward that is in effect for all students. When teachers use an independent group-oriented intervention, they must first determine the reward that will be in effect for the entire classroom and the criteria necessary for the student to receive the reward. Every student who reaches the criteria is eligible for the reward. This type of group-oriented intervention is unlike the dependent or interdependent group-oriented intervention, because the students do not depend on each other. In the following example, Ms. Dickinson uses an independent group-oriented intervention to increase in-seat behavior in the morning before class starts and before lunch:

> At the beginning of the school day, Ms. Dickinson notices that her students are wandering around the classroom talking rather than sitting quietly and waiting for class to begin. She has had a similar problem with her students before lunch, resulting in lost instructional time and a chaotic classroom. Sometimes, she becomes frustrated and engages in scolding or reprimanding, with no positive results, so she eventually decides to implement an independent group-oriented intervention.
>
> Ms. Dickinson explains to her students that they can earn check marks to earn extra afternoon recess if they walk into the class quietly, sit at their desk, and begin reading in the morning and before lunch. When students walk into the room quietly, Ms. Dickinson will put a check mark by their name on a poster in the front of the room. They will also get a check mark if they go directly to their seat, and another if they take out a book and began reading. Students can earn up to three check marks in the morning before class starts and also before lunch. Extra recess will be available for students who earned five of the six possible points.

Interdependent Group-Oriented Interventions   In an interdependent group-oriented intervention, the group is treated as a single entity. The teacher determines (a) what the group reward will be and (b) the criteria that the group must meet to earn the reward. Teachers may sometimes require that every student exhibit the targeted behavior at the specified criterion level to earn the reward. An advantage of the interdependent group-oriented intervention is that the students must work together to reach the goal. In the following example, Ms. Dickinson uses an interdependent group-oriented intervention to control student answering during social studies:

> When Ms. Dickinson has social studies, she asks a variety of questions to stimulate discussion. Her students, however, generally compete to see who can answer the question first and in the most boisterous way, thus making the class chaotic and noisy. Ms. Dickinson decides to see if an interdependent group-oriented intervention can reduce student competition and allow a more manageable social studies class.

(continued)

Ms. Dickinson instructs her students to raise their hands to be called on rather than calling out answers. She says she will ask approximately 20 questions during the 40-minute lesson and put check marks on the board when students raise their hand. Conversely, every time students call out without raising their hand, she will erase a check mark. She explains that if the class can get 15 checks during the period, they will get extra recess.

The second day of the intervention, the students earn the 15 check marks and receive the extra recess. As the students become successful for a few days, Ms. Dickinson increases the criteria to 18 check marks, and then to 20 a few days later. After a few weeks of the class earning the reward, she alters the strategy by providing the extra recess only on a secret and random day, and she also counts the hand raising to herself so that no one will know the total count. After several more weeks of using the intervention successfully, Ms. Dickinson discontinues it.

An interesting variation of an interdependent group-oriented intervention is the Good Behavior Game developed by Barrish, Saunders, and Wolf (1969). The Good Behavior Game has shown effectiveness with many different student behaviors in a variety of settings (see, e.g., Tankersley, 1995; Tingstrom, Sterling-Tuner, & Wilczynski, 2006). In the game, a class is divided into two or more teams. Competition occurs within the teams and against the criterion to receive the reward, not across groups.

In the study by Barrish and colleagues (1969), the students were told, before the game started, that the team with the fewest check marks against it at the end of the game would win the reward and that if a team had less than a specified number of check marks that team would win an additional privilege or reward. In a similar study, Lannie and McCurdy (2007) implemented the Good Behavior Game in first-grade urban settings to reduce disruptive behavior and increase on-task behavior. Both studies showed that the Good Behavior Game was an effective method for increasing desired behaviors in the classroom and, as such, for preventing disruptive behavior.

Q: *What should I do when I am using a group-oriented intervention and one of my students behaves poorly in a deliberate attempt to sabotage the group?*

A: Group-oriented interventions work best when students find peer attention and encouragement to be reinforcing. When peer attention is not reinforcing to students, they may be less likely to buy into the intervention, and they may not care if they ruin it for the other students. Interestingly, some students may find the negative attention from other students to be reinforcing and deliberately try to sabotage the intervention. There are three actions you can take when you set up the group-oriented intervention that may prevent these problems. First, do not assign a student to a group in which it may be difficult for them to earn the reward, because at some point, the student will just give up. Second, do not punish the group for the behavior of one student. Third, teach the class how to prompt and encourage each other to engage in the expected behaviors. If these three ideas do not solve your problem, you can remove the offending student from the lager group and make him or her a group of one. In this way, other students are not affected by this one student's misbehavior.

ESTABLISHING A GROUP-ORIENTED INTERVENTION   We mentioned that group-oriented interventions are ways to reduce chronic behavior problems in the classroom, but they can also be viewed as a way to prevent behavior problems. To plan and establish a group-oriented intervention in a classroom, teachers can use a six-step procedure to ensure that the intervention operates as a viable and effective strategy to reduce problem behaviors and increase more appropriate ones:

1. Determine the type of group-oriented intervention to use, and assign students.
2. Identify the target behaviors.
3. Choose group rewards.
4. Define the criteria for earning a reward.
5. Teach students how the group-oriented intervention will work.
6. Collect data to determine the effectiveness of the program.

Step 1: Determine the type of group-oriented intervention to use, and assign students.   This is an easy first step, but the teacher should think carefully about the type of behavior problems in the classroom and the goals to be achieved. The teacher can select from independent, dependent, or interdependent types of group-oriented interventions, each of which has its own variation. Once the type of intervention has been determined, the teacher can select students to make each group as equal as possible in skills and abilities and make sure that students are capable of performing the target behavior.

Step 2: Identify the target behaviors.   Teachers should consider what behaviors need to increase (e.g., on-task behavior, hand raising, homework completion) and what behaviors need to decrease (e.g., off-task behavior, talk outs, incomplete homework assignments). Teachers also should think carefully about how to reward behaviors that are incompatible with those behaviors for which reduction is desired. For example, if the student obtains a reward in the group-oriented intervention, there should be a comparable decrease in out-of-seat behavior. In a similar way, if a student obtains a reward for homework completion, there should be a comparable reduction in incomplete homework.

Step 3: Choose group rewards.   Teachers should select rewards that they believe will have reinforcing value for each member of the group. The reward should be simple and nonintrusive, and teachers can survey students to discover which rewards, such as additional recess time, structured free time, a Friday popcorn party, or watching a cartoon, may be most desirable.

Step 4: Define the criteria for earning a reward.   The teacher must decide what criteria students should reach to earn the group reward. For example, teachers could use percentage earned (e.g., 75 percent of possible behavior points earned daily) or reaching a designated point total (e.g., 40 behavior points earned daily). Finding the right criteria threshold may take some time, but if it is set too high, the group-oriented intervention may not work as intended. When the teacher finds success using the group-oriented intervention, the criteria can be adjusted for the group reward to encourage more student commitment and effort.

Step 5: **Teach students how the group-oriented intervention will work.** Before starting the intervention, teachers should explain the system to their students, including:
- The purpose of the intervention.
- The behaviors that are targeted for improvement.
- The specifics of the system that will be used (e.g., the reward, how students earn points, the criteria for acceptable performance).
- The ways that students can prompt and encourage other students.

One good idea is to post the rules for the intervention in the classroom to clarify the agreed-upon procedures and act as a reminder of what students have to do.

Step 6: **Collect data to determine the effectiveness of the program.** Teachers should collect data on the target behaviors of their students to see if the group-oriented interventions are effective. If teachers are unsure of which group-oriented intervention to use, they could try each one and then determine the respective effectiveness by examining the data.

In summary, group-oriented interventions are powerful systems designed to increase students' appropriate behaviors and reduce inappropriate ones. The distinguishing feature of group interventions is that rewards are delivered, contingent on their behaviors, to a group rather than a single student. The behavior of one student, a group of students, or all the students in a classroom determines the reward earned by the classroom as a whole. A basic idea behind the use of group-oriented contingencies is that they exert control over student behavior by using peers to influence the behavior of other students in the group.

Student Behavioral Contracting

In 1969, Homme, Csanyi, Gonzales, and Rechs wrote an excellent small book to assist teachers in developing behavioral contracts with their students. As contracts are implemented today, Homme and colleagues believed that contracts should require students to exhibit the appropriate behaviors called for in the contracts, and if the terms were fulfilled, students would receive a reward. Specifically, a behavioral contract is a written agreement between a student and teacher that specifies how a student's behavior will change and what rewards will be available to him or her for his or her success. Since the publication of their book, contracting has become a frequently used individual student intervention that teachers employ to teach and reward appropriate behavior. Similar to group-oriented interventions, developing a behavioral contract with a student can be viewed as an intervention to reduce chronic and troublesome behaviors, but it can also be viewed as a way to prevent behaviors.

Although contracts are most often an arrangement between a teacher and a student, they can also include a student's parents, peers, other teachers, counselors, or administrators. Contracts can also be developed with groups of students and are appropriate for a variety of age levels, but students should be old enough to understand fully the terms of the agreement and have the ability to carry out the requirements. A contract outlines what each participant must do to satisfy the contract's terms. Researchers

have demonstrated that contracting is an effective intervention for many types and ages of students and has been used successfully for a wide variety of behaviors in many different settings (Alberto & Troutman, 2009; Cooper et al., 2007).

A behavioral contract is based on the principle of positive reinforcement so that the student earns a specified reward upon successfully completing the contract. Homme and colleagues (1969) specified several guidelines for teachers to follow when developing a contract with a student or students that are still helpful today:

- **The terms of the contract must be clear.**   That is, the expectations for each of the parties in a contract (e.g., parents, teachers, students) must be specified clearly. Ambiguity may lead to disagreement, but this is avoided when the terms of the contract are in writing.
- **The contract must be fair.**   For example, the reward specified in the contract must be fair considering the amount and difficulty of the task to be completed.
- **The contract must be honest.**   That is, when the contract is complete, it must be carried out in accordance with the specified terms.
- **The reward delivered must be exactly as described in the terms of the contract and be delivered as specified.**   That is, it is best to deliver the reward immediately upon the successful completion of the contract.

Although developing, writing, and implementing a contract takes a substantial amount of time, there are five primary advantages to using this type of intervention, especially for children with more significant problem behavior:

1. When students help to negotiate the terms of the contract and collaborate with others to specify the terms, they are more likely to commit when carrying out the contract.
2. Formalizing a contract in writing increases the likelihood that students will engage in the behaviors specified in the contract, especially if their parents are also involved.
3. A contract is a way to intervene with chronic behavior problems that is positive in nature and rewards accomplishments rather than just obedience.
4. Behavioral contracts can be an intervention to reduce behavior problems and, at the same time, can act as a preventive technique.
5. Contracts can be written to improve behaviors both at home and at school. Parents and teachers work together to support a student's academic and social learning. Including parents in a contract may improve the parent–child relations, because parents have greater involvement in the child's school program and, when the contract is complete, parents can recognize their child's efforts.

ESTABLISHING A CONTRACT   There are five steps that teachers can follow when designing behavioral contracts:

1. Select the target behaviors.
2. Identify the reward for fulfilling the terms of the contract.
3. Identify the criteria for earning the reward.
4. Establish a record-keeping system.
5. Continuously monitor the contract.

Step 1: **Select the target behaviors.**   When teachers establish a contract, they must first select the target behaviors that will be reinforced. It is important that the behaviors be defined in observable and measurable terms. A vague and immeasurable behavior is "Maria will show more respect throughout the day." A more specific and observable behavior is "Maria will address peers and adults using appropriate language." All parties involved in the contract must agree on the definition of the behaviors so that everyone is clear about what the contract requires.

Step 2: **Identify the reward for fulfilling the terms of the contract.**   Clearly specify the reward that a student will earn after successfully completing the contract. Rewards can include being line leader for the day, getting a homework pass, skipping a class assignment, wearing a favorite hat in class, or having lunch with the teacher or principal. What students earn must be fair considering the parameters and difficulty of the task, and teachers should include the student when choosing the reward. The contract should also include how and when the reward will be delivered, with an understanding that the reward be delivered immediately upon successful completion of the agreement.

Step 3: **Identify the criteria for earning the reward.**   The parties in the contract must determine, in collaboration, what students need to do to earn the reward. The criteria for earning the reward must be realistic and should not require that students do something they are not likely to achieve. If the behavior change is difficult, the teacher should set up a number of contracts that reward growth toward the ultimate goal. For example, if a student turns in homework infrequently, an initial contract could establish a realistic goal of turning in homework on two out of five days, and when this goal is reached, subsequent contracts eventually could lead to an ultimate criterion of 100 percent of homework assignments (five out of five days) being handed in.

Step 4: **Establish a record-keeping system.**   A teacher may develop a recording sheet to attach to the contract and, if appropriate, record data on the form. It may also be an effective strategy to allow the student to self-record as well. Students can then determine whether they met the behavioral expectations for the specified period of time or task specified in the contract.

Step 5: **Continuously monitor the contract.**   After the contract is implemented, teachers need to monitor continuously how well it is working. If students meet the terms of the contract, they should be given the reward immediately. If the contract does not seem to be working as intended, it can be revised until the behavior improves.

AN EXAMPLE OF A BEHAVIORAL CONTRACT   Ms. Jones noticed that Madison has difficulty staying in her seat during instruction, so she decides to use a behavioral contract to increase Madison's in-seat behavior. First, Ms. Jones determined that the target behavior was for Madison to stay in her seat during whole-group instruction. Ms. Jones knew that Madison would be motivated to be class helper for a day, so with Madison in agreement, she set a criteria level of 20 thumbs up a week to earn being class helper for a day. Ms. Jones broke the day into periods in which Madison must sit in her seat during instruction and used a system of thumbs up and thumbs down on her data collection sheet. Ms. Jones was sure to include the target behavior, criteria, and reward on the behavioral contract. She then had a discussion with Madison about the expectations and behavior that must be exhibited to earn the reward. Ms. Jones monitored Madison's in-seat behavior throughout the week by marking on the chart after each time block, as shown in Figure 7.1, and followed up with a discussion about her progress. At the end of the week, Madison had earned 21 thumbs up and was able to be the class helper for a day.

Table 7.2 is an example of an upper elementary behavioral contract. Similar to the way that Ms. Jones used a contract for Madison, a teacher can use this contract with upper elementary students who can negotiate elements of the contract. For this level of contracting, the agreement becomes formal when all parties sign the document.

In summary, a contract is an agreement between a teacher and a student, and sometimes other parties, that specifies each party's responsibilities in fulfilling the terms of the contract. Student behavioral contracts can be effective interventions to reduce problem behaviors, but they can also prevent problem behaviors from happening in the first place. The contract includes a description of the target behaviors and the reward for fulfilling the terms of the contract. Contracts rely primarily on positive rewards to increase appropriate behaviors, and they can be effective procedures to teach and improve a variety of behaviors and skills.

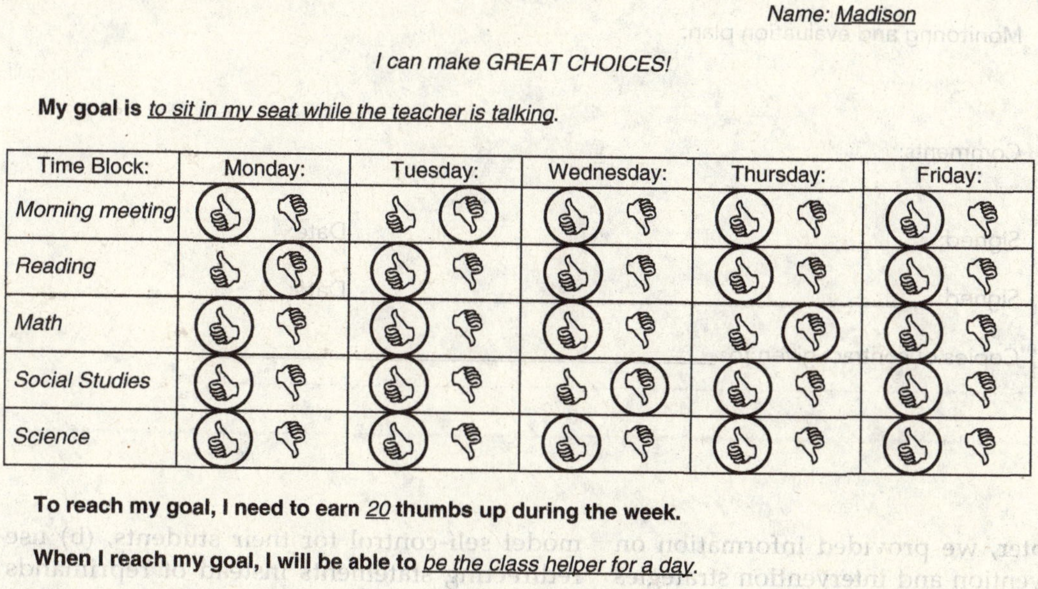

Name: _Madison_

I can make GREAT CHOICES!

My goal is _to sit in my seat while the teacher is talking_.

Time Block:	Monday:		Tuesday:		Wednesday:		Thursday:		Friday:	
Morning meeting	👍	👎	👍	👎	👍	👎	👍	👎	👍	👎
Reading	👍	👎	👍	👎	👍	👎	👍	👎	👍	👎
Math	👍	👎	👍	👎	👍	👎	👍	👎	👍	👎
Social Studies	👍	👎	👍	👎	👍	👎	👍	👎	👍	👎
Science	👍	👎	👍	👎	👍	👎	👍	👎	👍	👎

To reach my goal, I need to earn _20_ **thumbs up during the week.**

When I reach my goal, I will be able to _be the class helper for a day_.

FIGURE 7.1 A behavioral contract for lower elementary school

TABLE 7.2	A Behavioral Contract for Upper Elementary School

Behavioral Contract

Student: _____

Teacher: _____

Description of current behavior:

Description of desired behavior:

Plan for change:

Consequences of continued current behavior:

Rewards for desired behavior:

Monitoring and evaluation plan:

Comments:

Signed: _____   Date: _____

Signed: _____   Date: _____

Copies of contract given to: _____

Summary

In this chapter, we provided information on specific prevention and intervention strategies that teachers may use in their classrooms to prevent behavior problems, increase appropriate behavior, and maintain order. We discussed how teachers should (a) use self-discipline to model self-control for their students, (b) use redirecting statements instead of reprimands when addressing student misbehavior, and (c) allow students greater choice in activities as a way to prevent unwanted and inappropriate student behavior. We also examined two specific types of interventions that teachers may use to increase appropriate student behaviors: group-oriented interventions and behavioral contracting. While these two interventions can increase appropriate behaviors, they can also prevent inappropriate behaviors. Group-oriented interventions and behavioral contracting involve students who are acknowledged and rewarded for learning and exhibiting appropriate behaviors.

Group-oriented interventions involve all students in the classroom who are encouraged and rewarded for the behavior of a student, small group of students, or the entire group. Student behavioral contracts, on the other hand, are written agreements between a student and teacher that specify how a student's behavior will change and what rewards will be available to him or her for his or her success.

Additional Resources

On the Web

Page Title	Annotations	Web Address
Behavior Contracts	Printable behavioral contracts	http://worksheetplace.com/index.php?function=DisplayCategory&showCategory=Y&links=2&id=87&link1=31&link2=87
Least Restrictive Behavioral Interventions (Utah State Office of Education; click on Group Reinforcement Response Contingency)	Step-by-step directions for establishing and troubleshooting group interventions	http://www.iseesam.com/teachall/text/behavior/LRBI.htm
How to Redirect Off-Task Behavior in the Classroom	Directions for redirecting behavior in the classroom on the individual and group levels	http://www.ehow.com/how_2330253_redirect-offtask-behavior-classroom.html
Offering Students Choices from Day One	Ideas for integrating choice in the classroom	http://www.teachervision.fen.com/teaching-methods/classroom-management/6710.html

In the Literature

Anderson, J. (2002). Individualized behavior contracts. *Intervention in School & Clinic, 37*(3), 168–172.
This article focuses on the use of behavioral contracts in the classroom. The author recounts the purposes of contract development, discusses how to select an appropriate contract, and offers sequential steps for developing individualized behavioral contracts.

Tankersley, M. (1995). A group-oriented contingency management program. *Preventing School Failure, 40*(1), 19–24.
This article discusses a group-oriented intervention management program for the behavioral change of students. The author explains use of the Good Behavior Game, its implications for the classroom, and how to use it appropriately.

References

Alberto, P. A., & Troutman, A. C. (2009). *Applied behavior analysis for teachers* (8th ed.). Upper Saddle River, NJ: Merrill/Prentice-Hall.

Bandura, A. (1986). *Social foundations of thought and action: A social cognitive theory.* Englewood Cliffs, NJ: Prentice-Hall.

Bandura, A. (1997). *Self-efficacy: The exercise of control.* New York: Freeman.

Barrish, H. H., Saunders, M., & Wolf, M. M. (1969). Good Behavior Game: Effects of individual contingencies for group consequences on disruptive behavior in a classroom. *Journal of Applied Behavior Analysis, 2*, 119–124.

Cooper, J. O., Heron, T. E., & Heward, W. L. (2007). *Applied behavior analysis* (2nd ed.). Upper Saddle River, NJ: Pearson/Merrill Education.

Cullinan, D. (2007). *Students with emotional and behavioral disorders: An introduction for teachers and other helping professionals* (2nd ed.). Columbus, OH: Pearson Merrill Prentice-Hall.

Deci, E. L. (1992). The relation of interest to the motivation of behavior: A self-determination theory perspective. In A. Renninger, S. Hidi, & A. Krapp (Eds.), *The role of interest in learning and development* (pp. 43–70). Hillsdale, NJ: Lawrence Erlbaum.

Dunlap, G., dePerczel, M., Clarke, S., Wilson, S., Wright, S. White, R., & Gomez, A. (1994). Choice making to promote adaptive behavior for students with emotional and behavioral challenges. *Journal of Applied Behavior Analysis, 27*, 505–518.

Fabiano, G. A., Pelham, W. E., Karmazin, K., Kreher, J., Panahon, C. J., & Carlson, C. (2008). A group contingency program to improve the behavior of elementary school students in a cafeteria. *Behavior Modification, 32*, 121–132.

Flowerday, T., & Schraw, G. (2000). Teacher beliefs about instructional choice. *Journal of Educational Psychology, 92*, 634–645.

Homme, L., Csanyi, A., Gonzales, M., & Rechs, J. (1969). *How to use contingency contracting in the classroom*. Champaign, IL: Research Press.

Hoy, A. W., & Weinstein, C. S. (2006). Student and teacher perspectives on classroom management. In C. M. Evertson & C. S. Weinstein (Eds.), *Handbook of classroom management: Research, practice, and contemporary issues.* (pp. 439–460). Mahwah, NJ: Lawrence Erlbaum.

Jolivette, K., Wehby, J. H., Canale, J., & Massey, N. G. (2001). Effects of choice making opportunities on the behaviors of students with emotional and behavioral disorders. *Behavioral Disorders, 26*, 131–145.

Kaplan, J. S. (1995). *Beyond behavior modification: A cognitive–behavioral approach to behavior management in the school*. Austin, TX: Pro-Ed.

Lane, K., Falk, K., & Wehby, J. (2006). Classroom management in special education classrooms and resource rooms. In C. M. Evertson & C. S. Weinstein (Eds.), *Handbook of classroom management: Research, practice, and contemporary issues* (pp. 439–460). Mahwah, NJ: Lawrence Erlbaum.

Lannie, A. L., & McCurdy, B. L. (2007). Preventing disruptive behavior in the urban classroom: Effects of the Good Behavior Game on student and teacher behavior. *Education and Treatment of Children, 30*, 85–98.

Schraw, G., Flowerday, T., & Lehman, S. (2001). Increasing situational interest in the classroom. *Educational Psychology Review, 13*, 211–224.

Stage, S. A., & Quiroz, D. R. (1997). A meta-analysis of interventions to decrease disruptive classroom behavior in public education settings. *School Psychology Review, 26*, 333–368.

Smith, S. W., & Daunic, A. P. (2006). *Managing difficult behavior through problem solving instruction: Strategies for the elementary classroom*. Boston: Allyn & Bacon.

Tankersley, M. (1995). A group-oriented contingency management program: A review of research on the Good Behavior Game and implications for teachers. *Preventing School Failure, 40*, 19–24.

Thorne, S., & Kamps, D. (2008). The effects of a group contingency intervention on academic engagement and problem behavior of at-risk students. *Behavior Analysis in Practice, 1*, 12–18.

Tingstrom, D. H., Sterling-Tuner, H. E., & Wilczynski, S. M. (2006). The Good Behavior Game: 1969–2002. *Behavior Modification, 30*, 225–253.

CHAPTER 8

Responding to Problem Behavior in the Classroom

GOALS

- Explain the classroom conditions that reduce the likelihood of student problem behavior.
- Describe guidelines to follow when responding to problem behavior.

- Provide a plan that will allow teachers to respond effectively to minor and severe problem behavior.

SCENARIO

Art period is over, and Mr. Cleveland asks his students to put away their art supplies and get out their math books. While his students should be getting ready for the next activity, Mr. Cleveland notices that the students are getting noisy and few are making a successful transition. He announces to the class, *Be quiet while I find my math book.* After finding his math book, he instructs the students to turn to page 24 and begin working on the even-numbered problems. Mr. Cleveland sits down after that and starts marking the daily attendance chart while a few students begin talking, and then more and more join in. Mr. Cleveland stands up and loudly announces that unless everyone is quiet, they will have to do both the even- and the odd-numbered problems. Then Mr. Cleveland notices that Robbie, a student in the back of the class, is still working on his art. Mr. Cleveland walks toward Robbie. *Didn't you hear me?* he asks. *I said take out your math book.* Robbie mumbles, *Just a minute; I'm busy.* Mr. Cleveland raises his voice and says, *The other students are busy too, but they're doing what they are supposed to be doing. Now get your math book out!* Robbie notices the other students looking at him, and he replies, *I am sick of you always picking on me. I'm not going to do it!* Mr. Cleveland, however, has had it with Robbie's defiance. He opens Robbie's desk, takes out his math book, and slams it on the desk. *I've had it with you. Open your book and start working!* Instead, Robbie shoves the math book on the floor and screams, *Don't you touch me or I'll sue! You can't make me do anything!* At this point, the clearly exasperated Mr. Cleveland throws up his hands and says, *Fine, do whatever you want. Just sit there but be quiet. Just see if you pass this class. We'll see what the principal and your parents have to say about this.*

S o far, we have discussed the importance of proactive or preventive classroom management. When teachers set up their classes to maximize student on-task behavior and learning, they also minimize the likelihood of student misbehavior. Nevertheless, even in the most well-run classrooms, students will occasionally engage in misbehavior (e.g., noncompliance, refusing to follow directions, talking out, insubordination, defiance), and teachers must be prepared to respond effectively and efficiently.

Student misbehavior is a significant barrier to academic achievement and is one of the most frustrating problems that teachers face. Such problems lead to a loss of instructional time, disrupt the teaching and learning process, and can undermine the teacher's authority. Unfortunately, because teachers frequently are not prepared to deal with student misbehavior, they react in ways that may actually exacerbate the problem behavior and lead to power struggles such as the one between Mr. Cleveland and Robbie in the scenario above. Moreover, ineffective teacher response to student misbehavior, and the resulting loss of instructional time, may significantly reduce student achievement.

This chapter examines how teachers can respond to problem behavior in ways that will (a) stop misbehavior before it gets out of control, (b) ensure that the classroom environment remains focused on teaching and learning, and (c) minimize threats to safety and classroom order. We first examine the classroom conditions that make it less likely students will engage in problem behavior. If teachers understand these classroom variables, they can act to ensure that such conditions are present in their classrooms. Second, we examine three goals that teachers should consider when managing student problem behavior, including what teachers should *not* do when a student misbehaves. We believe that when teachers confront student misbehavior in inappropriate and ineffective ways, they may actually make misbehavior more likely to occur. Finally, we present guidelines for addressing student misbehavior, which in effect give teachers a game plan to follow when faced with problem behavior, and then discuss specific responses to problem behavior. When teachers have a preset plan for responding to problem behavior, they will be much more likely to respond to that behavior confidently, quickly, and effectively.

CLASSROOM CONDITIONS THAT REDUCE THE LIKELIHOOD OF STUDENT PROBLEM BEHAVIOR

Teachers can prevent student problem behavior by establishing and maintaining a proactive classroom management system, which encourages appropriate behavior and helps to ensure an optimal learning environment. As Kounin's (1970) research clearly demonstrated, an efficient and well-managed classroom will prevent the majority of student problem behaviors (see Chapter 1). Thus, the management systems and teacher behaviors that we discuss throughout this book are critical components in decreasing the likelihood of having to respond to student misbehaviors.

We have found that students are most likely to misbehave when they (a) do not understand what behaviors are expected of them and the rules they need to follow, (b) have too much time during which they are not actively involved in classroom activities, (c) are bored, or (d) are required to complete academic activities that are too difficult for them. We next briefly discuss strategies that teachers may follow that will help to ensure that these conditions do not occur in their classrooms.

Develop Classroom Rules and Procedures

Teachers should develop classroom rules that specify what student behavior is desired. When students understand clearly what behaviors are expected of them, and when these behaviors are consistently acknowledged and reinforced, students are much more likely to engage in appropriate actions. As we discussed in Chapter 6, having classroom procedures that are understood by all students will increase the overall efficiency in which the class operates and reduce the opportunities for student misbehavior.

Keep Students Busy

When students have down time during which they are not involved in academic activities, problem behavior becomes much more likely. On the other hand, when students are actively and productively engaged in interesting learning activities, the likelihood of problem behavior decreases. Kounin (1970) found that the most effective classroom managers kept their students engaged in learning activities, whereas ineffective classroom managers tended to have boring and repetitive learning activities that did not keep students engaged. In Chapter 6 we address how teachers can maximize the amount of time in which students are actively engaged in learning and minimize the time that students spend in transitioning from one activity to another.

Plan Lessons at the Appropriate Level of Difficulty

Teachers should plan a variety of interesting lessons at the appropriate level of difficulty for their students. If students are placed in a curriculum that is too easy for them, they are likely to become bored and, possibly, disruptive. On the other hand, if students are placed in a curriculum that is too difficult, they are likely to become frustrated and, possibly, disruptive. Thus, it is important that teachers use a curriculum and plan instructional activities that are at their students' academic level. Darch and Kame'enui (2004) suggested that teachers should modify task structure and selection if the learning tasks are too difficult for students and they become frustrated. If students are successful at completing the modified task, they are less likely to become disruptive. Similarly, teachers may often preempt problem behavior by allowing students to make choices in their activities (see Chapter 7), because such activities heighten student engagement in the task selected (Jolivette, Wehby, Canale, & Massey, 2001). For example, during a reading class a student could be given a choice among a variety of reading materials (Yell, Meadows, Drasgow, & Shriner, 2009). Additionally, teachers should use evidence-based teaching strategies that increase academic engaged time and student learning.

Monitor Student Behavior

In Chapter 1, we described the research of Jacob Kounin (1970), who coined the term "withitness." Withitness refers to teachers who are constantly aware of what is going on in their classrooms and what students are doing at all times. Kounin found that teachers who regularly moved around their classroom and monitored students had less problem behavior than teachers who did not successfully monitor students. Moreover, this finding was true for students with serious problem behaviors, because a teacher who was withit was more aware of student misbehavior in the early stages and, thus, able to "nip most of them in the bud" (Good & Brophy, 2008, p. 153). On the other hand, when teachers ignored misbehavior or failed to intervene until a problem behavior became more serious, they inadvertently communicated to their students that they did not know what was happening in the classroom or that they did know but would not address it.

Use Precorrection Strategies

Colvin (2004) noted that some students engage in unwanted behavior when there is something in the classroom that acts as a trigger. Colvin defined triggers as specific events that occur at school and that set the stage for problem behaviors. Teachers should systematically observe their students and the conditions in their classrooms that may serve as triggers. Darch and Kame'enui (2004) suggested that teachers should assess possible triggers (a) in the classroom organization, (b) among students and their interactions with each other, (c) in instructional tasks or activities, and (d) when scheduling activities.

Precorrections are actions that teachers take to prevent student problem behavior (Colvin, 2004). Precorrections are different from corrections, because the latter refers to consequences that teachers apply after problem behavior. Precorrections, however, are efforts to ensure that the problem behavior does not occur in the first place (Colvin, 2004). To use a precorrection strategy, teachers must identify the context or conditions that may be serving as triggers for problem behavior. When teachers know what these triggers are, they can act in a proactive manner and take steps to foster the appropriate behavior before the student has the opportunity to misbehave (Walker, Ramsey, & Gresham, 2004). In the scenario that opened this chapter, Mr. Cleveland could have identified a trigger in the classroom that contributed to Robbie's acceleration of behavior and saved himself from the inevitable poor outcome.

Colvin (2004) outlined seven steps that teachers should follow when using precorrection strategies:

Step 1: *Identify a trigger.* Teachers must identify the context or situation in which problem behavior is likely to occur. This can be an event, task, condition, or environment that has set the stage for problem behavior in the past.

Step 2: *Specify the desired behaviors.* Teachers should clearly specify the behaviors that they want the student to exhibit when these conditions occur. The objective of this step is to eliminate the problem behavior while establishing the appropriate behavior that will replace it.

Step 3: *Modify the environment.* Teachers should increase the likelihood that the appropriate behavior will occur by changing the trigger in the classroom environment. For example, if a student's problem behavior is most likely to occur when seated close to another student, the teacher may rearrange the seating so that the student is farther away from the trigger. When teachers change the context, they should make the change before the student has an opportunity to exhibit problem behavior. Moreover, these changes should be minimal and unobtrusive.

Step 4: *Conduct behavioral rehearsals.* Teachers should conduct behavioral rehearsals to allow the student to become fluent in the new skill. These behavioral rehearsals should be conducted before students enter the environment where the problem behavior often occurs.

Step 5: *Prompt the correct behavior.*   Teachers should prompt the appropriate replacement behavior when the student is in the context in which the problem behaviors tend to occur. Colvin (2004) suggested that teachers use gestures to prompt the correct behavior and acknowledge the student immediately for the appropriate behavior.

Step 6: *Provide reinforcement for desired behavior.*   Teachers should provide reinforcement when the student exhibits the replacement behavior in the particular context. In precorrections, teachers instruct and rehearse the appropriate behavior and acknowledge students when they behave appropriately.

Step 7: *Collect data.*   Teachers should monitor the success of the precorrection plan by collecting data on the implementation of the plan and the student's behavior. The purpose of assessing the teacher's implementation of the plan is to ensure that it is carried out correctly. To accomplish this, a checklist can be developed that describes each step of the precorrection plan and has a check off for each step as it is completed. As with any type of data collection, the system must be teacher-friendly and easy to complete.

As an example of using a precorrection strategy, Ms. Simmons helps a student reduce running in the hallway:

Ms. Simmons has noticed that Billy frequently runs when he is in the hallway, so she decides to use a precorrection strategy when transitioning to other classrooms or from the lunchroom. First, she will collect data over a few days to record the number of times Billy walks and the number of times Billy runs in the hallways.

Ms. Simmons: Billy, I noticed that you sometimes run in the hallway when we are leaving the classroom and sometimes going to lunch. We need to remember how to walk safely in the hallways. (*Step 1: Identify a trigger.*)

Billy: I know, I just forget sometimes that we are supposed to walk. I just can't remember.

Ms. Simmons: Instead of running in the hallway, I would like you to walk and keep your hands to yourself. To help you, I will remind you before you leave the classroom, and I will also place a sign on the classroom door for you to look at to remind you. I will also remind you before we all leave for the cafeteria. Do you think you can remember to walk in the hallways? (*Steps 2 and 3: Specify the desired behaviors, and modify the environment, respectively.*)

Billy: Yeah, I think I can do that.

Ms. Simmons: Billy, why don't we practice walking down the hallway appropriately? Don't forget, Billy, use walking feet in the hallway.

Billy: Okay.

Ms. Simmons and Billy practice walking down the hallway a few times before the class gets ready to leave for lunch. Billy successfully walks down the hallway a few times. (*Step 4: Conduct behavioral rehearsals.*)

(continued)

Before lunch, Ms. Simmons has students line up and prepare to leave for the lunchroom. She reminds the class to walk in the hallway and is sure to tell Billy personally. Ms. Simmons monitors the students while they walk in the hallway.

Ms. SIMMONS: Let's remember that we need to walk in the hallway on our way to the lunchroom. Billy, I know you can do it! *(Step 5: Prompt the correct behavior.)*

BILLY: Yep, I can do that.

As the class settles down in the lunchroom, Ms. Simmons thanks Billy for remembering to walk in the hallway.

Ms. SIMMONS: Billy, I noticed that you remembered to walk in the hallway on the way to the lunchroom. I appreciate you remembering to use walking feet. *(Step 6: Provide reinforcement for the desired behavior.)*

BILLY: Thanks, Ms. Simmons.

Ms. Simmons continues to remind Billy to walk in the hallway when transitioning from class to class. *(Step 6: Prompt the correct behavior.)*

Ms. Simmons continues to collect data for a few days. She wants to make sure that Billy walks in the hallway and reduces his running. *(Step 7: Collect data.)*

For keeping track of her use of precorrection, especially if she is working with several students, Ms. Simmons could use a checklist similar to the one in Table 8.1, which is teacher-friendly and easy to complete.

TABLE 8.1	Precorrection Plan Checklist	
Completed	**Not Completed**	**Component**
		Identify the trigger for possible problem behavior.
		Specify the appropriate behavior expected of the student.
		Modify the environment to increase appropriate behavior.
		Conduct behavioral rehearsals with the student.
		Reinforce the student for engaging in the appropriate behavior.
		Prompt the student to perform the appropriate behavior in situations where the inappropriate behavior may occur.
		Collect data to monitor the effectiveness of the precorrection plan.

(continued)

CONSIDERATIONS WHEN ADDRESSING PROBLEM BEHAVIOR

At some point, every teacher will face students who engage in problem behaviors. When determining how to address these problem behaviors, it is important that teachers keep in mind three considerations. First, teachers need to maintain the flow of instruction in the classroom and not divert students' attention from classroom activities to the problem behavior as they simultaneously stop the inappropriate behavior. Second, teachers must avoid ineffective responding to student problem behavior. Third, the teachers must take actions to prevent the problem behavior from recurring.

Maintain the Flow of Instruction

A teacher's first priority when confronted with student problem behavior is to stop the problem behavior while maintaining the flow of classroom activities. As Kounin (1970) found in his research, the teachers who were the most effective classroom managers noticed and addressed student misbehavior in its earliest stages (withitness) while simultaneously keeping classroom activities running smoothly. Kounin called this teacher attribute overlapping. He also found that the poorest classroom managers stopped classroom activities to address student problem behavior. Ensuring that instruction runs smoothly is important, because it allows teaching and learning to continue and it does not attract attention to the problem behavior. We talk in detail about procedures for maintaining classroom activities and instruction that flows smoothly and briskly in Chapter 6.

Avoid Ineffective Responding to Problem Behavior

Unfortunately, when teachers respond to problem behavior, they often do so in an ineffective and overly intrusive manner. Sometimes, teachers respond to problem behavior in a way that seems intended to (a) show the student who is boss, (b) enable the teacher to get revenge, or (c) embarrass the student (Savage & Savage, 2010). Responding in such a manner is not ethically consistent with the educational role of the teacher, and it will not help students to control their own behavior (Yell et al., 2009). Most of these procedures will simply not work, and sometimes, they may even escalate minor misbehavior into serious problem behavior. This was certainly the case with Mr. Cleveland and his student Robbie.

In this section, we explore ineffective responses to problem behavior. These include (a) ignoring, (b) questioning and nattering, (b) yelling, (c) issuing directions when a student is agitated, and (d) engaging in power struggles.

IGNORING   Teachers may think that ignoring student misbehavior is an effective procedure for eliminating misbehavior. This is rarely the case, however, because other students in the class often reinforce a student's misbehavior through their own attention or, sometimes, encouragement. If the problem behavior is brief, unintentional, and not noticed by other students (e.g., a student stares out a window at an inappropriate time), teachers may safely ignore the behavior, but otherwise, ignoring behavior is usually going to be ineffective.

In behavioral terms, ignoring may be a form of extinction, which is an attempt to reduce or weaken a behavior by withdrawing a reinforcer that was maintaining it (Alberto & Troutman, 2012). When a teacher's attention is the maintaining consequence for a student's behavior, and the teacher ignores the student's behavior, if the student's behavior decreases that means that the ignoring operated as extinction. Under the right circumstances, using extinction procedures can reduce behaviors, but this requires sophisticated knowledge of behavioral contingencies and expertise in using behavioral principles. Suffice it to say that under most situations, ignoring student behavior can come with a number of surprises, one of which is an increase in the student's problem behavior called extinction burst.

Consider the teacher who wants to ignore students who tattle on their classmates about benign situations they experienced at recess (e.g., being called a name, not being allowed in a game, not sharing). Because the tattling behavior has been reinforced with teacher attention over a period of time, the teacher may not expect that students will continue to seek attention by accelerating or intensifying their behavior to get the attention they received previously. As the students become frustrated by not receiving attention—because the teacher is ignoring them—there may be increasing levels of inappropriate behavior and, possibly, aggression. Sometimes, teachers have to ignore behaviors for a long period to see results, and there is risk of inadvertently reinforcing the inappropriate behavior through teacher attention. For example, it may be difficult to ignore a student who continues to engage in the behavior while the teacher is trying to complete a task in the classroom. After ignoring the behavior for a period of time, the teacher may end up maintaining, or even increasing the behavior at greater intensity, by saying, out of frustration, *Jalanda, what could you possibly want?* or *Please stop, I can't take much more of this!* Thus, when the teacher eventually attends to the behavior, the behavior can again become reinforced through the teacher's attention.

Also, when teachers ignore obvious student misbehavior, they may inadvertently send a message to the other students that they are not witit enough to notice the behavior or that they choose not to address it. Moreover, in many cases, student misbehavior cannot be ignored for any length of time, because it will disrupt the classroom environment. When it does cause a disruption, the teacher will have to respond, which may reinforce the misbehaving student, thus strengthening the problem behavior that the teacher is attempting to ignore.

Additionally, if students' misbehaviors are allowing them to escape from task demands in the classroom, then simply ignoring their problem behavior may be ineffective, because the students are getting what they want. For all these reasons, ignoring student misbehavior will most likely not be an effective strategy.

QUESTIONING AND NATTERING When a student is disrupting the classroom and the teacher wants to stop the misbehavior and get on with the normal classroom activities, it is an ineffective strategy to ask the student counterproductive questions, such as *What is the matter with you?* or *Why do you have to misbehave all the time?* Such questions convey to students that a teacher is not in control of the situation, and they may be interpreted as an attack or an attempt to embarrass them, which may then provoke a power struggle. Additionally, when teachers ask students why they are engaging in inappropriate behavior, they will typically just get excuses. It is always a good rule to never ask a question about an obvious misbehavior.

Engaging in scolding in an effort to persuade a student to stop his or her misbehavior, which Gerald Patterson (1982) called nattering, is also an ineffective practice. Nattering involves ineffective, and irritating, nagging that is repeated a number of times. Additionally, there is often no consequence administered by the teacher who is doing the nattering. In addition to being ineffective, nattering may also provide a student with attention from the teacher and peers, which may reinforce the inappropriate behavior. Nattering often results in a conflict between the teacher and misbehaving student. The best strategy is to move quickly to stop the behavior rather than dwelling on it.

In general, it is preferable to spend less than five seconds when interacting with students about their misbehavior (Sprick, Borgmeier, & Nolet, 2002). Interactions that last longer than five seconds break the pace of instruction and can actually reinforce the student's inappropriate behavior through teacher attention.

YELLING   A particularly ineffective, and possibly damaging, way in which teachers sometimes try to eliminate student misbehavior is through yelling, threatening, issuing increasingly harsh reprimands, or making a public display of authority (e.g., *I am the teacher here, and I am in charge, not you!*). Again, the student may interpret such behavior as an attack, which may lead to a power struggle, a series of negative exchanges between the teacher and student, which usually makes the situation worse. Additionally, other students in the class may see teachers who yell and threaten misbehaving students as being unsure if they can get the student to obey, or the other students may believe that the teacher is acting unfairly.

ISSUING DIRECTIONS WHEN A STUDENT IS AGITATED   Walker and Walker (1991) advised teachers not to make demands of students when those students are agitated or upset. When students are agitated, directions from the teacher, especially if delivered publicly, are likely to be perceived as an aversive, provocative event, which may serve to make misbehaving students' behavior worse (Walker et al., 2004). That is, students may perceive the teacher's commands as an attack and then respond in kind.

Students will usually have their own unique ways of showing when they are agitated or upset, and teachers need to be able to recognize these signs. By carefully observing their students' behaviors, teachers can often recognize when they are becoming agitated. In such cases, the teacher should attempt to calm the student down and speak softly to determine the source of the problem. For example, a teacher could quietly ask the student what the problem is and then assist in identifying some possible solutions. Walker and colleagues (2004) suggested that these supportive procedures should be attempted at the earliest indication that the student is agitated and that the teacher should not issue a direction until the agitated mood has passed.

ENGAGING IN POWER STRUGGLES   Walker and colleagues (2004) pointed out that some students will attempt to engage in a power struggle when a teacher issues a directive or command to which they do not want to comply. These students may then escalate the noncompliance to ever-higher intensity levels until the teacher withdraws the directive. Unfortunately, the students may learn that this in an effective method of getting their way. Patterson (1982) referred to this aversive behavioral escalation pattern as pain control, because continuing to engage can become so painful to teachers that they give in to the student. Most teachers have seen, or even participated in, power struggles, and as Colvin (2004) has warned, teachers cannot win these complex interactions with students and should try to not get involved in them.

Unfortunately, one of the most common mistakes that teachers make is attempting to control a student's problem behavior by using what Walker and colleagues (2004) called escalating interactions, which occur when teachers and students engage in a series of coercive interactions. Such interactions, which are often also referred to as power struggles, usually involve a teacher arguing, shouting, or otherwise attempting to force a student to behave and, as shown in Figure 8.1, a student responding to the teacher's coercive interactions. Power struggles can be frustrating to teachers, because the harder they try to control students' problem behavior, the less effect their efforts will have and the more likely that students will be reinforced in their use of coercion (Walker et al., 2004). Moreover, such interchanges totally disrupt teaching and learning in the classroom.

Colvin (2004) noted that a power struggle is actually an escalating behavior chain that begins with low-level misbehavior and eventually leads to serious acting-out behavior. For example, the chain may begin with talking out and end with physical assault. Specifically, the chain consists of a series of interactions between a student and another person, usually the teacher, in which each ensuing behavior in the escalating behavior chain is more serious and disruptive than the preceding behavior. Colvin (2004) referred to these successive interactions between a student and teacher as my turn–your turn. In my turn–your turn, a teacher's response leads to a student's response; which in turn leads to another more assertive teacher response; followed by a more coercive student response; and so on. Thus, each response serves as a signal for the next response in the chain. Continuing to argue or attempting to reason with students in such confrontations will make the situation worse, as Mr. Cleveland experienced in the scenario that began this chapter. His interactions and my turn–your turn argument with Robbie made the problem worse.

Teachers need to avoid escalating interactions like the one between Mr. Cleveland and Robbie. Fortunately, there are a number of suggestions to reduce these negative exchanges, such as (a) do not make demands when students are agitated; (b) do not respond to a student's series of questions, comments about a situation, or attempts to argue; and (c) do not try to force students to comply by threatening them (Yell et al., 2009). When a student with a history of using behavioral coercion refuses to comply with an initial teacher request (e.g., a task assignment), the teacher should wait a reasonable amount of time (e.g., five seconds) for a student to respond to the request instead of directly confronting the student. When a student does not respond but, instead, intends to wait until the teacher withdraws the request, the teacher will have to address the situation. Rather than using direct confrontation in such instances, however, the teacher should speak in a low voice so that the situation is kept private. If a student begins to escalate the behavior by arguing, the teacher should disengage, tell the student to sit quietly, and move away from the confrontation. The teachers should then leave the student alone and allow him or her to cope with the situation. At an

Teacher	Student

"Okay, everyone put away your art projects, and take out your math books."
(*Gives direction*)

(*Robbie ignores the teacher's direction.*)

"Robbie, didn't you hear me? Take out your math book."
(*Repeats direction*)

"Just a minute, I'm busy"
(*Robbie makes an excuse.*)

"The other students are busy, too! Now, take out your math book!"
(*Raises voice and repeats direction*)

"I'm sick of you always picking on me!"
(*Robbie gets defiant.*)

"I've had it with you. Take out your book and get working!!"
(*Opens Robbie's desk and takes out his math book*)

"If you touch me, I'll sue! You can't make me do anything!!!!"
(*Screams and throws book on the floor.*)

"Fine, do whatever you want. Sit and be quiet and see if you pass this class!!"
(*Teacher withdraws request*)

(*Robbie mutters.*)

"What did you call me? Do you want to go to the principal?"
(*Gets in Robbie's face and shouts*)

"I don't care where I go as long as it is away from you!!"
(*Robbie gets up and leaves the classroom.*)

FIGURE 8.1 Example of a coercive power struggle.

appropriate point, the teacher should make it clear to the student that he or she must comply with the request, either now or later, and that the lost time will have to be made up (Walker et al., 2004). What is important is that the teacher do what is necessary to avoid a direct confrontation.

In summary, whenever teachers are confronted by student problems, they must avoid the ineffective practices of ignoring, questioning and nattering, yelling, issuing directions when a student is agitated, and engaging in power struggles. These teacher behaviors will most likely not be successful in eliminating the problem behaviors, and they may actually result in an escalation of the very behaviors that the teacher wants to reduce. First and foremost, the best way that teachers can avoid ineffective practices that can increase rather than prevent behavior problems is to be aware of them.

> **Q:** *Sometimes, I find myself in a power struggle with a student, and I don't know how I got into it. Once I realize that I am in a power struggle, how can I escape? Just walking away is often easier said than done. Also, shouldn't the student still have to comply with my request?*
>
> **A:** The best way to escape a power struggle is to avoid being drawn into the struggle in the first place. Being aware of how a power struggle can start is the first step to avoid getting trapped in one, but once you are in a power struggle, there is no positive way out except to walk away and not pursue the request. Yes, walking away or disengaging from the struggle is not easy, but think of it as a skill that, over time, you can get better at as you practice. To avoid a power struggle, you can provide choices to the student, give the student time to comply with a request, and refrain from asking the student "why" questions (e.g., *Why are you acting this way?*), unless you are willing to accept the inevitable *I don't know* answer. Preventing the power struggle is the best way to ensure that you are not left searching for an exit.

Prevent the Problem Behavior from Recurring

A specific procedure that a teacher may use to prevent problem behaviors from recurring is to implement a debriefing activity. Debriefing activities are short, proactive, preplanned interactions between students and their teacher (see Table 8.2). The purpose of debriefing is to (a) help the student identify the conditions that triggered the problem behavior and (b) provide feedback to teach or remind a student to use socially appropriate behavior when confronting similar conditions (Colvin, 2004). Debriefing should not be conducted during classroom activities; rather, the teacher should debrief students privately when the class is not in session (e.g., during lunchtime, after school).

Debriefing is not a negative consequence, and it should not include nagging, reprimanding, or threatening a student. Rather, the debriefing session should be a brief and positive encounter between a student and teacher. Colvin (2004) provided the following guidelines for conducting the debriefing session: First, the teacher explains the purpose of the debriefing session to the student (e.g., *Rodney, you had to serve time out for cursing at Stacey. Now, let's put that behind us and talk about what we can do to prevent this behavior in the future so we can get you back to class*). Second, the teacher asks the student a few questions about the incident to help identify the antecedents of the problem

TABLE 8.2   Debriefing Questions
What happened, and what did you do?
What happened to you because of your actions?
What could you have done instead that would not have caused this problem?
The next time this happens, what will you do?
Will you do this?
Remember to end the session on a positive note, and encourage the student to assist in the transition to the next activity.

behavior, including what and when the incident occurred (e.g., *Rodney, will you tell me what happened and what you did?*). Third, the teacher asks the student what could happen next time instead of the problem behavior (e.g., *Rodney, tell me what can you do next time Stacey bothers you so that you will not get in trouble*) and gets a commitment from the student (e.g., *Good, you know what to do; now, can you do it?*). Fourth, prepare the student to successfully reenter the normal classroom activity (e.g., *Good work, Rodney. Remember what you will do the next time this occurs. Now, let's go back to class*).

GUIDELINES TO FOLLOW WHEN RESPONDING TO PROBLEM BEHAVIOR

When teachers respond to a student's problem behavior, their goal should be to (a) stop the inappropriate behavior, (b) maintain the flow of instruction, and (c) reduce the likelihood that the problem behavior will reoccur. Teachers can use a number of strategies to achieve these goals, such as (a) respond privately rather than publicly if possible, (b) be consistent, (c) use alpha commands, (d) maintain a calm and detached manner, (e) have a plan, and (f) acknowledge and reinforce students for appropriate behavior. When responding to minor or serious misbehavior, teachers should adhere to these suggested behaviors, which often will be successful in eliminating the problem behaviors and may defuse potentially explosive problems.

Respond Privately Rather Than Publicly if Possible

In the scenario that opened this chapter, Mr. Cleveland approached Robbie and engaged in a public exchange in the classroom. This type of interaction often serves to escalate a situation and may force students to "save face" in front of their peers. Teachers should instead respond privately, if possible, to a student who is exhibiting problem behavior (see also Chapter 7).

If a teacher publicly reprimands or attempts to correct a student and the student becomes noncompliant, the teacher is put on the spot with the entire class watching. Because the teacher has been challenged and the class is waiting to see what the teacher will do, the teacher often escalates his or her behavior to force the student to comply (Savage & Savage, 2010). Thus, a power struggle ensues in front of an attentive audience. This situation is one to be avoided if at all possible and these interactions kept private, because (a) it lessens the chance that other students in the class will become an audience for the misbehaving student; (b) private responding does not disrupt classroom order, and it allows learning activities to continue without interruption; and (c) it reduces the likelihood of a power struggle between the student and teacher.

Unfortunately, there are situations in which private correction is not possible (e.g., verbal or physical aggression), but teachers should always use private correction when possible and attempt to respond to problem behavior unobtrusively. Use a soft voice, and be in close proximity to the student when responding to that student's misbehavior. Additionally, when delivering a direction to a student, the teacher should (a) use initiating directions rather than terminating ones (e.g., *John, take out your math book* as opposed to *John, stop goofing around, and where is your math book?*), (b) give only one direction, (c) give the student a few seconds to comply, and (d) do not engage in talk with the student.

Be Consistent

Teachers should always to attempt to respond to student problem behavior in a consistent manner. This means that a teacher should respond to all incidences of problem behavior, whenever they occur and with whomever they occur, using the same measured response. If a teacher ignores problem behavior one day but responds to it the next, or if a teacher ignores a problem behavior when exhibited by one student but responds to the same behavior when exhibited by another, students will perceive that teacher as inconsistent or unfair. This will undermine a teacher's credibility with his or her students, thus making it more likely the students will test the teacher by engaging in problem behavior. As Savage and Savage (2010) noted, classrooms that are characterized by students' constantly testing the rules are usually classrooms in which a teacher is inconsistent in responding to violations of those rules. The same can be said of problem behavior; classrooms that are characterized by students who exhibit problem behavior are usually classrooms in which a teacher is inconsistent in responding to problem behavior.

Use Alpha Commands

According to Walker and Walker (2001), when teachers respond to student problem behavior, they should do so with short and clear directions, or alpha commands. Teachers should avoid responding with wordy and unclear directions, which Walker and Walker called beta commands. As shown in Table 8.3, alpha commands give students specific information on what they need to do, whereas beta commands do little more than convey teacher frustration. This is because alpha commands are precise, direct, and to the point (Walker et al., 2004). In fact, alpha commands are associated

TABLE 8.3   Examples of Alpha and Beta Commands

Alpha Command	Beta Command
Take out your language book, and turn to page 48.	Jeremy, can't you hear me? I told students to take out their language book. Can't you follow directions?
Pick up the papers around your desk, and throw them in the wastebasket.	Stacey, you are always so messy. Do you always expect people to clean up after you? You need to learn to clean up after yourself.
Michelle, you need to stop talking.	Michelle, you are always talking without permission. If I've told you once, I've told you a thousand times to not talk so much. This is a warning.
Jerome, move your chair away from Jennie.	Young man, teasing is disrespectful. Leave Jennie alone. How do you think she feels? I do not like your attitude. Unless I see an attitude adjustment you are going to be in trouble.

with higher levels of compliance in both preschool and K-12 settings; in contrast, beta commands are associated with lower rates of compliance and, therefore, should be avoided (Walker et al., 2004).

Maintain a Calm and Detached Manner

When responding to students exhibiting problem behavior, teachers should maintain a calm and detached manner. This can be difficult, especially in situations involving serious incidences of misbehavior. Nevertheless, if teachers do not remain calm and respond with a businesslike attitude, it is more likely that a student will escalate his or her behavior. According to Colvin (2004), teachers should remember the following guidelines when approaching a problem situation:

1. Move slowly and deliberately.
2. Speak calmly, using a flat and controlled voice.
3. Keep a reasonable distance, and avoid crowding a student.
4. Establish eye contact.
5. Use brief, simple, and direct language.
6. Stay with the agenda, and do not get sidetracked.
7. Acknowledge cooperation if a student follows directions.

Walker and colleagues (2004) echoed these guidelines. According to those authors, the teacher must approach problem behavior in a calm, detached, unhurried, respectful, and step-by-step manner. When teachers respond in a frenetic manner and students believe that their dignity is being challenged and a teacher is attempting to humiliate them, the natural tendency of students is to strike back (Savage & Savage, 2010). Additionally, Colvin (2004) asserted that when students perceive a teacher is trying to embarrass or ridicule them, they often resort to more serious problem behavior in an attempt to maintain their dignity. Teachers, therefore, should never attempt to ridicule or embarrass a student. Rather, when they respond directly to a student's misbehavior, they should do so in a respectful and businesslike manner. It also bears mentioning again that when a teacher responds to problem behavior privately, the likelihood that a student will perceive that his or her dignity has been challenged is greatly diminished.

Have a Plan

Responding to student problem behavior in an appropriate and efficient manner will be much easier if teachers have a preset plan. Teachers will also face such situations with greater confidence if they have a consistent manner of responding when confronted with problem behavior. When teachers don't have a consistent way of responding, they are more likely to respond in an emotional and ineffective manner (Yell et al., 2009). Moreover, when students know that teachers will consistently respond to misbehavior and cannot be negotiated with or intimidated, they will be less likely to test their teacher's resolve.

Acknowledge and Reinforce Students for Appropriate Behavior

Unfortunately, teachers often ignore students who are calm and on task but provide attention when those same students are displaying problem behavior (Walker et al., 2004). If students receive more attention when they are acting out than when they are behaving appropriately, it is much more likely that they will continue exhibiting the problem behaviors (Colvin, 2004). To increase students' appropriate behavior, teachers need to reinforce students when they follow school rules and comply with teacher directives. An intervention that applies consequences only for misbehavior will fail (Sprick et al., 2002).

Teachers need to catch students behaving appropriately and reinforce them. This is especially true for students with behavior problems. Curwin and Mendler (2000) suggested that teachers catch students being good every 15 to 20 minutes and then give the student positive feedback in private. Because many students with behavior problems seldom receive attention for appropriate behavior, teachers need to apply contingent attention consistently so that it will have the desired effect (Walker et al., 2004). Colvin and Lazar (1997) asserted that frequently acknowledging and reinforcing appropriate student behavior is one of the most powerful strategies available to teachers. Such procedures call attention to appropriate behavior and provide a model for students. Colvin also suggested that teachers develop a system to remind themselves to frequently look for and reinforce students who are displaying appropriate behaviors.

RESPONDING TO PROBLEM BEHAVIOR

Often, teachers have difficulty responding to student problem behaviors, because they are uncertain how to respond in an effective and efficient manner. As previously mentioned, teachers sometimes overreact to incidences of misbehavior (e.g., shouting) or even sometimes don't respond at all (e.g., ignoring). When a teacher responds to student misbehavior, it is important to keep the aforementioned guidelines for effective responding in mind while avoiding the ineffective responses to problem behavior. Teachers can use the do's and don't's of teacher responding to student problem behavior as shown in Table 8.4 to ensure that appropriate responses are practiced.

Effective responding to student problem behaviors requires that teachers have a game plan for responding to both minor and major incidences of problem behavior. The other option, randomly choosing a response on the spot, usually will not work. It

TABLE 8.4 **The Do's and Don't's of Teacher Responding to Student Problem Behavior**

Do	Don't
Address the behavior privately.	Ignore the misbehavior.
Maintain class attention on the lesson.	Provide attention to the misbehaving student.
Use proximity control.	Yell or threaten.
Talk in a quiet, businesslike voice.	Humiliate or be sarcastic.
Use alpha commands.	Use beta commands.
Give only one command at a time.	Question or natter.
Deliver initiating commands.	Issue a command when a student is agitated.
Be calm and respectful.	Argue or verbally punish.
Use a precision request.	Engage in power struggles.
Reinforce compliance.	Ignore noncompliance.

also is crucially important that when responding to problem behaviors, teachers do so in a timely and effective manner (Colvin, 1997). Certainly, a prerequisite for responding in a timely and effective manner is that the teacher must be withit.

Responding to Minor Problem Behavior

According to Yell and colleagues (2009) it is crucial that teachers know how to effectively respond to minor misbehavior for four primary reasons. First, much of the student misbehavior that occurs in classrooms is of a minor nature (e.g., talking, leaving the seat without permission, inattention). Second, minor misbehavior, if not addressed, will often lead to more severe problem behavior (Rozalski, Drasgow, Drasgow, & Yell, 2001). Third, ineffective responding to minor incidences of misbehavior can actually escalate minor misbehavior into a severe problem behavior. Fourth, effective teacher responding to minor misbehavior may stop misbehavior before it escalates into severe problem behavior.

When minor behavior problems occur, a teacher should focus on eliminating the problem behavior quickly and with a minimum amount of classroom disruption (Evertson & Emmer, 2009; Good & Brophy, 2008; Savage & Savage, 2010). By eliminating the problem behavior quickly, a teacher ensures that the problem behavior does not spread to other students (see the discussion of the ripple effect in Chapter 1), does not escalate into more severe problem behavior, and does not interfere with classroom learning. When minor student problem behaviors occur, therefore, teachers should respond immediately using unobtrusive methods and continue with instruction.

LOW-PROFILE APPROACHES   Figure 8.2 presents three low-profile strategies to use when responding to minor problem behaviors:

1. Praise the appropriate behavior of a student (or of other students near the student) who is engaged in the minor problem behavior.
2. Use proximity control.
3. Use a brief verbal redirect.

The fourth strategy shown in Figure 8.2 (i.e., use a precision request) may be necessary when these low-profile strategies are not effective and will be discussed later in this chapter.

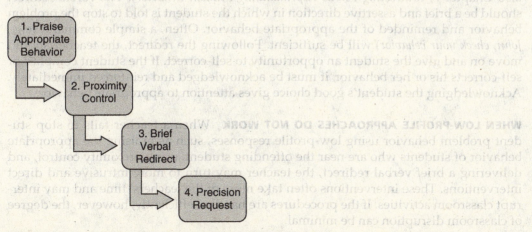

FIGURE 8.2 Responding to student behavior problems.

Praise Appropriate Behavior The first strategy, praising the appropriate behavior of students who are near the offending student, has the following four advantages. First, the praise lets the students who are behaving appropriately know that the teacher recognizes and appreciates their behaviors. Second, it may alert the misbehaving student of the need to stop the inappropriate behavior. Third, if offending student stops the misbehavior, this allows the teacher to acknowledge the student for appropriate behavior. Fourth, if this strategy works, it allows classroom instruction to continue uninterrupted.

Use Proximity Control If praising appropriate behavior is unsuccessful, the teacher should use proximity control. To use proximity control, the teacher moves near the offending student or students during the course of classroom instruction. For example, if students are talking in the back of the room, the teacher could move toward them while continuing the instructional activity. Proximity control is a powerful classroom management procedure that will often stop minor student misbehavior. The advantages of this procedure are that it (a) alerts misbehaving students that they must stop the inappropriate behavior in a direct manner that does not focus attention on the problem behavior, (b) communicates that the teacher is withit enough to recognize the inappropriate behavior that is occurring, and (c) does not disrupt the classroom activities. Proximity control may be accompanied by a brief glance at any offending student to show that the teacher is aware of the misbehavior and that it needs to stop. The teacher should not linger but, rather, move on after the student corrects the misbehavior. The teacher should deliver a brief and quiet compliment to students who correct their own behavior.

Deliver a Brief Verbal Redirect If neither of the first two strategies is successful, the teacher will need to let the misbehaving student know that he or she is unruly by using a slightly more intrusive verbal procedure, such as a brief command made privately to the student. Again, it is important that when using such procedures the teacher does this in an unobtrusive manner so as not to focus attention on the misbehavior or disrupt the classroom activities. Thus, it is important that the verbal response be made privately and in an unemotional manner to a student who is misbehaving. When teachers deliver a verbal redirect, they need to focus on the misbehavior by walking directly to the offending student, making eye contact, and delivering the verbal redirect (see also Chapter 7, *Redirecting versus Reprimanding Student Behavior*). The verbal redirect should be a brief and assertive direction in which the student is told to stop the problem behavior and reminded of the appropriate behavior. Often, a simple command (e.g., *John, check your behavior*) will be sufficient. Following the redirect, the teacher should move on and give the student an opportunity to self-correct. If the student complies or self-corrects his or her behavior, it must be acknowledged and reinforced immediately. Acknowledging the student's good choice gives attention to appropriate behavior.

WHEN LOW-PROFILE APPROACHES DO NOT WORK When a teacher fails to stop student problem behavior using low-profile responses, such as praising the appropriate behavior of students who are near the offending student, using proximity control, and delivering a brief verbal redirect, the teacher may turn to more intrusive and direct interventions. These interventions often take more of the teachers' time and may interrupt classroom activities. If the procedures are handled efficiently, however, the degree of classroom disruption can be minimal.

In a direct intervention like delivering a precision request, a teacher essentially demands appropriate behavior from the student. It is important when making direct commands that teachers do not use any of the ineffective responses discussed earlier (e.g., yelling, nattering, engaging in power struggles). Teachers can take a number of actions to increase the likelihood that students will comply with commands. These actions include:

1. Issuing an alpha command (direct and unambiguous).
2. Making a statement not asking a question.
3. Speaking firmly but not shouting or nattering.
4. Issuing one command, and repeating it only once.
5. Giving a student adequate time to comply.
6. Standing close to a student, and making eye contact.

Use a Precision Request   Morgan and Jenson (1988) reported on a procedure they termed a "precision request" to provide an effective method that teachers could use when issuing directions to students. As shown in Figure 8.3, a precision request is a simple, easy-to-implement format that teachers can use when low-profile strategies have not stopped student problem behavior.

Specifically, a precision request involves the following steps:

Step 1: The teacher issues the request or command in a quiet, but firm, voice while standing close to a student (e.g., *Robbie, return to your seat*).

Step 2: After making the request, the teacher waits for five seconds. During this time, the teacher does not interact with the student and does not reissue the request.

Step 3: If the student complies, the teacher reinforces the behavior.
OR

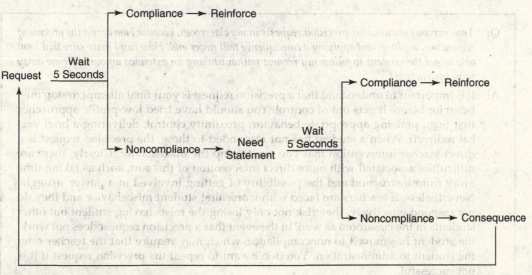

FIGURE 8.3 The precision request.
Adapted from Morgan and Jenson (1998).

Step 3: If the student does not comply with the request, the teacher repeats the request using the word "need" (e.g., *Robbie, you need to return to your seat*). Adding the word "need" to the initial statement is important, because it signals the student that this is the last chance before a consequence is delivered.

Step 4: After repeating the request, the teacher waits for 5 seconds. During this time, the teacher does not interact with the student and does not reissue the request.

Step 5: If the student complies, the teacher reinforces the behavior.

OR

Step 5: If the student does not comply with the second request, the teacher delivers a mild consequence. This consequence must be delivered as soon as the student has failed to comply with the teacher directive. Teachers must not allow students to plea, whine, negotiate, or bully their way out of the consequence. By allowing a student to escape the consequence, teachers will be demonstrating to the offending student, and to the other students, that they will not follow through when they are confronted with student noncompliance.

Step 6: After the consequence is delivered, the teacher must reissue the request.

If teachers decide to use a precision request, it is important that they follow the procedure consistently and reissue the request after the consequence has been applied. If the request is not reissued, students' problem may be reinforced, because they are allowed to escape from the original command. Morgan and Jenson (1988) noted, however, that if the procedure is applied consistently and correctly, students will usually respond appropriately.

Consequences When teachers deliver a precision request, they must have a pre-planned consequence to use if students do not comply. The worst time to select a consequence for misbehavior is during an argument or power struggle with a student.

Q: *I am nervous about using precision requests in my classroom, because I am afraid the process of requesting, waiting, and applying a consequence will never end. How can I make sure that I am able to get the student to follow my request without taking an extended amount of time away from instruction?*

A: It is important to understand that a precision request is your final attempt to stop misbehavior before it gets out of control. You should have tried low-profile approaches first (e.g., praising appropriate behavior, proximity control, delivering a brief verbal redirect). When a student has not responded to these, the precision request is a direct teacher intervention that you use to stop the misbehavior. Clearly, there are difficulties associated with more direct intervention of this sort, such as taking time away from instruction and the possibility of getting involved in a power struggle. Nevertheless, if teachers are faced with worsening student misbehavior and they do not respond effectively, they risk not only losing the misbehaving student but other students in the classroom as well. In the event that a precision request does not work, the student has moved to noncompliance, which may require that the teacher refer the student to administration. You don't want to repeat the precision request if it is not successful.

It is also important that teachers deliver consequences in an appropriate manner. In other words, deliver the consequence privately, in a calm manner, and in such a way as to preserve the student's dignity. Students are more likely to accept negative consequences when teachers consistently apply logical consequences without publicly criticizing them.

When administering a consequence, it is very important that teachers (a) remind the student of the rule being broken, (b) state what the consequence will be in a matter-of-fact manner, (c) implement the consequence, and (d) return to whatever they are doing (e.g., teaching a lesson). Canter and Canter (1992) suggested that following administration of a consequence, teachers look for the first opportunity to recognize the student's positive behavior.

When deciding on consequences, teachers should consult their school's discipline or behavior plan, if one exists. Frequently, school discipline plans will include lists of suggested or mandated consequences that teachers may use. Consequences should be approved by school administrators and explained to parents and students before they are used (Walker et al., 2004). Implementing these consequences consistently is an important way to help students understand the association of behavior and consequences. Examples of negative consequences include time out, loss of points or privileges, in-school suspension, or an office referral.

In summary, many of the behaviors that students exhibit are minor forms of misbehavior. Nonetheless, it is important that teachers deal with these misbehaviors in an efficient and effective manner so that they do not spread to others and do not escalate into serious problem behavior. Teachers must be able to deal with minor misbehavior in a relatively unobtrusive manner that will communicate their withitness to students and maintain attention on the task at hand. The advantages of using the three low-profile strategies are that they (a) do not take much teacher time, (b) can fit well into the flow of classroom activities, and (c) can maintain the students' focus on classroom instruction. Using the fourth strategy, precision requests, may be appropriate for behaviors that are not responsive to the three low-profile techniques.

Responding to Severe Problem Behavior

Teachers occasionally find themselves having to respond to severe student problem behavior. By severe problem behaviors, we mean behaviors such as defiance, intimidation, property destruction, physical aggression, and fighting. Responding to severe misbehavior is one of the most challenging, difficult, and stressful situations that teachers face. Such behavior may (a) destroy the learning environment, (b) threaten student and staff safety, (c) involve issues of liability, and (d) cause emotional distress for students and teachers. For these reasons, it is crucial that teachers understand the basics of managing these serious behaviors (Colvin, 2004).

ASSESS THE SERIOUSNESS OF THE SITUATION AND POTENTIAL RISKS   Many, if not most, school districts have policies and procedures about crisis management of serious problem behavior, and teachers should become familiar with their district's procedures. When crisis situations occur, teachers should first assess the seriousness of the situation and the potential risks involved. According to Sprick, Sprick, and Garrison (1993), crisis situations include actions that threaten the physical safety of others (e.g., physical aggression, property destruction) as well as self-destructive behaviors (e.g., head banging, self-mutilation). Getting involved in a crisis incident is a trying and stressful experience, and teachers will be much more likely to respond in an appropriate manner if they have a plan. In crisis situations, teachers should (a) ensure the safety of students and staff, (b) call or send for assistance, (c) attempt to defuse the situation, (d) keep thorough records of the incident, and (e) notify the student's parents or guardians.

ENSURE THE SAFETY OF STUDENTS AND STAFF The teacher's first priority is to remove immediately students who may be injured by the severe problem behavior. Removing students from the classroom is important for several reasons: (a) it protects students from being involved in a situation in which they could be injured, (b) it deprives the student engaging in the problem behavior of an audience and possible reinforcement, and (c) it may make it easier for the teacher to calm down the student who is having the behavioral crisis.

When using room clears, teachers must determine where the class will go when an incident occurs (e.g., another classroom, hallway, gymnasium). Moreover, because the teacher must remain in the classroom to supervise the student engaged in the problem behavior, an arrangement should be made with the administration, a paraprofessional, or another teacher to take charge of the students being removed. If the incident happens on a playground or in a hallway, the teacher should disperse the students or move them away from the student who is engaging in the serious problem behavior. If it is not possible to remove the students, the teacher (or teachers) may have to physically restrain the out-of-control student. A teacher should not use restraint procedures, however, unless (a) a student presents a danger to himself, herself, or others and (b) the teacher has been trained to use restraint in a proper manner.

CALL OR SEND FOR ASSISTANCE When a student begins to engage in serious problem behavior, the teacher should have a prearranged procedure for summoning assistance. This procedure should include (a) who will respond (this person should also be trained in crisis intervention), (b) the chain of command in case the first person is unavailable, and (c) a communication process to ensure that everyone involved will be kept informed (Sprick et al., 1993).

If the school has an intercom, the teacher should call for assistance. The responder should then come immediately to the classroom to assist the teacher. Additionally, this person also will be a witness to the incident. If the person who comes to assist is not an administrator, the school principal or assistant principal should be notified and apprised of the situation as soon as possible.

If the school doesn't have an intercom to call for assistance, Sprick and colleagues (1993) suggested that the teacher have a prearranged crisis signal, called a red card, that a student messenger brings to the office, where an immediate response is initiated by the school administration.

> **Q:** *I do not have a paraprofessional in my classroom to help me in the event of a severe behavioral crisis. Our school has intercoms in most of the classrooms, but not in mine. The idea of having a student alert the administration with a crisis signal is a good one, but can you give me some idea of how to make that happen?*
>
> **A:** The students in your class are your best resource for calling for assistance during a crisis. During the first week of school, the procedures and signals for use during a crisis should be introduced and practiced with students. Teachers need to practice with their students how to seek out assistance in the same way that we talk about and practice classroom rules and routinely engage in fire and tornado drills. Students can engage in role plays in the classroom and practice using the emergency signal for clearing the classroom and finding assistance from another adult. Revisit the procedures and role plays periodically throughout the school year, and if ever used, evaluate the effectiveness of your plan.

ATTEMPT TO DEFUSE THE SITUATION   When a serious behavioral incident happens, the teacher needs to remain rational and composed. The teacher should attempt to calm the out-of-control student by speaking in a poised and neutral voice. The teacher should stay about three feet away from the student, not make sudden movements, and ignore any screaming, yelling, or questioning. Using the student's name, the teacher should give simple, clear, and reasonable directions (e.g., *Robbie, you need to return to your desk*) and not threaten, humiliate, or attempt to force the student to do anything.

KEEP THOROUGH RECORDS OF THE INCIDENT   When an incident of severe problem behavior occurs, teachers should thoroughly document it using a form similar to the one shown in Table 8.5. Documentation is important for a number of reasons. First, a record of the incident will exist if liability issues arise from the incident—for example, if a student is injured. Second, there will be documentation to dispute any false accusations the student might make about the incident. Third, the documentation of the incident provides information for administrators and teachers to evaluate the adequacy of their reaction to the incident.

The teacher should be responsible for completing the behavioral incident form. When teachers have paraprofessionals working with them, the paraprofessional may be assigned the duty of recording behavioral incidences. Several guidelines should be followed when completing the behavioral incident form:

1. *Complete the form as soon as possible after the behavioral incidence occurs.* This will ensure that the incident is fresh in everyone's mind, thus increasing the likelihood of accuracy.
2. *Include certain minimal information in the documentation form.* Information that must included would be (a) the date of the report; (b) the names of all persons involved (e.g., teacher, paraprofessional, student, witnesses); (c) the date, time, and location of the incident; (d) an objective and truthful description of the incident; (e) a description of the action taken by the teacher and the results of the teacher actions; and (f) the signatures of all persons involved.

TABLE 8.5   Behavior Incident Report

Behavior Incident Report

Student's name _____   Date _____   Grade _____

Teacher's name _____   Time of the incident _____

Location of the incident:

Description of the behavior incident (e.g., precipitating factors, students involved, incident description, etc.):

Did the student's behavior endanger the safety of the student or others? If so, how?

Description of interventions used to manage the problem:

Reason for actions taken:

Results of actions taken:

Reported to administrators and parents (incident must be reported to administrators and parents as soon as possible):

Signature of teachers: _____   _____

Signature of witnesses: _____   _____

Signature of parents _____

Signature of administrators _____

3. *Inform the school principal of the incident as soon as possible.* The principal should be involved in completing the documentation, including signing the completed behavioral incident form. Additionally, the student's parents or guardians should be given a copy of the report.

NOTIFY THE STUDENT'S PARENTS OR GUARDIANS   Whenever a serious behavioral incident occurs, the student's parents or guardians should be notified and asked to attend a conference in which (a) the teacher and administration communicate their willingness to work with the parents, (b) the severity of the problem is determined, and (c) a joint problem-solving process is begun (Sprick et al., 1993).

Summary

Students will engage in problem behaviors, and teachers must be prepared to respond effectively and efficiently. Unfortunately, teachers often do not plan how to respond to problem behavior effectively and, therefore, resort to ineffective and intrusive responses, such as ignoring, nattering and yelling, threatening, issuing commands when students are agitated, and engaging in escalating prompts. Proactive management strategies can serve to prevent problem behaviors from occurring, even with students who exhibit serious problem behavior. It is most important that teachers follow a plan when responding to student problem behavior. For Mr. Cleveland to have a successful interaction with his student Robbie, he should have a plan and follow it consistently to show his confidence. He could identify Robbie's possible triggers, avoid the public interaction, and not enter into the my turn–your turn coercion cycle.

Additional Resources

On the Web		
Page Title	**Annotations**	**Web Address**
4 Proven Strategies for Differentiating Instruction	Tips for differentiating instruction in the classroom as a way to prevent problem behaviors	http://www2.scholastic.com/browse/article.jsp?id=3747918
Debriefing Strategies	Activities and techniques that teachers can use with students during debriefing	http://www.supportrealteachers.org/debriefing-strategies.html
Reasons for Student Misbehavior Require Thoughtful Responses	Ideas about possible functions of student misbehavior in the classroom	http://www.advantagepress.com/newsletters/jun03news.asp
Ten Activities for Establishing Classroom Rules	Games and activities to use for teaching rules in the classroom	http://www.educationworld.com/a_lesson/lesson/lesson274.shtml
In the Literature		

Babkie, A. M. (2006). Be proactive in managing classroom behavior. *Intervention in School & Clinic, 41*(3), 184–187.

This article provides teachers with simple ideas for how to proactively manage behavior in the classroom through the use of rules and procedures. The author delineates developing and teaching rules in the classroom.

References

Alberto, P. A., & Troutman, A. C. (2013). *Applied behavior analysis for teachers* (9th ed.). Upper Saddle River, NJ: Pearson/Merrill Education.

Canter, L., & Canter, M. (1992). *Assertive discipline: Positive behavior management for today's classroom* (3rd ed.). Santa Monica, CA: Lee Canter & Associates.

Colvin, G. (2004). *Managing the cycle of acting-out behavior in the classroom*. Eugene, OR: Behavior Associates.

Colvin, G.T., & Lazar, M. (1997). The effective elementary classroom: Managing for success. Longmont, CO: Sopris West.

Colvin, G. T., & Sugai, G. M. (1988). Proactive strategies for managing social behavior problems: An instructional approach. *Education and Treatment of Children, 11,* 341–348.

Curwin, R. L., & Mendler, A. N. (2000). *Discipline with dignity* (2nd ed.). Upper Saddle River, NJ: Merrill/Prentice-Hall.

Darch, C. B., & Kame'enui, E. J. (2004). *Instructional classroom management: A proactive approach to behavior management* (2nd ed.). Upper Saddle River, NJ: Merrill/Prentice-Hall.

Evertson, C. M., & Emmer, E. T. (2009). *Classroom management for elementary teachers* (8th ed.). Upper Saddle River, NJ: Pearson/Merrill Education.

Good, T. L., & Brophy, J. E. (2008). *Looking in classrooms* (10th ed.). Upper Saddle River, NJ: Pearson/Merrill Education.

Jolivette, K., Wehby, J. H., Canale, J., & Massey, N. G. (2001). Effects of choice making opportunities on the behavior of students with emotional and behavioral disorders. *Behavioral Disorders, 26,* 131–145.

Kounin, J. S. (1970). *Discipline and group management in classrooms*. New York: Holt, Rinehart, & Winston.

Morgan, D. P., & Jenson, W. R. (1988). *Teaching behaviorally disordered students: Preferred practices*. Upper Saddle River, NJ: Merrill/Prentice-Hall.

Patterson, G. R. (1982). *Coercive family process: A social learning approach*. Eugene, OR: Castalia.

Rozalski, M. E., Drasgow, E., Drasgow, F., & Yell, M. L. (2009). Assessing the relationships among delinquent male students' disruptive and violent behavior and staff's proactive and reactive behavior in a secure residential treatment center. *Journal of Emotional and Behavioral Disorders, 17*(2), 80–92.

Savage, M., & Savage M. (2010). *Successful classroom management and discipline: Teaching self-control and responsibility* (3rd ed.). Thousand Oaks, CA: Sage.

Sprick, R. S., Borgmeier, C., & Nolet, V. (2002). Prevention and management of behavior problems in secondary schools. In M. A. Shinn, H. M. Walker, & G. Stoner (Eds.), *Interventions for academic and behavior problems II: Preventive and remedial approaches*. Bethesda, MD: National Association of School Psychologists.

Sprick, R., Sprick, M., & Garrison, M. (1993). *Interventions: Collaborative planning for students at risk*. Longmont, CO: Sopris West.

Walker, H. M., Ramsey, E., & Gresham, F. M. (2004). *Antisocial behavior in the school: Evidence-based practices* (2nd ed.). Belmont, CA: Thomson/Wadsworth.

Walker, H. M., & Walker, J. E. (1991). *Coping with noncompliance in the classroom*. Austin, TX: Pro-Ed.

Walker H. M., & Walker, J. E. (2001). *Coping with noncompliance in the classroom: A positive approach for teachers*. Austin, TX: ProEd.

Yell, M. L., Meadows, N. B., Drasgow, E., & Shriner, J. G. (2009). *Evidence-based practices for educating students with emotional and behavioral disorders*. Upper Saddle River, NJ: Pearson/Merrill Education.

CHAPTER

9

Providing Students with Skills to Independently Make Wise Behavioral Choices

with Erika Nicsinger

GOALS

- Present a rationale for preventing problem behavior by teaching students to manage their own behavior.

- Explain how teaching self-management is a way of teaching students to be their own change agent.

- Describe how social problem solving is one of the most important life skills.

- Describe the essential steps students can use to be effective problem solvers.

SCENARIO

Mr. Claudio has several problems in his class that he would like to fix. Unfortunately, his efforts so far have been unsuccessful.

One problem is with Rubin, a student who has a difficult time finishing his work in class. Rubin spends a great deal of classroom time looking around the room, talking with other students during seatwork, fidgeting at his desk, and making noises. Too often, Mr. Claudio has to remind Rubin to stay on task by saying *Rubin, get to work* or *Keep your eyes on your paper*, or by asking *Are you done yet?* or *Why can't you get your assignment finished on time?* The constant reminders to Rubin seem to exhaust Mr. Claudio, and he would like to find a way to help Rubin complete his work without having to remind him so often. For his part, Rubin, who generally is compliant and well liked by his peers, has started to react negatively to Mr. Claudio's reminders to get his work done. Mr. Claudio has had several talks with Rubin about the way he reacts and how his behavior could lead to some more serious problems. Mr. Claudio also has had a conference with Rubin's mother to see if she could help, but the situation seems to be getting worse.

Another problem Mr. Claudio wants to address is the negative and the disrespectful ways that his students treat each other. He often sees students talking in an angry and threatening manner to each other, pushing and shoving when they are standing in line, and constantly pestering each other until someone gets upset. Additionally, there have been two incidences of pushing and throwing objects in class that have resulted in suspensions from school. Mr. Claudio has had several talks with his class about getting along with each other better and how they need to solve their social problems in a more effective manner. During one of these talks, Mr. Claudio was surprised to find that a good number of his students do not seem to think they have any social problems. In fact, Mr. Claudio has heard his students say that the reason they engage in such behavior is because someone "deserves" it. Despite Mr. Claudio's effort, it seems as if his students are arguing and behaving inappropriately toward each other more frequently.

Throughout this book, we have described frameworks, approaches, specific strategies, and suggestions to prevent student behavior problems in the elementary classroom. Problem behaviors can cause disruptions that consume large amounts of a teacher's instructional time and energy, and these disruptions can distract other students, which negatively affects the learning environment. It is understandable how teachers can react ineffectively to these student behaviors and even engage in power struggles (see Chapter 8), and as we emphasized in Chapter 2, teachers need to focus on preventing behavior problems before they occur. Managing a classroom through a preventive approach can create a positive atmosphere and increase appropriate student behavior, thus allowing teachers to concentrate more on planning and teaching academic content, monitoring student achievement, and targeting attention on severe and critical behavioral issues.

Our focus in this book has been on the many fundamental components of preventing problem behaviors that we believe can be systematically managed, thus allowing teachers to direct their energy toward other important classroom issues. Moreover, assisting students to control their own behavior is also a type of prevention, as well as an important component of providing a positive learning environment (see also Chapters 7 and 8). In this chapter, we describe two strategies that can be used as a means of prevention: self-management and social problem solving. Unlike many interventions that are designed to change student behavior through external controls, helping students to engage in appropriate behavior through self-management and learning to solve their own social problems is more likely to result in long-term behavior change and to prevent student problem behavior in the classroom.

SELF-MANAGEMENT

Self-management is used to assist students to become their own change agents by teaching them to observe, record, and reinforce their academic or social behavior (Polsgrove & Smith, 2004). Teaching students to manage their behavior by using a self-management approach can be an effective intervention to help students replace inappropriate behavior with more appropriate and wanted behavior, and it can also be a way to prevent problem behavior. Teaching a self-management technique may, for example, be a way for Mr. Claudio to help Rubin increase his on-task behavior, thus increasing his work completion while, at the same time, decreasing Mr. Claudio's constant monitoring and reminding. As a component of an overall preventative approach in the classroom, self-management can teach students like Rubin to be aware of and manage their own behavior.

Teaching students self-management provides them with a precise understanding of their problematic behavior and helps them observe, monitor, and reinforce their own behavior when they achieve a goal. When students engage in self-management, they become more invested in their personal behavior, because they are more aware of their actions. According to Rafferty (2010), teaching students self-management has many benefits, including increased student self-efficacy, motivation, and academic achievement.

In their review of the literature on the effects of self-management for students with emotional and behavioral disorders, Mooney, Ryan, Uhing, Reid, and Epstein (2005) found that there were large positive effects on academic outcomes and that these results maintained over time. Moreover, Kaplan (1995) argued that a student-operated system, such as self-managment, frees up valuable teacher instructional time, can be used with a wide variety of students, and moves a student from external controls over their behavior to self-control. Menzies, Lane, and Lee (2009) pointed out that in contrast to teacher-operated systems (e.g., token reinforcement), self-management supports student independence and acceptance of responsibility for behavior.

Steps of Self-Management

Typically, students can take control of their own behavior using self-management in the following areas: (a) self-assessment, (b) self-monitoring, and (c) self-reinforcement. In a teacher-operated system, the teacher usually assesses the student's behavior, observes and monitors the behavior using a data collection procedure, and reinforces the student if the behavior is changed in the desired direction. Self-management, however, is student operated, because students assess or define the problematic and desired behavior, monitor their own progress, and determine whether there has been enough behavior change to warrant reinforcement. When students control their own behavior, not only are inappropriate behaviors prevented, there is a greater likelihood of the learned behaviors transferring or generalizing to special classes, such as art, music, and physical education, and less unstructured situations, such as at lunch, at recess, and on the bus (Martin & Pear, 2010). Generalized behaviors may also transfer to situations outside of school, such as the home, neighborhood, and community.

SELF-ASSESSMENT   Before students like Rubin can manage their own behavior, they need to be aware of what behaviors are appropriate and what behaviors are inappropriate. Mr. Claudio can have a discussion with Rubin about why a certain behavior needs to be replaced. Additionally, however, students must understand *why* they are assessing themselves and *what* behavior they are assessing. Teachers need to be active in teaching students how to monitor and evaluate their own behavior and in identifying strategies that will help them exhibit appropriate behavior in the classroom (McMillan & Hearn, 2009).

During self-assessment, students judge their own behaviors and then, with the teacher's collaboration, determine if those behaviors are in line with the expectations of the classroom. Together, the teacher and student should determine a target behavior for the student to self-assess (e.g., on task, in seat, raising hand to speak, work completed). Students must be able to define these behaviors precisely so that measurement is accurate and reliable. Students also must be aware of their behavior before self-monitoring can occur and have the ability to determine if the behavior is present or absent. For example, Rubin understands that he is often off task, and in conversations with Mr. Claudio, he can identify when he is on task. This target behavior is the desired behavior and should be defined clearly and in positive terms to increase accuracy and reliability during assessment (e.g., be on task during math instruction, be in the seat facing forward with both feet flat on the floor).

To define the behaviors further, teachers can have students give examples as well as nonexamples of the behaviors. Mr. Claudio, for instance, has devised a "Help Sheet" rating appropriate for an upper elementary student to assist Rubin in thinking about whether he is on or off task at the moment that data are being collected on his behavior. As shown in Table 9.1, Rubin can assess his own behavior by referring to what is on task and what is off task. At the time when data are collected, Rubin can determine for himself whether he is on task, such as by looking at his materials, thinking about what he has to do to complete the assignment, or using his pencil to complete his work, indicating on-task behavior. Conversely, he can also use his Help Sheet to determine if he is off task, such as by looking out the window, talking to others, or out of his seat without permission, indicating off-task behavior. For lower elementary students, the teacher can provide drawings of on- and off-task behavior for the student (e.g., a simple sketch of a student attending to material or a student looking away from material and daydreaming).

TABLE 9.1   Rubin's Help Sheet Rating System for Self-Assessment

I am on task when...	I am off task when...
...I look at my materials, book, or worksheet.	...I look away from my materials, book, or worksheet. For example:
...I pay attention to what I have to do.	looking out the window, looking at things inside my desk, or talking to other students.
...I think about what I have to do to complete the assignment.	...I think about things not related to my work. For example:
...I use my brain to figure out what to do.	What is for dinner tonight?
...I think carefully about how to approach my work.	Will my Dad fix my bike soon? What should I be for Halloween?
...I use my pencil to complete work.	...I am not using my pencil or keyboard to complete the assignment.
...I use the keyboard to finish the math computer game.	
...I raise my hand to ask for help.	...I am out of my seat without permission, bothering other students, or looking inside my desk to play.
...I wait patiently for the teacher to provide assistance to complete an assignment.	

Recording Systems   Implementing a student assessment system also requires that teachers devise and teach students to use a recording system. A recording system allows a student to collect data about his or her behavior. The easiest method for collecting data is to have the student count the number of times the behavior occurs during a specified time period. This is called frequency or event recording. Taking simple frequency data may be helpful when counting discrete behaviors (e.g., behaviors that have a clear beginning and end) like the number of items completed during independent seatwork. For example, suppose that a student has difficulty completing a sufficient number of math problems when working independently due to out-of-seat or off-task behaviors. In this case, frequency data on the number of items completed over time can be an appropriate data-gathering approach to determine if the self-management strategy is having the desired effect.

In contrast, time sampling provides an estimate of how much the student is engaged in the target behavior. Sampling behavior using defined periods of time (e.g., 15 seconds, 5 minutes, 20 minutes) is a realistic procedure in the classroom, because data only need to be gathered intermittently. A system to prompt data collection, however, is needed, yet prompting systems can be as simple as using a kitchen timer or a smart phone that is set to provide an audible tone at regular intervals. After hearing the prompt, students indicate on a recording sheet whether or not they are engaged in the target behavior. As shown in Figure 9.1, Rubin can record a + or 0 in the appropriate box to indicate his assessment of whether he was on or off task during five-minute intervals when cued by the teacher or when using his own prompting device.

As shown in Figure 9.2, having younger students circle a happy or a frowning face to indicate a target behavior can simplify the process and allow them to take part in assessing their own behavior. The teacher can have the student count the number of happy faces (target behavior), or with help from the teacher, the student can determine the percentage of time that he or she engaged in the target behavior for the session.

Baseline   Before any self-management project is to begin, the teacher must gather some baseline data so the student and teacher can compare data before and after the procedure starts. Mr. Claudio can use the behavior definitions in the Help Sheet and the data-recording sheet over several sessions or days to get an idea of the amount of on-task behavior in which Rubin is engaging. He can set his smart phone to produce an audible tone or to vibrate at a certain interval (e.g., 1 minute, 5 minutes, 20 minutes) and, at the prompt, look to see if Rubin is on or off task and mark on the recording sheet a + or a 0 as needed. To visually estimate of the amount of time Rubin is on task during an instructional period, Mr. Claudio can create a graph, as shown in Figure 9.3.

The following steps would help Mr. Claudio prepare Rubin for his self-assessment:

- *Determine, along with the student, a target behavior (the appropriate and wanted behavior) that will replace the maladaptive behavior.*   For example, excessive and disruptive out-of-seat behavior can be replaced with in-seat behavior.
- *Develop a rating and recording system that includes a description of the expected behavior and when/how the student will assess behavior.*   Teachers should make sure the rating and recording system is easy for students to use once they are assessing their own behavior.

Rubin's Data Sheet

Date: _____   Subject: _____

+ = On Task

0 = Off Task

Total Intervals for Session = _____

Total On Task (+) = _____

Percentage On Task for Session = _____

FIGURE 9.1 Data recording sheet for Rubin.

- ***Explain, model, and guide the student through assessing behavior.*** Make sure to include the target behavior, rating approach, and recording system in the teaching process. Again, make sure the student understands when, how, and why he or she is assessing the behavior. Be sure to use student-friendly vocabulary throughout the process, typical to what is used during academic instruction.

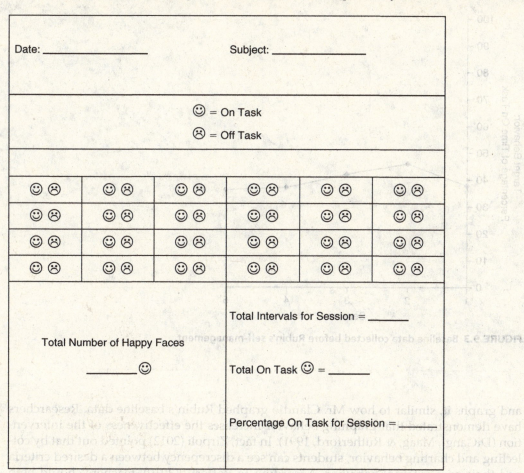

Date: _____   Subject: _____

☺ = On Task

☹ = Off Task

☺ ☹	☺ ☹	☺ ☹	☺ ☹	☺ ☹	☺ ☹
☺ ☹	☺ ☹	☺ ☹	☺ ☹	☺ ☹	☺ ☹
☺ ☹	☺ ☹	☺ ☹	☺ ☹	☺ ☹	☺ ☹
☺ ☹	☺ ☹	☺ ☹	☺ ☹	☺ ☹	☺ ☹

Total Intervals for Session = _____

Total Number of Happy Faces

_____ ☺

Total On Task ☺ = _____

Percentage On Task for Session = _____

FIGURE 9.2 Data rating and recording sheet for younger elementary students.

- *Monitor the student's use of the rating and recording system to ensure that the student is using it correctly.*   Teachers should make sure to not correct any data that the student has recorded to reflect how that student perceived the situation. The purpose is to raise a student's awareness about behavior and promote self-efficacy, not to pinpoint each success or mistake.

- *Brainstorm ideas and strategies useful in the classroom to improve results.*   This step should be taken when students mature and become proficient at using self-assessment. Students need to be active participants in this discussion to promote ownership of the assessment process.

Self-Monitoring   The second component of self-management involves self-monitoring. Self-monitoring is an extension of the assessment process that requires students to observe and evaluate their own behavior and self-record when the target behavior is being displayed. In self-monitoring, the student takes the data from the recording sheet

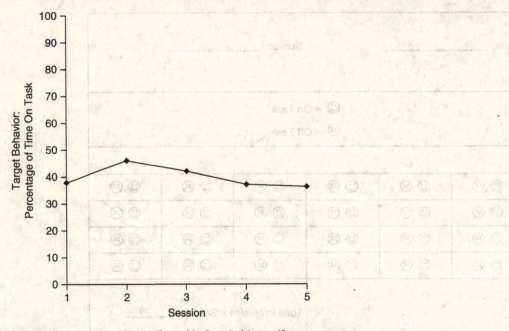

FIGURE 9.3 Baseline data collected before Rubin's self-management.

and graphs it, similar to how Mr. Claudio graphed Rubin's baseline data. Researchers have demonstrated that graphing behavior increases the effectiveness of the intervention (DiGangi, Maag, & Rutherford, 1991). In fact, Zirpoli (2012) pointed out that by collecting and charting behavior, students can see a discrepency between a desired criteria and their own external behavior. According to Rafferty (2010), teachers should help students use their own graphing procedures as part of self-monitoring to help students develop self-regulatory processes. Including a graph to show the results in the rating and recording system will aid students in becoming better and more experienced self-monitors and increase the opportunities for teachers to use the data for instructional purposes (Kaplan, 1995).

Implementing self-monitoring in the classroom follows the same basic procedures as using self-assessment. Implementation is a multistep process that requires teachers to work with students to establish the monitoring plan and assess the effectiveness of the plan throughout its use. As with self-assessment, teachers should begin by defining a target behavior, designing a rating and recording system, and assisting students to graph or chart their own behavior (Rafferty, 2010).

As with self-assessment, Mr. Claudio could refer to the following list of helpful hints to help Rubin self-monitor his target behavior:

• *Before students self-monitor, teachers must collect baseline data to ensure that the target behavior is appropriate for remediation and is properly defined.* The teacher needs to ensure that the behavior is actually maladaptive in the classroom environment and that students have the self-awareness to monitor their behavior.

- *Teachers must establish the procedures for self-monitoring and construct the data collection model for the student to follow.* It is essential that the data collection method be easy for students to use independently of the teacher and with minimal interruption of the class.
- *Once all of the preliminary data and materials are in place, teachers must instruct students in the proper use of the data collection tools.* As with self-assessment, explain, model, and guide students in charting their data accurately. Students will need opportunities for practice and feedback using the rating and recording system and graphing it to provide a visual display of the effectiveness of the self-management procedure. Again, place emphasis on why the behavior is being monitored, how it is appropriate for the classroom, and how it contributes to the overall classroom community.
- *After students begin to chart their behavior independently, the teacher must check their process.* Teachers need to be sure that students are using the rating and recording system correctly and are being accurate and proficient in graphing their own behavior.

As an example, Rubin can use his rating and recording sheet to compute his time on task at the end of each session (e.g., independent seatwork during math time) and then chart the percentage on a graph. Over time, this graph (see Figure 9.4) can be used to compare the baseline to Rubin's use of self-management and make determinations about how well the system is working to increase Rubin's target behavior. When graphed, Rubin's data can be used to judge whether self-reinforcement is to be delivered.

Q: *I teach elementary students in the lower grades, so I am not sure they can graph their own behavior. Is it necessary that students graph their behavior?*

A: Self-management may not be for every student. Students do need to be able to understand the process and have the capabilities to engage in the rating, recording, and graphing of their behavior. For those students who have the ability, graphing or charting behavior is a necessary ingredient in self-management. When students graph the data they collect during self-monitoring, they are giving themselves visual feedback about their progress. When more positive behaviors begin to replace the unwanted behavior, students will be able to "see" how much better they are doing in relation to where they started (i.e., baseline). For the lower elementary grades, teachers can have students record happy/frowning faces on a recording sheet, as shown in Figure 9.2. Students can draw their own face or, more simply, circle a happy or a frowning face according to their behavior at the time of the prompt and then record the number of happy faces on the graph at the end of the recording period. For example, a student self-assesses her target behavior (on task) every 5 minutes during a 30-minute period.

SELF-REINFORCEMENT The final phase of self-management is self-reinforcement. In self-reinforcement, the student has access to sources of positive reinforcement in the classroom when meeting some predetermined criteria. Through an interview, interest survey, or observation, the teacher can determine what reinforcer can motivate the

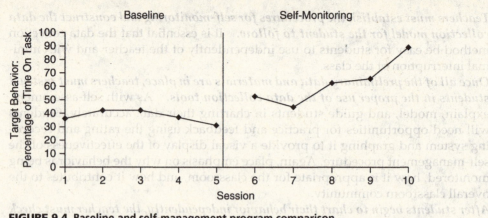

FIGURE 9.4 Baseline and self-management program comparison.

student to agree to participate in self-management and to be his or her own agent of change. Reinforcers can be tangible rewards for reaching some predetermined criteria, but they can also include other types as well. As shown in Table 9.2, there are multiple types of reinforcers for the student to self-administer based on success in the self-management project.

While Table 9.2 is not an exhaustive list, it does provide some ideas of possible reinforcers other than the traditional tangibles often used in the classroom. When using self-reinforcement, teachers need to transition students into identifying reinforcers to which students can have easy access, and there should be an attempt, over time, to move from tangibles, privileges, and tokens to more internal or natural reinforcers, such as those listed in Table 9.2 under social praise and self-praise.

According to Polsgrove and Smith (2004), when a teacher and student agree collaboratively on a behavioral goal but the student fails to reach it, the student should go

TABLE 9.2 List of Reinforcers for Self-Reinforcement

Self-Reinforcement List

Tangibles	Tokens	Privileges	Social Praise	Self-Praise
• Small toys	• Checks	• Board games	• Thumbs up	• Positive self-talk
• Notebooks	• Stars	• Art supplies	• Clapping	• Journaling
• Posters	• Chips/tokens redeemable for tangibles/ privileges	• Line leader	• Pat on back	• Relaxing breathing
• Books		• Listening to music	• High fives	
• Candy		• Class helper	• Positive note home	
• Soda		• Extra computer time	• Teacher/peer verbal approval	
• Chips		• Elective break		
• Other sweets				

unrewarded. Other guidelines that will help teachers make self-reinforcement a powerful self-management component include:

- Self-reinforcement requires competency in self-assessment and self-monitoring, so the teacher should observe the student's fluency and accuracy before moving into self-reinforcement.
- Even though the goal is for the student to manage his or her own behavior, the teacher should continue rating and recording the student's behavior after baseline to match with the student's data. In this way, the teacher can continue a conversation with the student about the rating, recording, and graphing process and reward the student for improvements in fluency, accuracy, and honesty.
- The teacher should start out by providing the access to the agreed-upon reinforcer, then slowly allow the student to self-reinforce.
- Gradually, students should be provided opportunities to increase control over evaluating their behavior and establishing criteria for and selecting reinforcers as they demonstrate competency in the self-management process.

Q: *I have started using self-management techniques with one of my students, and it is going well so far. I am ready to introduce self-reinforcement into the student's repertoire, but I am concerned that my student will take advantage of free access to the reinforcers we agreed on. How can I make sure my student only gets the reinforcer after reaching the agreed-upon criteria?*

A: When you are first using self-reinforcement in the classroom, it is important to manage your students' access to reinforcers. Start by having students submit their self-monitoring data, and then determine if students have met the required criteria for access. Give students a choice of reinforcer from predetermined options. In this way, students have access to a desirable reinforcer, but the teacher is able to monitor if students are accurately meeting the criteria. Gradually, transition students toward having free access to reinforcers. Once students have mastered accurately monitoring and reinforcing their own behavior, encourage them to move toward more internal forms of reinforcement, such as positive self-talk or self-praise.

Key Tips

Self-management is typically taught to individual students the teacher judges as being capable of and motivated to use the strategy to control their behavior. It would be best to start with one student to get comfortable with the procedures and for both teacher and student to learn the process. Also, start with a behavior problem that is relatively easy to correct, and make sure that the student views the opportunity to work on this behavior as a positive one. It is possible that when one student is able to demonstrate some mastery over his or her own behavior and accrue rewards for exhibitng the replacement behavior, others may also want to learn the process.

Whole-Class Self-Management

Whereas self-management is used most efficiently with individual students, there are also opportunities to use the technique as a whole-class strategy. Every student in a class can benefit from a whole-class approach to managing behaviors using the components of self-managment. In the following scenario, Ms. Sandy uses self-management techniques to help her students increase their hand raising during whole-class discussions:

Ms. Sandy has noticed that a few of her students are having difficulties following the rules of the classroom. In particular, students are not remembering to raise their hands before talking. Ms. Sandy believes that students know the hand-raising rule and have had sufficient practice following it but are simply not aware they are calling out. Ms. Sandy has decided to use a self-management strategy with her students to help make them more aware of the calling-out behavior and to increase their hand raising.

Before she discusses her strategy with the students, Mrs. Sandy defines her target behavior and collects some initial data. She determines that she is looking for students to raise their hand and wait to be called on during instruction. She collects data about the number of times that students raise their hands and wait to be called on and the number of times that students call out. She also defines call outs as those students who raise their hand and then call out. During her data collection, Ms. Sandy finds that students are able to raise their hands every two out of five times during instruction.

Ms. Sandy discusses the calling-out problem with her students. She explains the classroom rule again and tells them they are able to follow the rule. Then, she discusses why they need to raise their hand in the classroom. Ms. Sandy decides that students now are aware of their behavior and should be able to accurately self-monitor it. Because students can follow the rule, she believes that her students can raise their hands every four out of five times during instruction. She devises a rating and recording system to record the number of times they raise their hand during instruction. She also remembers to set up a graphing system so that students can see their collective classroom hand raising data.

Each student has a chart to record tally marks during instruction, marking on the left when they raise their hands and on the right when they call out. Ms. Sandy models how to use the rating and recording system. Students practice with Ms. Sandy using the system and take turns recording for each other. Before Ms. Sandy has students begin using the rating and recording system, she has another discussion with students about why they need to raise their hands in the classroom. Students continue to return to why they are monitoring their behavior and practice using the marking system until they are able to use the system independently. Ms. Sandy also discusses possible reinforcers that her class would be excited to receive when they reach the agreed-upon criteria.

After instruction, Ms. Sandy sets aside five minutes for students to transition to independent work and chart their data, and she monitors her students as they use the rating and recording system. She is careful not to correct her students' data based on her own beliefs but, rather, checks to make sure they are using the system correctly and honestly. Each week, Ms. Sandy looks at the data her students collect, and after a few weeks, Ms. Sandy notices that her students are raising their hands without calling out more often in class. Based on the data, she decides to continue using the self-monitoring strategy with her students but, over time, will gradually fade out the whole-class management system.

Summary

Teaching self-management skills to students consists of (a) self-assessment, (b) self-monitoring, and (c) self-reinforcement. Teachers can break these tasks into small and manageable parts so that students can learn to become managers of their own behavior. Teachers should first define a target or desired behavior and focus on student-generated data collection. Teachers should make sure that students have opportunities for adequate practice at each step and time during the entire process to truly master self-management. According to Kaplan (1995), teachers should focus continuously on the reason for students to be able to manage their own behavior throughout the entire self-management process. Using self-management in the classroom can help to prevent behavior problems, increase students' sense of efficacy, and promote awareness about appropriate behavior in the classroom.

SOCIAL PROBLEM SOLVING

Most people understand the need for solving problems, because everyone is challenged by problems throughout the day that need to be solved. For school-aged children, youth, and even adults, finding an effective solution for difficult social problems is often complex, confusing, and sometimes, overwhelming. According to Smith and Daunic (2010), when children first enter the educational system, they should be taught the skills to be effective and efficient social problem solvers. The ability to get along well with others in a variety of settings, such as within the family, in the neighborhood, at school, during recreational and structured activities, and employment, requires skillful and effective problem solving.

Problem solving is a cognitive process that can generate a rational response to a problematic situation and increases the likelihood of generating an appropriate and effective solution (Smith & Daunic, 2006). Similarly, D'Zurilla and Goldfried (1971) and D'Zurilla and Nezu (1980) defined problem solving as a cognitive–behavioral process that generates a variety of alternative responses to a problem and promotes the evaluation of consequences to employ the most appropriate option. Basically, effective problem solving is what happens when a person learns to dissect a problem and then select a solution that has a good chance to achieve the desired outcome.

Substantial evidence demonstrates the effectiveness of using a cognitive strategy like social problem solving to assist students in developing self-control. Smith, Graber, and Daunic (2009) state that teaching children social problem-solving skills can have significant effects on reducing anger, aggression, antisocial behavior, classroom disruption, and hyperactivity/impulsivity in school-aged populations and they can strengthen pro-social behaviors as well (see also Daunic, Smith, Brank, & Penfield, 2006; Daunic et al., 2012; Smith & Daunic, 2004).

Everyone can benefit from instruction on how best to apply problem-solving skills in everyday social situations. When students become skillful at applying problem solving in social situations that make them frustrated, angry, or even enraged, they become proficient in self-control. When students gain self-control, they rely less on adults to help them, which, in turn, can prevent social problems from becoming more significant problems in the future. Thus, students like those in Mr. Claudio's class need to learn how to think deliberatively and carefully, especially about their social problems, rather than relying on adults to "think" for them. Often, teachers expect their students to behave appropriately and make thoughtful and constructive choices when they encounter a social conflict, yet even the best problem solvers need guidance, instruction, and support to achieve a successful outcome. For some students, however, their social problems are rarely resolved successfully, and for them, explicit instruction in the skill of social problem solving is crucial.

In the scenario that opened this chapter, Mr. Claudio talked to his students about getting along better with each other, and he was troubled by the fact that many of the students did not recognize they have social problems. Apparently, some of his students stated that when their peers get pushed, are pestered, or are talked to in mean ways, they probably deserved it. For Mr. Claudio, this indicates a need for problem-solving instruction that can, over time, prevent behavior problems.

Steps of Social Problem Solving

A variety of steps are found in various problem-solving curricula, and they are suitable for a variety of contexts. For example, there are intrapersonal problems that people encounter and struggle to solve, such as how to set up a new computer, planning for an international vacation, or balancing expectations about family visits during special holidays. Teachers certainly understand that students need to enlist problem-solving skills, in a step-by-step process, to accurately and completely solve math problems. Students also need to enlist those same skills when faced with interpersonal problems or those issues that come up as a result of social interactions on a daily basis. Generally, the steps in problem solving include:

1. Recognizing that there is a problem.
2. Defining the problem, and setting a goal.
3. Generating a number of possible solutions.
4. Evaluating the solutions.
5. Designing a plan and carrying it out.
6. Evaluating how well the plan worked.

Teachers frequently use a similar step-by-step process during math instruction. When approaching a word problem in math, students must first recognize that there is a problem that needs to be solved (step 1). Next, the student needs to determine what the problem is asking for (step 2: Defining the problem) and what information is needed to solve it (step 2: Setting a goal). The student would then generate solutions to the problems, evaluate which solution might be the best to try, and carry it out (steps 3 to 5). The last step of the process would involve the student evaluating the solution by checking the answer in the book or when the problem was reviewed in class (step 6).

Skilled problem solvers use the same step-by-step process when they encounter intrapersonal or interpersonal problems. *Oh no, what am I going to do? My car will not start, and I need to make the meeting on time. I was late last week, and I cannot be late again!* or *Okay, that is it! I need to talk to her about how she hurt my feelings by talking about my best friend* are problematic situations that demand solution generation, careful evaluation of the array of solutions possible, and a plan to carry it forward. For teachers like Mr. Claudio, teaching social problem solving to his students is the same process whether he is teaching how to approach a math problem, a personal problem, or a problem with other people. Teachers can also help their students learn to apply a systematic approach to those social situations that are anger provoking. If Mr. Claudio teaches his students to solve their social problems more effectively, they should be better able to manage their everyday situations, reduce their disruptive or aggressive behavior through better self-control, and be contributors to a positive classroom climate. In this way, teaching social problem solving prevents future problem behaviors from occurring.

How to Teach Social Problem Solving

Schools may want to adopt a "packaged" program for teachers to use with their lower or upper elementary students, or teachers may want to develop their own lessons to teach the problem-solving sequence. A number of curriculum-based instructional packages are available through commercial sources, and some are undergoing rigorous research to determine their effectiveness. There are curricula for whole-class instruction, such as *I Can Problem Solve* (Shure, 2001) and *Tools for Getting Along: Teaching Students to Problem Solve* (Smith & Daunic, 2006), that are focused exclusively on social problem solving for school-aged children and youth. Other well-known curricula, such as *Second Step* (see, e.g., Cooke, Ford, Levin, Bourke, Newell, & Lapidus, 2007) and *Promoting Alternative THinking Skills* (*PATHS*) (see Conduct Problems Prevention Research Group, 1999), include problem-solving skill instruction but also provide explicit instruction in other areas, such as emotional literacy, impulse and self-control, social competence, positive peer relations, empathy, and anger management.

Mr. Claudio could use a curriculum appropriate for whole-class instruction like *Tools for Getting Along*, or he could design his own social problem-solving curriculum that would cover the essential problem-solving steps. First, we describe using the *Tools for Getting Along* curriculum and then explain how Mr. Claudio could inform his own lesson creation in the steps of problem solving. Regardless of how Mr. Claudio would approach problem-solving instruction, he would be investing in preventing the problem behavior of his students, because they would be equipped to recognize (a) when they have a problem and (b) what steps they need to take to arrive at an effective and efficient solution that can help them achieve their social goals.

TOOLS FOR GETTING ALONG Teachers can use *Tools for Getting Along* to work with upper elementary students to apply a step-by step problem-solving framework, especially in frustrating or anger-provoking social situations. The instructional focus is on understanding and dealing with frustration and anger, because anger is a frequent companion of disruptive and aggressive behavior and is often preceded by frustration. The *Tools . . .* lessons help students recognize and manage anger, clarify how anger may lead to or make social problems worse, and illustrate the use of an approach to generate, implement, and evaluate solutions to problems students face every day. The overall intent of *Tools . . .* is to provide students with efficient cognitive problem-solving skills, enhance their use as self-statements to guide their decision making, and ultimately, foster automaticity in how to approach successfully a challenging social situation at school or in other venues.

TABLE 9.3	Comparison of the Steps of *Tools for Getting Along* and General Problem Solving

Tools for Getting Along Steps	General Problem-Solving Steps
1. I know I'm angry.	1. Recognizing that there is a problem.
2. I calm down.	2. Defining the problem, and setting a goal.
3. I think about the cause.	3. Generating a number of possible solutions.
4. I think about what I could do.	
5. I try a solution.	4. Evaluating the solutions.
6. I think about how it turned out.	5. Designing a plan, and carrying it out.
	6. Evaluating how well the plan worked.

A total of 20 lessons, delivered about two or three times per week, focus on six problem-solving steps, which are compared with general problem-solving steps in Table 9.3. Fifteen content lessons cover the six problem-solving steps, and five strategically placed role-play lessons provide opportunities to practice steps as they are learned. Each lesson begins with a review of the previous lessons, and there is direct instruction, modeling, guided practice, and independent practice to maximize skill development and generalization. After the 20 lessons are six booster lessons, taught approximately every two weeks, to allow additional skill practice and students to get involved in group problem solving. Throughout the *Tools . . .* curriculum are numerous role-play activities that become more complex as students continue to learn the sequence of steps.

The first step, *I know I'm angry*, is recognizing that anger is the problem, and the second step, *I calm down*, is included to teach a stop-and-think strategy to calm down to approach a social problem in a rational rather than an irrational way. The third step, *I think about the cause*, is basically defining the problem and trying to figure out what students would like to achieve or what their goal is. The fourth step, *I think about what I could do*, is learning how to generate a number of possible solutions, and the fifth, *I try a solution*, is evaluating each solution, designing a plan, and carrying it out. The last step, *I think about how it turned out*, includes lessons that teach students to evaluate how they implemented their solution and if they achieved their goal.

Incorporated throughout the curriculum are three features to facilitate generalization of the problem-solving strategies:

1. *Tool Kit.* The Tool Kit helps students practice the strategies they learn and acts as a self-monitoring device. Each Tool Kit includes practice in skill development that builds on each preceding lesson, thus providing cumulative practice and review. Teachers who use *Tools . . .* sometimes instruct their students to complete their Tool Kits at home to increase the generalization of learned skills.
2. *Paired or small group learning.* Frequently, teachers use small groups (three to four per group) so that students can share responsibility for learning the problem-solving strategies. Teachers are reminded to group students with differing levels of social skill development and reading ability.

3. *Point system:*   After each lesson, there is a point system which can aid generalization. By rewarding completion of the Tool Kit and cooperation with others, students are reinforced for generalizing the cognitive skills they are learning during the lessons.

If Mr. Claudio used *Tools . . .*, he might be able to get his students to see that their behavior toward one another is creating problems. Additionally, over time, he might be able to prevent many of the behavioral issues, because his students would be better equipped to manage their own social disputes. In the following example, Mr. Claudio is weeks into teaching *Tools . . .* and is now teaching a lesson about how to generate a number of possible solutions that may solve a social problem:

Box 9.1	Lesson: I Think About What I Could Do

Objective: Students will practice generating alternative solutions.

Mr. Claudio shows the *What's Good About Problem Solving?* slide and asks, *Who can remember what is good about problem solving?*

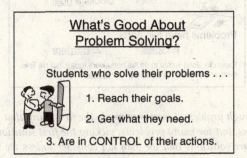

Mr. Claudio prompts the students, allows response time for student answers, and provides a rationale for becoming an effective problem solver.

Great! You guys obviously remember the "whys" (i.e., rationale) behind problem solving. Now, I want to make sure that I still have your commitment to learn more about problem solving? . . . Awesome! Now, just to recap, since school started this year, we have been learning the steps of problem solving. We have learned the first three, so who can tell me what they are?

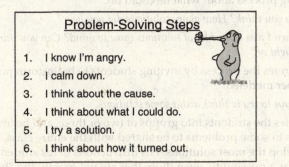

(Continued)

Box 9.1   **Continued**

Mr. Claudio reviews the previously learned problem-solving steps (1: *I know I'm angry*; 2: *I calm down*; 3: *I think about the cause*) with students using the *Tools . . .* slides and class discussions.

Excellent thinking, guys! In our last lesson, we talked about the third step: I think about the cause. *What are the two parts to most problems?*

Mr. Claudio directs a class discussion about the two parts of most problems, goals and barriers, while reinforcing student answers.

When we remember to calm down (step 2), we are able to think about our goal *and identify the* barriers *that may be causing the problem (step 3). Today, we are going to talk about the fourth step:* I think about what I could do.

Mr. Claudio shows the *Barriers Cause Problems* slide and says, *After we figure out what the barriers are, we need to think about how we can remove the barriers, reach our goal, and have the "Tools for Getting Along."*

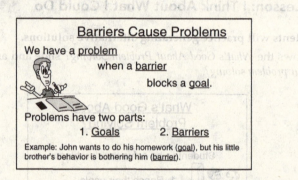

When confronted with a tough problem, sometimes we do the first thing that pops into our heads. This may work for easy decisions, but for many problems, picking the first solution we think of might make the problem worse. There are solutions that we may not consider unless we take time to examine all the possibilities.

Mr. Claudio reveals possible strategies to use (e.g., talk to a trusted friend or adult, think about what they may do, think about what you have done in similar situations that seemed to work) when thinking about what to do to solve a problem (i.e., generate possible solutions). He then leads the class in a discussion of possible solutions for realistic problems.

After examining possible problems and solutions, Mr. Claudio models for the students possible solutions based on several of his real-life problems using think alouds so his students can "hear" his thinking process about what he could do.

Well, guys, what do you think? How many solutions did you hear?

Did you see how when I was calm a lot of solutions came to mind? Can you think of any other ones that I may not have thought of?

Mr. Claudio continues the process by inviting students to brainstorm possible solutions to the problem the teacher modeled.

Now, I want you guys to try to think about some solutions.

Mr. Claudio divides the students into groups of two or three, and he instructs them to record possible solutions to some problems to be shared with the entire class. He poses this activity as a game to develop the most solutions. His instructions to his students are to generate any realistic solution as a possibility, even those that are not exactly the "best."

Box 9.1	**Continued**

When all have finished, Mr. Claudio goes over the suggested solutions. He evaluates each solution with the class, and the class determines whether it is appropriate and feasible. He explains to his students that some ideas may be good solutions but not feasible to carry out. He also helps them dismiss the completely inappropriate or impossible solutions, and he keeps a total for each group.

Finally, Mr. Claudio wraps up the lesson with a recap and preview of the next lesson. He is sure to assign meaningful homework to reinforce the concepts learned in class.

Okay, everybody, you did great work, and I'm very proud of everyone. The bell is about to ring, so for our next lesson, we'll be playing the "What can I do?" game again, coming up with more solutions for a different problem. The more we practice thinking of solutions to problems, the more Tools . . . *we will have to help us solve our problems in real situations.*

The homework for tonight is to think of a problem that's going on in your life and play the "What can I do?" game. I'd also like you to share your solutions with a family member and/or friend and then bring your list of solutions into class tomorrow. Again, you guys were awesome. I'm proud of you!

GENERAL SOCIAL PROBLEM-SOLVING INSTRUCTION   Whether teachers want to use packaged programs or institute their own curriculum to better fit the level and circumstances of their students, teaching problem solving can be a great asset in the classroom to prevent behavior problems. Lower elementary teachers should teach more of the skills needed for problem solving, including self-awareness and social awareness, basic self-management, building relationships, and some initial problem-solving skills, such as imbedding the learning intervention into early literacy instruction using books that are aligned with social and emotional themes. Social and emotional themes foundational to social problem solving can consist of:

- Recognizing and expressing feelings.
- Feeling angry or afraid.
- Understanding the feelings of others.
- Understanding jealousy and being upset.
- Knowing that feelings can change.
- Being aware that other people have feelings, too.
- Understanding that actions have consequences.
- Understanding the value of friendships.

If students in the early grades can get substantive and systematic instruction in these areas, there will be a firm foundation to provide more explicit, step-by-step social problem solving in the middle and upper elementary grades. For teachers to put together lessons of their own to teach social problem solving, they could build their instruction by following the general problem-solving steps shown in Table 9.3.

Recognizing That There Is a Problem   At first glance, this step may seem like a meaningless and unnecessary one, because of course, anyone would know when a problem exists. Yet sometimes, adults can deliberate about whether some social interaction, event, or situation is truly a problem to solve. Some situations can simply be ignored or not acted upon, because the situation does not merit further deliberation. Other social incidents or situations that are more complex may require some sorting out to determine what, exactly, the problem might be. In Mr. Claudio's case, he has students who fail to see how their actions toward others constitute a problem. To them, there is no problem to solve when they believe that saying mean things and pushing or pestering each other happens because someone deserves it. The first step of recognizing that there is a problem to solve is particularly difficult for some students, especially those with chronic behavior problems who have difficulty attributing the consequences of their actions to their own behavior. These students often think of themselves as the victims and that nothing they do will change anything.

Mr. Claudio would need to help his students understand that their actions in some social situations do, indeed, constitute a problem to be solved. His students might also need assistance to understand that their peers' emotional reaction to their actions might exacerbate a problem or create future problems. Using classroom situations to illustrate what happens when students are not good problem solvers, or what happens when problems go unresolved, is an easy way to introduce this concept. Teachers can also use examples from their own experience to illustrate how to recognize a problem.

One good vehicle to recognizing that there is a problem is using anger, as in *Tools for Getting Along*, because many problematic social interactions involve strong emotions, starting with frustration, which can lead to anger and rage. Some students may think that when shoved, poked, or made fun of, shoving back angrily or retaliating with verbal aggression is the *only* way to respond. When students react this way, they bypass the first steps of taking the time to figure out if there is a problem and what the problem might actually be. Understanding that anger can precede (but not always) inappropriate behavior is a necessary first step. Teachers can develop lessons that describe what triggers angry feelings. Topics such as how to recognize and describe anger and how anger can impede good judgment all constitute possible lesson content. Once students realize that there is a problem to be solved, especially when they are frustrated, getting angry, or otherwise upset, they are in a better position to take the next step of defining the problem and determining a goal.

Defining the Problem, and Setting a Goal   After recognizing that there is, indeed, a problem, the next step is to understand the problem clearly by breaking down its parts and setting a goal. In some cases, the problem is clear and straightforward. For example, someone cuts in line and is in clear violation of the rules for the lunch line, or someone shoves a peer off of a swing with intent to be mean for no apparent reason. In these situations, the problems are obvious, and the goal would be to right the wrong. More often, though, problems are more complex, and they come with a host of historical factors or complicated situational nuances that are not easily sorted out. One way to help students define problems is to design lessons about goals and barriers. If students can learn to accurately identify the barriers that prevent what they want to achieve (i.e., their goal), they are well on their way to solving their problem.

When teachers talk to their students about defining a problem, it is a continuation of the problem-solving process that can lead to a successful outcome. Teachers need to spend considerable time teaching the idea that students have control over some of the barriers (i.e., those things that stand in the way of reaching our goals) without placing blame on another person. As in the first step, students need to understand the role of frustration and anger as barriers that can aggravate a problem.

Teachers can help their students recognize that the occasional small incidents can become larger problems if they are unable to control their frustration or anger appropriately. Some students, however, fail to recognize that the problem they are experiencing is related to a goal they have, and sometimes, they want to view others as the barriers. Students need to define the problem for themselves, because they will have little success controlling other people's behavior. For example, if Monique defines her goal as wanting to repair and keep a friendship after an argument with her best friend and she recognizes her anger or hurt feelings as the barrier, then it makes it easier for her to find a solution.

Defining a problem involves determining what goal is being blocked. Teachers can provide instruction to their students about how feelings and emotions can become connected to what they want out of the problem situation. For some situations, like someone cutting in the cafeteria line or getting pushed off the swing, keeping emotions in check and thinking about the goal (e.g., place in line, time on the swing) can continue the process toward generating a number of possible solutions to achieve the goal.

Generating a Number of Possible Solutions For almost all students, and even for adults, generating a number of possible solutions to solve a problem can be difficult. When a person's strong emotions are involved in a social problem, solution generation is limited, because the ability to engage in rational decision making is compromised. Generating viable solutions to solve a problem requires rational decision making based on an assessment of the existing barriers and the person's goals. One reason why a student would act impulsively when engaged in a social problem may stem from not knowing that there may be more than one course of action they can take to achieve their goal.

When developing lessons for this step, it is crucial that teachers provide students with opportunities for constant practice in generating solutions within the context of existing barriers and what students want to achieve. Brainstorming is one way for students to create solutions, but they will inevitably come up with some nonviable and immature solutions that are not useful and will not facilitate a logical outcome. Teachers need to resist initially judging these ideas as *will not work*, *not a good idea*, or *cannot do that*. Students should first think for themselves, and the teacher can provide guidance later to learn how to think about evaluating the solutions. For this step, the skill of generating a number of solutions to solve a problem emerges through the *thinking* process and seeing that there may be *many* ways to act.

The point of being able to develop solutions is for students to be as self-sufficient as possible, yet there are times when support is needed. For example, in adult life, problems come along for which, despite great cognitive effort, solutions are not forthcoming. When this happens, adults might seek the advice of a trusted friend, family member, or spouse. By doing so, the realm of possible solutions might expand. If students get stuck and are seemingly at a stopping point, the teacher should resist providing specific solutions but, rather, help by providing ideas about how to get past the block. For example, a teacher could start by asking, *Is there another way you could think about this?* Teachers might also share how they came up with some solutions to problems they have solved in the past by including the barriers they faced and their goals in the situation. By going through the process of generating solutions, students develop critical thinking and self-control skills as they decide for themselves what they could do.

Q: *I am teaching problem solving to my students, and they are coming up with some pretty crazy and inappropriate solutions. Some of the solutions include fighting, yelling, or social exclusion from the group. I know clearly that they are not acceptable solutions to problems. How can I explain to my students that they cannot discuss inappropriate solutions during brainstorming?*

A: The point of generating numerous possible solutions is for students to have many options to think about when deciding how to problem solve. It is, in fact, the case that hitting, yelling, or being mean are possible ways to solve a problem, but they would most likely be solutions that would not help the students achieve their goals. The goal of brainstorming solutions is to develop a list so that students understand that there is *more than one way* to solve a problem. When students throw out crazy or inappropriate solutions, they are often trying to be funny or get attention. Refrain from judging the quality or appropriateness of the solution (the evaluation step comes next). The goal of *this* step is simply to brainstorm ideas. Teachers need to remember that students are usually accustomed to reacting quickly in problem situations. It will take continued practice and repetition before students learn to problem solve rationally.

Evaluating the Solutions Students will need to select a solution to try that is both effective and feasible. A solution would be effective if it could help them achieve their goal, and to be feasible, it should be a solution that the students can actually implement. One solution to constantly being called a name, for example, is to learn a martial art for self-defense, which could be highly effective (although fighting back may not be a solution that achieves a goal), but it would not be feasible in the short term. Another solution might be for the student to yell at the other person and call him or her a name as well, which would be feasible but, perhaps, not effective. Still another solution might be for the student to practice using I-messages. I-messages state a problem simply, without asserting blame or criticizing anyone (e.g., *I feel sad when you call me names because I thought we were best friends*, or *I feel angry when you boss me around because that is not how we are supposed to act*). Students can practice I-messages with an adult when conflict among students occurs and report incidents immediately, which could be an effective and feasible strategy.

Similar to the previous step, every time students practice evaluating solutions to use, they become more skillful, because they have to predict, using if-then thinking, what will happen for themselves and the others involved. This type of thinking requires that students have the capability to (a) identify and acknowledge their own feelings, (b) anticipate the feelings of others, and (c) anticipate the future feelings of all involved. If students lack these essential skills, teachers should make sure they have a clear understanding about the nature of feelings and the connection to social problem solving.

An additional aid to evaluating solutions that would be the most effective and feasible is to answer each of three evaluation questions:

1. What is the worst thing that could happen?
2. What is the best thing that could happen?
3. What is most likely to happen?

For the best results, teachers can instruct their students to think through the answers using real-life social situations they encounter on a regular basis. When students practice the three questions for situations that they may actually experience, it will help them generalize their problem-solving skills across a number of settings, such as in the classroom, at recess, in the cafeteria, at home, or in the neighborhood.

DESIGNING A PLAN, CARRYING IT OUT, AND EVALUATING HOW WELL IT WORKED The final steps involve the how, when, and where of implementing the chosen solution. Teachers can use role plays in the classroom to show examples of designing and carrying out a plan to implement a solution. The role plays may also consist of non-examples to show how a poor plan of action (the how, when, and where) can lead to undesired outcomes. This last step also consists of evaluating how well the plan worked. As with any social interaction, there can be a variety of outcomes, but generally, when the problem-solving steps are followed, there can be predictable outcomes. When a plan does not work as intended, however, or when the results are not what were expected, teachers should resist telling students why they were not successful. If students are praised for following the step-by-step procedure and not necessarily for the outcome, they will be more comfortable about making mistakes and the learning that comes with it. What is important is that the student went through a deliberative process to select and carry out a thoughtful solution. Students should be encouraged to tell themselves *Hey, I did it!* or *It didn't work like I thought, but I did the best I could do.*

Finally, teachers can also have students share real-life problems (those appropriate for sharing) with the class, brainstorm and evaluate solutions as a group, design a plan, carry it out, and report back to the class about how well it turned out. This will allow teachers an opportunity to discuss with students how actions have consequences and whether or not they would do the same again in a similar situation.

KEY TIPS When setting up instruction in social problem solving, teachers should keep in mind that adequate instruction will require weeks, with ample review sessions to make sure learned skills are maintained. Teachers will want to devise a number of lessons for each step consisting of content knowledge, discussion, activities, and grouping arrangements. Most importantly, teachers should provide abundant practice opportunities while students are learning the basic steps. This can be accomplished by writing role plays for students to act out or having students in small groups develop their own role play situations. Generalization of learned skills is accomplished when students practice learned skills in a variety of situations and settings, with varying problems and complexity, and are provided with ample teacher guidance and support.

For each step, teachers can use classroom situations or personal examples to make the process relevant. One important thing to do is show students how adults use the steps to work through a situation by overtly modeling the thinking process at each stage in the sequence. Teachers can also ask students to share some situations that they recently experienced, what they did, how it turned out, and what they might have done differently. When building a social problem-solving curriculum, teachers need to

(a) cover each step sufficiently, (b) provide an abundance of practice, (c) teach students to evaluate how they perform along the way, and (d) help students transfer or generalize their skills to a variety of situations.

Chaplain and Smith (2006) provide a number of reminders when teaching problem solving:

1. Present a general overview of the need for problem solving.
2. Dedicate multiple lessons to each problem-solving step in detail.
3. Use a variety of activities, such as discussion, role play, completing worksheets, games, and contests.
4. Integrate various grouping activities, such as whole class, small group, student dyads, individual work, throughout.
5. Use the students' own personal experiences (those that are appropriate to share) as much as possible to maximize the generalization of learned skills.
6. Practice, practice, practice, because only through constant review and repetitive exercises will problem solving for students become an organized way of thinking.

Summary

Teaching students to solve their own problems with other people is an intervention used to equip students with the skills to independently make wise behavioral choices and to prevent future behavior problems in the classroom. Problem solving teaches a process to help students make their own choices about how to act and to connect their actions to the subsequent consequences. When processing social problems using a step-by-step problem-solving framework, students are able to predict the outcomes of their actions. The more students can make careful and deliberative behavioral choices independently, the more control they have over their social relationships and, thus, can prevent problem behaviors from occurring in the first place.

In this chapter, we presented a rationale for preventing problem behavior by teaching students to manage their own behavior through self-management and social problem solving. These skills can be taught using a step-by-step procedure, but they do take significant teacher effort because of the need to practice the learned skills. Despite the amount of teaching involved, the results can be significant, because students become equipped to be their own agent of change.

For students with behavior problems, their inability to adequately manage their own behavior or solve their social problems obstructs their relationships with the peers and adults around them, and it can undermine their future adolescent and adult adjustment. If students continuously have behavior problems and cannot get along with others, the lack of effective self-management and problem-solving strategies can create a variety of ever-increasing problems. If left untreated, these problems can lead to dropping out of school, poor employment histories, or adult mental health problems. Self-management and problem solving are powerful strategies that can create for students a sense of control over their daily activities. Ultimately, teaching students to self-manage and solve their social problems will help empower students to take control of problem situations and make decisions to achieve their goals.

Additional Resources

On the Web

Page Title	Annotations	Web Address
Self-Management: The Ultimate Goal	Basic information for educators about self-management for children	http://www.education.com/reference/article/teaching-social-skills-self-management/
Create a Graph	Site for students to develop graphs	http://nces.ed.gov/nceskids/createagraph/
Rewards and Positive Consequences: Strategies for Students with Behavioral Disorders	Ideas for classroom reinforcers beyond traditional tangibles	http://specialed.about.com/cs/behaviordisorders/a/rewards.htm
Managing Student Behavior in Today's Schools	Elementary and middle school social problem-solving curriculum	http://education.ufl.edu/conflict-resolution/
Problem-Solving Games	Creative and fun games for kids to play that require problem solving	http://pbskids.org/games/problemsolving.html

In the Literature

Donham, J. (2010). Creating personal learning through self-assessment. *Teacher Librarian, 37*(3), 14–21.
This article discusses the role of teachers in developing self-assessment habits in students. The author explains the role, importance, and numerous opportunities for self-assessment throughout the day.

References

Chaplain, R., & Smith, S. W. (2006). *Challenging behaviour*. Cambridge, UK: Pearson.

Conduct Problems Prevention Research Group. (1999). Initial impact of the Fast Track prevention trial for conduct problems: II. Classroom effects. *Journal of Consulting and Clinical Psychology, 67*, 648–657.

Cooke, M. B., Ford, J., Levine, J., Bourke, C., Newell, L., & Lapidus, G. (2007). The effects of citywide implementation of Second Step on elementary school students' prosocial and aggressive behaviors. *The Journal of Primary Prevention, 28*(2), 93–115.

Daunic, A. P., Smith. S. W., Brank, E. M., & Penfield, R. D. (2006). Classroom based cognitive–behavioral intervention to prevent aggression: Efficacy and social validity. *Journal of School Psychology, 44*, 123–139.

Daunic, A. P., Smith, S. W., Garvan, C. W., Barber, B. R., Becker, M. K., Peters, C. D., Taylor, G. G., Van Loan, C. L., & Li, W., & Naranjo, A. H. (2012). Reducing developmental risk for emotional/behavioral problems: A randomized controlled trial examining the Tools for Getting Along curriculum. *Journal of School Psychology, 50*, 149–166.

DiGangi, S. A., Maag, J. W., & Rutherford, R. B. (1991). Self-graphing of on-task behavior: Enhancing the reactive effects of self-monitoring on on-task behavior and academic performance. *Learning Disability Quarterly, 14*, 221–230.

D'Zurilla, T. J., & Goldfried, M. R. (1971). Problem solving and behavior modification. *Journal of Abnormal Psychology, 78*, 107–126.

D'Zurilla, T. J., & Nezu, A. M. (1980). A study of the generation-of-alternative process in social problem solving. *Cognitive Therapy and Research, 4*, 67–72.

Kaplan, J. S. (1995). *Beyond behavior modification: A cognitive–behavioral approach to behavior management in the school* (3rd ed.). Austin, TX: Pro-Ed.

Martin, G. L., & Pear, J. (2010). *Behavior modification: What it is and how to do it.* Upper Saddle River, NJ: Pearson.

McMillan, J. H., & Hearn, J. (2009). Student self-assessment. *Education Digest, 74*(8), 39–44.

Menzies, H. M., Lane, K. L., & Lee, J. M. (2009). Self-monitoring strategies for use in the classroom: A promising practice to support productive behavior for students with emotional or behavioral disorders. *Beyond Behavior, 18*(2), 27–35.

Mooney, P., Ryan, J. B., Uhing, B. M., Reid, R., & Epstein, M. H. (2005). A review of self-management interventions targeting academic outcomes for students with emotional and behavioral disorders. *Journal of Behavioral Education, 14,* 203–221.

Polsgrove, L., & Smith, S. W. (2004). Informed practice in teaching self-control to children with emotional and behavioral disorders. In R. B. Rutherford, M. M. Quinn, & S. R. Mathur (Eds.), *Handbook of research in emotional and behavioral disorders* (pp. 399–425). New York: Guilford.

Rafferty, L. A. (2010). Step-by-step: Teaching students to self-monitor. *TEACHING Exceptional Children, 43*(2), 50–58.

Shure, M. B. (2001). *I can problem solve: An interpersonal cognitive problem-solving program.* Champaign, IL: Research Press.

Smith. S. W., & Daunic, A. P. (2004). Research on preventing behavior problems using a cognitive–behavioral intervention: Preliminary findings, challenges and future directions. *Behavioral Disorders, 30,* 72–76.

Smith, S. W., & Daunic, A. P. (2006). *Managing difficult behavior through problem solving instruction: Strategies for the elementary classroom.* Boston: Allyn & Bacon.

Smith, S. W., & Daunic, A. P. (2010). Cognitive–behavioral interventions in school settings. In R. Algozzine, A. P. Daunic, & S. W. Smith (Eds.), *Preventing problem behaviors: A handbook of successful prevention strategies* (2nd ed., pp. 53–70). Thousand Oaks, CA: Corwin Press.

Smith, S. W., Graber, J., & Daunic, A. P. (2009). Cognitive–behavioral interventions for anger/aggression: Review of research and research-to-practice issues. In M. Mayer, R. Van Acker, J. Lochman, & F. Gresham (Eds.), *Cognitive–behavioral interventions for emotional and behavioral disorders: School-based practice* (pp. 111–142). New York: Guilford.

Zirpoli, T. J. (2012). *Behavior management: Positive applications for teachers.* Boston: Pearson.

Putting It All Together

GOALS

- Describe the elements of a positive classroom culture that is foundational to a proactive classroom.
- Explain the importance of the first days of school in developing a proactive classroom.

- List activities in which the effective classroom manager engages on the first days of school.
- Describe how teachers can maintain an effective classroom management system over the course of the school year.

Successfully managing the behaviors of a variety of students in a classroom can be rewarding for teachers, yet as most teachers will agree, that success does not come without significant effort, patience, reflection, and skill. Being a skilled manager of behavior and working to prevent behavior problems can be even more difficult when a teacher's efforts are compromised by students who experience poverty, neglect, and harsh treatment. Simply put, managing student behavior can strain the personal and professional resources of even the most experienced teachers.

What is well-known by experienced teachers is that students of all ages can sometimes engage in difficult behaviors, such as noncompliance, impulsivity and inattention, poor self-control, and aggression. For some students, however, their chronic behavioral excesses and deficits detract in a significant way from their learning opportunities and their behavior prevents them from gaining appropriate friendships and other positive peer relationships. Preventing behavior problems that, over time, can result in poor school adjustment, juvenile delinquency, and school drop out should be a teacher's primary focus and drive a teacher's approach to classroom management. Our purpose in this book has been to provide a guide to help elementary teachers manage student behavior in ways that will create a proactive classroom envionment in which learning is maximized and student problems are minimized. Proactive classrooms are better places to teach and learn because teachers who emphsize prevention of behavior problems experience fewer discipline problems. We contend that the most effective and efficient way to achieve a proactive classroom is by structuring a positive classroom culture that is foundational for preventing misbehavior.

POSITIVE CLASSROOM CULTURE

There has always been a need for a positive classroom culture that reinforces and maintains certain values, such as respect, fairness, and openness, and provides students with a safe and secure environment that makes them feel welcomed and successful. Prevention strategies like those introduced in this book provide the foundation for a positive classroom culture, yet even though such a culture may sound simple to create, it is a lot more challenging than just being nice to students. Students bring many complicated issues to school, and many come from home environments where they are not receiving enough appropriate support to acquire the social interaction skills necessary for school success. With these challenges in mind, teachers need to make creating a positive classroom culture a daily priority. Throughout this book, we have detailed many strategies to create a positive classroom environment, that can be accomplished through many of the practices we suggest, especially those we talk about in some of the beginnning chapters.

The first approach to creating a positive classroom culture that can prevent many behavior problems is to always remember that student discipline is not necessarily punishment to correct misbehaviors but, rather, is a means to provide students opportunities to learn. For a long time in education, there has been a tension between creating positive classroom cultures through kindness, caring, and reinforcing the positive and using punitive techniques to reduce aberrant student behavior. For some teachers and administrators, student discipline is administered by taking away privileges, writing sentences, placement in time out, and dispensing in-school and out-of-school suspension. Yet, discipline is more synonomous with training, teaching, instructing, regulating, and directing students in a way that educates them to manage themselves appropriately.

As we also detailed in Chapter 2, teachers can take on an authoritative teaching style as opposed to a laissez-faire or authoritarian one. An authoritative teaching approach can lead to a positive classroom culture, because it is characterized by a student-centered approach that holds high expectations of maturity and compliance with classroom rules and directions while allowing an open dialogue about behavioral issues. An authoritative teacher encourages students to be independent but also places limits and controls on student actions. Although most teachers set limits and demand maturity, authoritative teachers explain the reasons that underly outcomes of behavior so that students are aware before their actions. Further, teachers can explore what constitutes their teaching philosophy through a variety of mechanisms. Understanding the importance of developing an explicit teaching philosophy is one of the foundational aspects of teaching and providing a positive learning environment. When teachers have an understanding of their teaching philosophy as a guiding foundation, effective and positive teaching behaviors will most likely follow.

As we discussed in Chapter 7, teachers can model appropriate behavior on a daily basis so that students can see how adults solve problems and conduct their social interactions successfully. Teachers can practice self-discipline and increase their self-control to add to the positive culture in the classroom. Also, teachers can use redirecting rather than reprimanding behavior. In this way, minor problem behaviors are simply redirected toward more acceptable ones, and a negative interaction through reprimanding students is averted. Increasing choice making is another powerful strategy that can empower students to take control of some aspect of their learning and create a positive learning environment, and using a precorrection strategy to prevent behaviors can add to a more positive classroom culture as well. As detailed in Chapter 8, precorrection is a specific, step-by-step preventive and positive approach to managing behavior. Rather than applying consequences after a behavior occurs, precorrection is an attempt to ensure that problem behavior does not occur in the first place.

Fostering good teacher–student relationships is another powerful determinant of academic and social outcomes and in maintaining a positive classroom culture. When we addressed forming healthy teacher–student relationships in Chapter 4, we wrote that without meaningful interpersonal relationships with students who have behavior problems, effective pedagogical techniques and behavioral interventions can become significantly compromised.

Finally, conducting structured meetings with students in the morning is an interesting, dynamic, exciting, and fun way to start the day and create a positive classroom culture. Chapter 5 illustrated how effective morning meetings to begin the school day can create a positive classroom community that, in turn, can reduce the chances for problem behaviors. A morning meeting can help to establish trust between teachers and students, improve student speaking skills and confidence, encourage cooperation, and establish respectful patterns of communication.

In this final chapter, we draw on the collection of themes throughout this book and apply them to what a teacher should do to:

- Prepare for the school year.
- Introduce the classroom management system to students on the first days of school.
- Maintain the system throughout the school year.

PREPARING FOR THE SCHOOL YEAR

Establishing and maintaining a proactive classroom requires that teachers spend time before the school year planning and organizing their management system. Successful classroom management requires that teachers introduce the system to their students on the first day of school and diligently maintain the system throughout the school year. Teachers of proactive classrooms spend time and effort preparing the environment before the start of school by:

- Arranging the physical environment.
- Establishing the classroom procedures and rules.
- Creating an acknowledgment-and-consequence system.
- Developing a plan for responding to student misbehavior.

Arranging the Physical Environment

As we explained in Chapter 3, the manner in which teachers arrange and organize the physical space in their classrooms can contribute to creating an environment that is conducive to teaching, learning, and appropriate student behavior. The most important principle is to arrange the physical parts of the classroom in a way that will benefit the teacher and prevent behavior problems (Marzano, Gaddy, Foseid, Foseid, & Marzano, 2005). Three ways to accomplish this are:

1. Arrange the classroom so that the teacher can see all the students at all times and the students can see the teacher.
2. Ensure that high-traffic areas are free from congestion and allow easy movement.
3. Organize student seating in ways that facilitate student involvement.

Arrangement of the physical environment is a critical component of teacher "withitness," which involves the teacher moving among students and scanning the environment, interacting with students, giving positive feedback for appropriate behavior, and correcting inappropriate behavior (see Chapters 1, 3, and 6). Teacher withitness is a critical teacher attribute for preventing student misbehavior. Thus, teachers must be able to see all events occurring in the classroom and be able to reach any student in the classroom within three or four steps from where the teacher spends the majority of instructional time (Marzano et al., 2005). In this way, a teacher can maximize proximity control, which we explained in Chapters 3 and 6.

Establishing Classroom Procedures and Rules

Teachers must outline the procedures and rules that they need for teaching and learning to occur in their classrooms (see Chapter 3). Because classrooms are comprised of a diverse group of students assembled in crowded conditions for long periods of time with specific tasks to accomplish, it is crucial that teachers have explicit, specific rules and procedures to guide student behavior.

Rules describe what is, and what is not, acceptable in the classroom, and they act as guidelines for appropriate classroom behavior that, if followed, allow teaching and learning to take place in an efficient manner. In Chapter 3, we described the process for establishing classroom rules, which generally entails developing a few positively stated rules that are clearly defined and objectively written.

Procedures consist of the prescribed ways of managing various activities and duties that occur day in and day out during the school year. The purpose of establishing procedures is to accomplish recurring tasks in the most efficient manner possible. In Chapter 3, we addressed how teachers should establish their classroom procedures by first determining the predictable events that occur frequently and then developing the procedures by which students can most efficiently accomplish these tasks.

Creating an Acknowledgment-and-Consequence System

A teacher's goal in establishing classroom procedures and rules is to have students not only know the procedures and rules but follow them. Unfortunately, simply listing and telling students the classroom rules will not always result in complete compliance. Teachers should monitor students' compliance with classroom rules and acknowledge and reinforce rule-following behavior. Additionally, consequences should be implemented when students break classroom rules. The types of consequences that teachers use, and the way in which they use them, can determine whether certain students follow the classroom rules and whether they respect the teacher.

As we explained in Chapter 3, planning acknowledgments and consequences in advance will help to ensure that procedures and rules, important components of the classroom management system, are used systematically and with confidence. Having to come up with acknowledgments and consequences on the spot often leads to inconsistency. When this happens, students may perceive the inconsistency as unfair and unreasonable, which may undermine the teacher's authority and effectiveness as a classroom manager.

Developing a Plan for Responding to Student Misbehavior

In Chapter 8, we presented numerous ideas and strategies to address both minor and severe student misbehavior. Students will occasionally engage in misbehavior, and teachers must be prepared to respond effectively and efficiently to the problem. In Chapter 8, we described how responding effectively to problem behavior is critical to a proactive classroom, because ineffective approaches to student misbehavior may increase the likelihood of additional student misbehavior, which, in turn, can lead to a loss of instructional time and a reduction in student achievement.

Teachers who have a plan to address problem behavior will be more consistent, confident, and likely to respond effectively when students engage in problem behavior. When teachers are setting up the proactive classroom, three actions are important:

1. Focus on maintaining the flow of instruction while simultaneously stopping the inappropriate behavior.
2. Avoid ineffective responding to student problem behavior, such as ignoring, questioning and nattering, yelling, issuing directions when a student is agitated, and engaging in power struggles (see Chapter 8).
3. Take actions to prevent the problem behavior from recurring.

THE FIRST DAYS OF SCHOOL

Researchers have investigated the importance of the first days of school in developing an effectively managed classroom (for reviews, see Evertson & Emmer, 2009; Evertson & Weinstein, 2006). The findings clearly indicate that the first few days are critical, because this is the period in which students learn the procedures and rules they will follow and the work habits and behaviors they should exhibit throughout the school year. Marzano and colleagues (2005) called the first day of school the linchpin for an effective classroom management system and the crux of effective learning for the entire school year. Marzano and colleagues also cited the frequently used expression "You have only one chance to make a first impression" as a fitting description of the importance of the first day of class.

In this section, we describe important steps that teachers should follow during the first days of school to set the stage for a proactive classroom, such as:

• Welcoming students to the classroom.
• Teaching classroom procedures, rules, acknowledgments, and consequences.
• Building positive relationships with students and parents.

Welcoming Students to the Classroom

Proactive classrooms are better places to teach and learn not only because there are fewer discipline problems but also because there is a positive classroom environment. Teachers can initiate this positive environment by welcoming their students on the first day of school. Teachers can accomplish this by standing at the door when students enter the classroom for the first time, greeting students, making eye contact, and behaving in a warm and kindly manner.

On the first day of class, students will likely enter quietly; however, if a student enters in a noisy or unacceptable manner, a teacher should provide correction and explain the proper procedure for entering the classroom. It is also best to have students go immediately to their desks and not allow them to congregate or wander about the room.

In addition, teachers should have nametags prepared for their students and taped to their desks. Simultaneously, the teacher should greet arriving students, monitor those who have entered the room, and provide an activity, such as an interesting questionnaire or puzzle, to keep students at their desks and busy. After all the students are in the room, Evertson and Emmer (2009) have suggested that the teacher take a position in the front and center of the classroom and provide a personal introduction. These authors also noted that the teacher should smile and present a friendly, confident manner. If students do not know each other, the teacher may also have a brief activity to acquaint the students with one another.

Teaching Classroom Procedures, Rules, Acknowledgments, and Consequences

Perhaps the most important first-day activity is to introduce students to the proactive classroom by teaching them the classroom procedures and rules. As we discussed in Chapter 3, teachers should not assume that students will understand classroom procedures and rules just because they are mentioned the first day or posted in the classroom. Essentially, the teaching process for classroom procedures and rules is similar to that for teaching any academic subject. That is, teach directly through presentation, modeling, practice, and feedback.

On that first day of school, teachers can present the rationale for the procedures and rules, and students should have opportunities to engage in a discussion and provide input. The teacher can provide examples of appropriate and inappropriate adherence to procedures and rules and provide opportunities to practice following them. Classroom rules should be posted in a conspicuous place where students can see them at all times and teachers can refer to them easily. Posting the rules serves as a constant reminder to students and the teacher, and it allows other staff, substitute teachers, and visitors to see what the expected behavior is in the classroom. Classroom procedures may also be posted in a free-time area, close to the reading corner, or at the learning centers. The end goal of having classroom procedures and rules is not that students merely know them but that students follow them. Teachers should monitor students' compliance with classroom procedures and rules and acknowledge when students adhere to them.

Throughout this book, we have stressed that teachers should always emphasize positive approaches for teaching and encouraging appropriate student behavior. Occasionally, however, students will violate classroom procedures or rules. When this happens, teachers must demonstrate a willingness to act by correcting the offending students quickly, efficiently, and consistently. When correcting a rule violation, teachers should give corrective feedback by describing the rule that was broken and the appropriate behavior that the student should have exhibited.

Building Positive Relationships with Students and Parents

Welcoming students, conducting a brief get-acquainted activity, and talking about hopes for the coming school year are good ways for teachers to begin to form positive relationships with students. In Chapter 4, we addressed methods to foster positive relationships between teachers and students. In that chapter, we discussed how relationships are bidirectional and how, because they are professionals, teachers are highly capable of reflection and change. This is good news, because it is much easier for teachers to adapt their patterns of interaction than it is for some of the students they teach. We further explained in that chapter that teachers should be mindful of the three relational dimensions during interactions, noting if interaction patterns are too conflictive, too distant, or under- or overdependent. For students with problematic behaviors, a mutually perceived high-quality relationship is key to accepting any intervention and then managing and changing their behavior.

It is also important that teachers communicate with the parents or caregivers of students on a regular basis. Along with sharing concerns, it is imperative that teachers share positive messages and acknowledgments about the student's accomplishments and behavior. It does not take long to send a positive e-mail or a note home, and it will set a positive tone and help to secure parental cooperation when problems do occur.

MAINTAINING THE PROACTIVE CLASSROOM

When Benjamin Franklin left Independence Hall in Philadelphia after the final session of the Constitutional Convention in 1787, he was asked if the country had a republic or a monarchy. He replied, "A Republic, if you can keep it!" Similarly, if teachers implement correctly the strategies and procedures we have discussed in this book, they will have created a proactive classroom, but they have to keep it going for the entire year! It takes effort to set up the classroom, but maintaining it requires effort as well. In this section, we talk about using withitness, evaluating academic instruction, and continuously assessing the classroom management system as strategies that teachers can use during the school year to continue their proactive classroom.

Using Withitness

Throughout this book, we have emphasized the importance of teachers exhibiting what Jacob Kounin (1970) called withitness in creating the proactive classroom. Withitness refers to teachers being aware of what is going on in their classroom at all times. According to Kounin, teachers need to constantly watch their students to ensure that students are (a) staying on task, (b) participating in learning activities, (c) behaving appropriately, and (d) complying with classroom rules and procedures. A teacher's withitness can help to evaluate and maintain an efficient and effective management system throughout the school year.

When teachers display withitness, they have higher rates of student involvement and lower rates of misbehavior in their classrooms. When teachers do not monitor student behavior, however, and communicate to their students that they are not withit, student inattention and misbehavior may increase, thus making it difficult for teaching and learning to occur. Withitness is an important skill for teachers to exhibit from the first day of school and throughout the school year.

Evaluating Academic Instruction

Although teachers may think that classroom management and academic instruction are separate elements, they are inextricably intertwined. Teachers cannot deliver effective instruction unless they have a well-managed classroom, and effective instruction facilitates good classroom management (see Chapter 6). When teachers plan for efficiency and deliver effective instruction, it is more likely that student academic achievement will be increased and on-task behavior promoted. On the other hand, poorly planned and delivered instruction will often lead to increased student off-task behavior and problem behavior as well as to lower rates of academic achievement. Thus, it is crucial that teachers maintain their focus on providing effective, engaging instruction at the correct level of difficulty throughout the school year.

Continuously Assessing the Classroom Management System

Teachers should continuously assess and evaluate their classroom management throughout the school year by carefully observing student achievement and behavior. When students are not making academic progress and classroom order is breaking down, the teacher may need to consider changes to the system. A typical part of academic instruction is ongoing evaluation, yet systematic assessment of the management system is often ignored. Teachers can take an overall look at their management system using the following questions to guide their evaluation:

IS THE CLASSROOM MANAGEMENT SYSTEM BEING IMPLEMENTED ACCORDING TO PLAN? Teachers can develop checklists of the major components of their management plan that we outline in this book as a way of thinking critically about, for example, classroom rules and procedures, transitions, teacher–student relationships, morning meetings, academic instruction, modeling appropriate behavior, and redirecting behavior. Other checklist items might include use of choice making, group-oriented interventions, student behavioral contracts, precorrections, and responding appropriately to student misbehavior. When teachers find that they are not implementing any element of the classroom management system to its potential, they should react accordingly and increase their efforts.

DO STUDENTS PERCEIVE THAT A MANAGEMENT PROBLEM EXISTS? Usually, students will be aware that classroom management problems are occurring. The teacher may address the problems during Morning Meeting, as discussed in Chapter 5, or in less structured class meetings by asking students about the nature of the problems and what might be working well. Engaging in conversation will allow students a forum to voice any concerns they may have about their community. Teachers should also be flexible and be open to changing their system if needed. Through constant review of the system with students, teachers can judge more accurately if the plan needs to be changed and, if so, what those changes might be.

ARE PROBLEM BEHAVIORS OCCURRING AT SPECIFIC TIMES OR IN SPECIFIC PLACES? Teachers should observe carefully when and where problems occur. Are there recurring problems during transitions or specific instructional times? Are there problems specific to the morning meeting time? If problems are occurring during a specific academic activity, teachers may review the suggestions outlined in Chapter 6.

DO PROBLEM BEHAVIORS OCCUR PRIMARILY WITH ONE OR A FEW STUDENTS?   If so, teachers may want to consider increasing choice making and using behavioral contracts (see Chapter 7). Teachers also may want to implement a self-management program or teach replacement behaviors by helping students to handle their social problems effectively (see Chapter 9).

ARE THE BEHAVIOR PROBLEMS OCCURRING WITH MORE THAN SEVERAL STUDENTS IN THE CLASSROOM?   If so, teachers should address their implementation of the classroom management system and instruction. Again, teachers should increase their efforts to implement the classroom management system as originally intended. Teachers should also ask themselves what is the current plan and what are its components? It may be that teachers need to provide students with more ongoing support and increase the review of the classroom management system with their students. Teachers should also consider using the group-oriented interventions outlined in Chapter 7 or whole-class self-management as described in Chapter 9.

Summary

Preventing behavior problems in today's classrooms should be a strategic effort of all teachers. Preventing problems, as we have discussed in this book, can be accomplished through the concerted efforts of teachers and administrators, yet putting all the components together to establish an efficient and effective classroom management system requires teacher and student commitment and attention to detail. Teachers must design positive classroom cultures that are foundational to proactive classrooms, be strategic about implementing management plans during the first days of school, and realize the necessity of maintaining effective classroom management systems over the course of the school year.

References

Evertson, C., & Emmer, E. (2009). *Classroom management for elementary teachers.* Upper Saddle River, NJ: Pearson/Merrill Education.

Evertson, C., & Weinstein, C. (2006). *Handbook of classroom management: Research, practice, and contemporary issues.* Mahwah, NJ: Lawrence Erlbaum.

Kounin, J. S. (1970). *Discipline and group management in classrooms.* Austin, TX: Holt, Rinehart, & Winston.

Marzano, R. J., Gaddy, B., Foseid, M. C., Foseid, M. P., & Marzano, J. S. (2005). *Handbook for classroom management that works.* Alexandria, VA: Association for Supervision and Curriculum Development.

INDEX